Paul Sullivan's journalism and photography work has been published in a variety of international publications including the *Guardian*, the *Sunday Times*, *BBC Travel* and more. He has written and contributed to over a dozen music and travel books for *National Geographic*, *Time Out*, *Wallpaper*, Rough Guides and Fodor's, and runs the popular Berlin website www.slowtravelberlin.com, through which he publishes Berlin-themed books and runs cultural-historical tours through the city.

Marcel Krueger is a writer and translator whose articles and essays have been published in the *Daily Telegraph*, *Süddeutsche Zeitung*, *CNN Travel*, the Matador Network and more, and who also works as a local Berlin expert or 'Spotter' for Spotted by Locals. He divides his time between Berlin, Cologne and Dublin and together with Seamus Heaney, Roddy Doyle and a team of other great Irish writers Krueger also holds the world record for 'Most Authors Reading Consecutively From Their Own Books'.

'A rich and learned companion for every lover of Berlin; bursting with anecdote and alive with history. A must.'

Rory MacLean, author of *Berlin: Imagine a City*

Literary Guides for Travellers
Listed in Fathom's 24 Best Indie Travel Guides

Andalucia by Andrew and Suzanne Edwards

Florence and Tuscany by Ted Jones

The French Riviera by Ted Jones

Scotland by Garry MacKenzie

Sicily by Andrew and Suzanne Edwards

Tangier by Josh Shoemake

Venice by Marie-José Gransard

Berlin

A LITERARY GUIDE FOR TRAVELLERS

Paul Sullivan and Marcel Krueger

I.B. TAURIS

LONDON · NEW YORK

Published in 2016 by
I.B.Tauris & Co. Ltd
London • New York
www.ibtauris.com

Copyright © 2016 Paul Sullivan and Marcel Krueger

ISBN: 978 1 78453 642 8
eISBN: 978 0 85772 864 7
ePDF: 978 0 85772 837 1

A full CIP record for this book is available from the British Library
A full CIP record is available from the Library of Congress

Library of Congress Catalog Card Number: available

Typeset by JCS Publishing Services Ltd, www.jcs-publishing.co.uk
Printed and bound in Sweden by Scandbook AB

CONTENTS

Illustrations

All photographs are by Paul Sullivan, 2016

Key to map (overleaf)

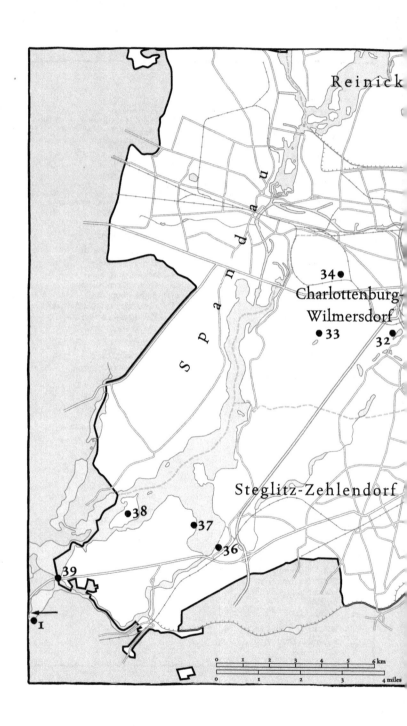

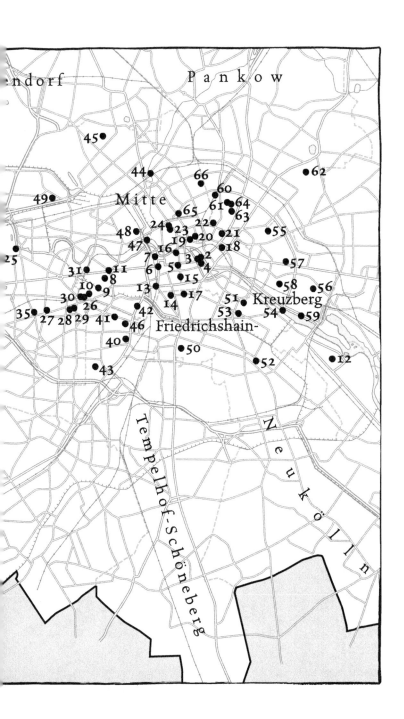

₭ 1 ₭

INTRODUCTION

*Berlin is a young and unhappy city-in-waiting. There is something
fragmentary about its history. Berlin's frequently interrupted, still
more frequently diverted or averted development has been checked and
advanced, and by unconscious mistake as well as by bad intentions; the
many obstacles in its path have, it would seem, helped it to grow.*

(Joseph Roth, 1930)

Approached via air or land across the seemingly endless wooded
plains of Brandenburg, Berlin manifests suddenly, almost magically:
a brick-and-concrete apparition caught between lakes and forests. It
seems to have no tangible connection to the surrounding landscape
and feels similarly distanced from the mega-sprawl of western
German cities such as Bonn, Cologne and Leverkusen, which creep
into each other to form part of the Manchester–Milan axis.

This idea of an island-city fits Berlin well. It has always been more
concerned with its own image and development than with looking
too far beyond its borders, and its detachment has undoubtedly
helped it serve as both canvas and laboratory over the centuries,
drawing artists and dreamers, city planners and megalomaniacs. In
turn, the rich blend of immigrants who have made the place home
since its birth have ensured that the city has never remained static:
in the famous words of arts historian Karl Scheffler, Berlin is a city
'destined forever to become and never to be'.

In fact, the city literally began as an island; two, actually – Alt
Berlin and Cölln – which lay side by side in the middle of the river
Spree, roughly where the Museum Island, the Fisher Island and

the Nikolaiviertel are located today. The surrounding landscape of Brandenburg, described in 1598 by travel writer and topographer Nicholas Leuthinger as a 'flat land, wooded, and for the most part swamp', meant that these riverside settlements, founded officially in the early thirteenth century and joined together in 1307, remained fairly obscure until the ambitious Hohenzollern dynasty entered the fray a couple of hundred years later.

In his book *Berlin: Imagine a City* (2014), Rory McLean paints a colourful picture of the city in medieval times:

> [A] dirty patchwork of squalid hovels and mean manors stitched to a low, lazy twist of the Spree. Along its sandy banks fisher-boys hawked the morning catch, their high voices lifting in a kind of babbling river music. Brawny lads stripped to the waist unloaded barrels of Rhenish wine and sacks of rice from Arborio. A matron from a noble house craned her neck to select the finest trout, the freshest loaf, the thickest wedge of cheese, tucking each prize into her willow basket. Urchins raced by the Mühlendamm mills like dogs on a scent. Blue-tunicked soldiers sauntered through the mêlée, plucking any ware that took their fancy.

By 1618, the first year of the Thirty Years War that would devastate the city, Berlin still only had around 10,000 inhabitants compared to London's 130,000. It was later in the seventeenth century, when Frederick William of Brandenburg, a.k.a. the Great Elector – the first to be named king in Prussia – worked to make Brandenburg-Prussia into a powerful northern German state, that Berlin began to gain more prominence. By the eighteenth century Frederick William I and his son Frederick the Great had managed to transform Prussia into a serious European power with an influence that far transcended its size.

As well as his renowned military victories, Frederick the Great – who ruled from 1740 until 1786 – was also famed for his patronage of the arts; as Kant once stated, he was more or less synonymous with the Enlightenment values that swept Europe during the eighteenth century. Frederick's own liberal ideals were admirable: not only was he notoriously tolerant towards other religions, he also suspended the use of judicial torture in his lands – a huge step at the time. In terms of the arts, he eased up considerably on censorship too, even allowing his critics – and critical publications like *The Berlin News* (*Die Berlinischen Nachrichten*) – to live and operate in the city. Scottish travel writer and physician John Moore, who visited the city in 1775, wrote about this exceptionally liberal atmosphere:

> Nothing surprised me more, when I first came to Berlin, than the freedom with which many people speak of the measure of government, and the conduct of the King. I have heard political topics, and others which I should have thought still more ticklish, discussed here with as little ceremony as at a London coffee house. The same freedom appears in the book sellers' shops, where literary productions of all kinds are sold openly. The pamphlet lately published on the division of Poland, wherein the King is very roughly treated, is to be had without difficulty, as well as other performances, which attack some of the most conspicuous characters with all the bitterness of satire.

By the end of the eighteenth century there were some 200 clubs and societies throughout Prussia dedicated to reading and writing, not to mention a burgeoning selection of bookshops and literary cafés. Berlin's own literary scene spanned societies like the Wednesday Club, a private club for high-profile society members, prominent local print publications like the *Berlin Monthly* (*Berlinische Monatsschrift*), and poets and writers such as Karl Wilhelm Ramler, Christoph Friedrich Nicolai, Gotthold Ephraim Lessing and Moses Mendelssohn.

Much of this literary activity was initially connected to the Prussian state in that the writing published and ideas discussed tended to come from noblemen, professors and civil servants. In this sense it was not particularly anti-establishment, but as the reading public grew and as more nuanced social strata began to emerge, different types of literature developed, ranging from more upper-class and critical (so called 'autonomous') publications to more egalitarian formats for the masses, often described as *Trivialliteratur*.

Another major literary network of the time, though, consisted of the more independent literary salons that brought together an array of writers, artists, scientists and thinkers. The Berlin salons emulated the established French formats – both the aristocratic and more modest bourgeois versions – and were similarly instigated and hosted by female intellectuals, often of Jewish heritage, such as Rahel Levin Varnhagen (1771–1833), Sara Levy (1761–1854) and Henriette Herz (1764–1847), as well as non-Jewish intellectuals and artists like Bettina von Arnim (1785–1859) and court lady Karoline Friederike von Berg (1760–1826).

Usually held in private homes, the salons became intimate forums for discussing the artistic and social issues of the day, facilitating new forms of literature such as cultural and travel works inspired by German Romanticism to politically charged poems and writings (for example, Heinrich Heine's anti-establishment poems of the 1840s). Many of these republican ideals directly informed the demands fought for in the German revolutions of 1848–9, as an 1847 Prussian surveillance report on von Arnim demonstrates:

> Social questions were discussed even at tea parties. The Political leaning at these tea parties is socialist, in that members of the gathering prefer to talk and debate how the substance and form of life could be improved. The female sex especially long for liberations from the bonds of tradition, fashion, convention. Among all the women of this type in Berlin who enjoy a public reputation, Bettina von Arnim is indisputably the chief and most prominent. It is generally known, even to the court, that her soirees have the character I just described. She is left in peace because she

is held in universally high regard here, and no fault can rightly be found in her.

After the failed revolutions (see Chapter 2), official censorship and control quashed the culture of politicised writing, at least in public, leading to a period of more conventional literature characterised by non-political, often late Romantic, themes such as historical fiction and country life. Hence the first internationally known Berlin-based writers – the Brothers Grimm, Heinrich von Kleist, E. T. A. Hoffmann, Adelbert von Chamisso – for the most part took on these broader themes rather than writing about the social and daily life of the Prussian *Hauptstadt* – its capital city.

It was only with the rise of realist writers such as Gerhart Hauptmann, Gottfried Keller, Theodor Fontane and Wilhelm Raabe that the social realities of the city – mass culture, accelerating modernisation – began to be addressed. Raabe was one of the first to engage with Berlin's increasingly urbanised surroundings in *The Chronicle of Sparrow Alley* (*Die Chronik der Sperlingsgasse*, 1856), a short novel that, by relating the tale of ordinary people's lives in a normal, if fictional, street, offered insights into the social and political situation of the era. Though not a particularly dark novel, it opens with the ominous line 'Es ist eigentlich eine böse Zeit!' ('These are actually rather evil times!').

Fontane, Germany's first travel writer, hiked extensively through and around rural Berlin and Brandenburg, relating its geographical and historical details in his famous five-volume *Ramblings through Brandenburg* (*Wanderungen durch die Mark Brandenburg*, 1862). But he also engaged with the emerging nuances of modern Berlin society and the quirks of Berliners themselves in fictional works like *Frau Jenny Treibel* (1892), and in *Trials and Tribulations* (*Irrungen, Wirrungen*, 1888):

> See here, Here Baron, while I, who am hardened to the weather, am still staying indoors because the east wind blows and the March

sun scorches, the Berliner already sits out of doors, lays his summer overcoat on the chair and orders pale ale. For if only the sun shines the Berliner speaks of beautiful weather. It is all the same to him if there is inflammation of the lungs or diphtheria in every wind that blows. It is then that he best likes to play grace-hoops, blistered from the reflected sunlight, my heart really aches for them, for there is not one among them whose skin will not peel off at least by the following day.

After 1871, the year in which Germany finally unified under Prussia's Kaiser William I and Otto von Bismarck, Berlin underwent even more intensive industrialisation. Financed by the proceeds of the Franco-Prussian War of 1870–1 and marked by a slew of grandiose buildings commissioned by the Kaiser to make Berlin into a real *Weltstadt* (world city), the now-German capital's burgeoning status began to attract the attention of high-profile literary visitors. In 1892 none other than Mark Twain penned a hyperbolic essay describing the city as a 'Chicago on the Spree', included in his *The Chicago of Europe*:

One is not allowed to build unstable, unsafe, or unsightly houses in Berlin; the result is this comely and conspicuously stately city, with its security from conflagrations and breakdowns. It is built of architectural Gibraltars. The building commissioners inspect while the building is going up. It has been found that this is better than to wait till it falls down. These people are full of whims. One is not allowed to cram poor folk into cramped and dirty tenement houses. Each individual must have just so many cubic feet of room-space, and sanitary inspections are systematic and frequent.

Twain's report was, however, blind to the harsher realities of the rapidly expanding city – inevitable, given that he was based in the wealthier centre of the city and hobnobbed with the city's social and cultural elite (including the Kaiser himself). The truth was that, with around 10,000 new inhabitants arriving each year from the 1850s onwards, Berlin had long struggled to provide adequate housing and infrastructure. The response to these challenges was the Hobrecht Plan of 1862, which was loosely inspired by Baron Haussmann's overhaul of Paris between 1850 and 1870. Named after urban planner James Hobrecht, the plan did away with the former customs wall that had defined the city limits for the previous couple of centuries, created many of the city's now-famous neighbourhoods and gave rise to the five-storey tenement buildings – nicknamed *Mietskaserne* or 'rental barracks' – that still dominate the cityscape today.

Built by property investors to accommodate as many new rent-paying workers as possible, these tenements, despite being planned with good and even Utopian intentions by Hobrecht, resulted in overcrowding and outbreaks of disease, especially in the denser, factory-filled neighbourhoods such as Kreuzberg, Neukölln, Prenzlauer Berg and Wedding. Journalist and politician Albert Südekum painted a very different picture from Twain's when writing about life in the industrial part of the city in his essay 'Impoverished Berlin Dwellings – Wedding', first published in his collection *The Desperate Housing Situation in Large Cities* (*Großstädtisches Wohnungselend*, 1908):

> How did the family sleep? Husband and wife in the only bed. The children were placed on laid-out pieces of clothing and could sneak into bed only when their father and mother – usually around five o'clock in the morning – got up. The smallest of the children slept occasionally in a basket but sometimes, too, when the woman had to leave the room for some purpose, slept in a half-open drawer in the commode.

The Kaiser's bid to bring the city to the same level of grandeur as other European capitals didn't convince everyone. As a reaction to Twain's Americanised description of the city, a young Walther Rathenau, who would become a prominent industrialist, writer and politician, penned an ironically titled essay – 'The Most Beautiful City in the World' (1899) – that declaimed its pompous and eclectic architecture and tendency towards modernity over tradition:

> Berlin is the parvenu among cities and the city of parvenus: and that is nothing to be ashamed of. After all, a parvenu in plain German, is a self-made man. Of course, we have no cross, no dinner hour, no fashionable suburbs, and no business district. [...] Carriages roll, share prices permitting, and the most venerable palaces go back no further than the 1870s. Strictly speaking, Berlin the metropolis does not exist.

Yet while it may have lacked the same cultural elan of Paris or the commercial diversity of London, Berlin's growing modernity was for many a cause for celebration and excitement. The grand Industrial Exhibition at Treptow Park in 1896 symbolised the prevailing mood of progress and innovation that, by the start of the twentieth century, had transformed the city into a bustling hub of entrepreneurism and consumerism. It was this mix of abundant neon advertising signs, ever-increasing population and non-stop parade of trams, trains and motor cars (by 1908 over 170,000 cars per hour crossed through Potsdamer Platz) that led sociologist Max Weber to describe the city as follows (at the first German sociologists' conference in 1910):

> The distinctive formal values of our modern artistic culture could only have come to be through the existence of the modern metropolis, the modern metropolis with its tramways, underground railways, its electric [...] lamps, display windows, concert halls, and restaurants, cafés, smokestacks, masses of stone, and the wild dance of impressions of sound and colour, impressions and experiences which have an effect on sexual fantasy, all variants of spiritual constitution, which brood voraciously over the seemingly inexhaustible possibilities of means to life and happiness.

This explosion of modern sights and sounds naturally drew artists, intellectuals and writers too. Swiss writer Robert Walser wrote his story 'Berlin and the Artist' in 1908, which praised the cultural milieu of the city and its inspirational tempo:

> Berlin never rests, and this is glorious. Each dawning day brings with it a new, agreeably disagreeable attack on complacency, and this does the general sense of indolence good. An artist possesses, much like a child, an inborn propensity for beautiful, noble sluggardizing. Well, this slug-a-beddishness, this kingdom, is constantly being buffeted by fresh storm-winds of inspiration. The refined, silent creature is suddenly blustered full of something coarse, loud, and unrefined. There is an incessant blurring together of various things, and this is good, this is Berlin, and Berlin is outstanding.

Expressionism was the main cultural movement in Berlin before the First World War, represented across many different cultural mediums from painting and poetry to architecture and literature. With its emphasis on subjective emotions and the 'inner life' rather than fixed natural or societal orders, Expressionism was perfectly primed to record all facets of the modern era, from its consumerist decadence to its angst and isolation. Plays such as Reinhard Johannes Sorge's *The Beggar* (*Der Bettler*, 1912) were joined by other works by the likes of Georg Kaiser, Ernst Toller, Walter Hasenclever and Reinhard Goering, plus Expressionist poetry from Georg Heym, Gottfried Benn and Else Lasker-Schüler, all of which portrayed the horrors of urban life in order to either satirise them or provoke political and social reforms.

As Austrian writer Hans Flesch von Brünningen wrote in a text accompanying an exhibition by expressionist painter Ernst Ludwig in early 1914: 'The year was 1913. You have to realise what Berlin meant to us back then in Vienna. It was everything to us, really. For us, Berlin was crazy, debauched, metropolitan, anonymous, gargantuan, futuristic. It was literary and political and artistic (the city for painters). In short: an infernal cesspool and paradise in one.'

This all changed drastically with the outbreak of the First World War in 1914 – an event that by many accounts was welcomed by many in Germany and Austria. 'Every face looks happy. We've got war!' wrote Austrian actress Tilla Durieux during a stay in Berlin in the same year: 'One's food gets cold, one's beer gets warm. No matter – we've got war!' The Association of German Jews proclaimed that every German Jew was 'ready to sacrifice all the property and blood demanded by duty', and even intellectuals such as Max Weber described the situation as 'grand and wonderful [...] worth experiencing'. English aristocrat Evelyn Fürstin Blücher von Wahlstatt (otherwise known as Princess Blücher) offered a more balanced view in her famous memoir on 9 August 1914:

> Exactly what was the real cause of the war no one seems to know, although it is discussed night and day. One thing grows clearer to me every day: neither the people here nor there wished for war, but here they are now being carried off their legs with patriotism, at seeing so many enemies on every side. It is said in England that Germany provoked the war, and here they emphatically deny it. To me it seems that Europe was thirsting for war, and that the armies and navies were no longer to be restrained. Certainly here, the militarists grew weary of the long lazy peace as they called it, and if the Kaiser had not proclaimed war, he would have been in a precarious position. There are two men at the head of affairs: one is called stupid and the other dangerous. The dangerous one has won the day, and brought the war to a head. Lord Northcliffe seems to be responsible on the other side.

Over the next four years many artists left the city, either fleeing the hunger and deprivation that marked the later stages of the Great War or fighting and dying in the trenches. Some writers continued publishing, either as part of the propaganda effort (for example,

Alfred Döblin's 1914 essay 'Reims', about the 'necessary' destruction of the cathedral of Reims), as part of an increasing pacifist movement (Heinrich Zille's anti-war cartoon *Iron Cross* in 1916 and Gottfried Benn's hospital-influenced poetry collection *Flesh*, 1917), or in neutral countries like Switzerland (Robert Walser's *The Walk*, 1917).

Towards the end of the war, new avant-garde art and literary ideas such as Dadaism and Surrealism were introduced to the city. German poet, psychoanalyst and member of Zürich's influential Cabaret Voltaire Richard Hülsenbeck moved to Berlin in 1917 and founded the local Dada group, which drew artists such as George Grosz, Raoul Hausmann, Hannah Höch, Johannes Baader and John Heartfield. Hülsenbeck's first Dada speech in the capital took place in February 1917 and described the city as a place of 'tightened stomachers, of mounting, thundering hunger, where hidden rage was transformed into a boundless money lust, and men's minds were concentrating more and more on questions of naked existence [...] Fear was in everybody's bones.'

In 1918 the defeat of the German army and the abdication of the Kaiser led to political chaos and bloody revolution in Berlin and, eventually, the foundation of the Weimar Republic. With the fixed social orders of the imperial era gone, Berlin's cultural life exploded again into a complex array of liberated lifestyles and ideas that contrasted with hyper-inflation, prostitution and high unemployment. After the war, the Dada group began publishing numerous political magazines and periodicals with titles such as *Club Dada*, *Everyman His Own Football* and *Dada Almanach*, and also organised the First International Dada Fair in 1920, which featured around 200 works by local artists and international guests such as Francis Picabia, Jean Arp and Max Ernst. Berlin intellectual Walter Benjamin paid tribute to the Dadaists in his 1936 essay 'The Work of Art in the Age of Mechanical Reproduction':

> The Dadaists attached much less importance to the sales value of their work than to its uselessness for contemplative immersion.

The studied degradation of their material was not the least of their means to achieve this uselessness. Their poems are 'word salad' containing obscenities and every imaginable waste product of language. The same is true of their paintings, on which they mounted buttons and tickets. What they intended and achieved was a relentless destruction of the aura of their creations, which they branded as reproductions with the very means of production [...] Dadaistic activities actually assured a rather vehement distraction by making works of art the centre of scandal. One requirement was foremost: to outrage the public.

A less surreal and more pragmatic reaction to the horrors of the First World War arose with New Objectivity, a German-centric movement whose key protagonists – including Otto Dix, George Grosz and Max Beckmann in Berlin – developed an eclectic array of techniques to represent the sober (and sordid) realities of the Weimar period: workers, prostitutes, street life and the garish contrasts between poverty and wealth. As writer and historian Arthur Eloesser writes in *German Literature from Baroque to Present* (*Die deutsche Literatur vom Barock bis zur Gegenwart*, 1930–1): 'Vienna was the city of talent, Berlin that of criticism, and unprejudiced, authoritative criticism, capable of grasping a subject rapidly, which was establishing a hierarchy of merit not among German writers alone.'

While the movement is usually connected with portraiture, other artistic realms from theatre and music to publishing and journalism succumbed to New Objectivity's pervasive influence. Anton Kaes, Martin Jay and Edward Dimendberg sum the situation up succinctly in their *Weimar Republic Sourcebook* (1994):

Subjective distortion and expressionistic pathos were no longer in fashion; fiction and fantasy yielded to sober and rational prose that was seen as both 'democratic' and 'international'. The ultimate mark of quality for a literary 'product' was its usefulness; even poetry adhered to this philosophy, as the usable poetry

(*Gebrauchslyrik*) of Bertolt Brecht's *Hauspostille* (1927) or Erich Kästner's *Herz auf Taille* (1929) demonstrated.

The Weimar period was an extraordinarily fertile time for books, newspapers and other print media: at its peak during the 1920s, the German newspaper industry was publishing some 25 million newspapers annually. Of the almost 5,000 daily and weekly newspapers – many printed three times a day in morning, lunchtime and evening editions – 147 were located in Berlin. Some became a rich source of employment for local writers, especially those that also published novels, books of poetry and other literary formats aside from journalism.

Ullstein – founded in 1877 by Leopold Ullstein – for example, published not only daily newspapers such as the *Vossische Newspaper (Vossische Zeitung)* and *Berlin Morning Post (Berliner Morgenpost)* but also mainstream literature and political and avant-garde works via its Propyläen Verlag imprint. With a head office in Friedrichstrasse (which is still in use today) and large modernist Ullsteinhaus printing plant and office in Tempelhof built in 1925 (today housing call centres and retail stores), the publishing house and its subsidiaries Propyläen and Arkadia circulated seminal works by the likes of Bertolt Brecht, Carl Zuckmayer and Lionel Feuchtwanger, and was also the first to publish Thomas Mann's *The Magic Mountain* (*Zauberberg*) to great acclaim in 1924. In her 1962 autobiography *It Was All Quite Different*, Vicki Baum – who worked at Ullstein for many years as an editor – wrote:

> If one speaks with old Berliners today, with those who led through the twenties and now live elsewhere, they will sigh with profound homesickness and tell you that there is no comparison anywhere to that lively, fascinating city of Berlin in those years. Yes, and one of the hearts of the inner city was the House of Ullstein. It was a focus of liberalism [...] To be known as a liberal and an intellectual was a high honor then, a goal infinitely desirable and worth working and

struggling for. At Ullstein's this liberalism meant that the doors were wide open for the widest variety of opinions, ideas, notions, and positions. Our authors included all the colors of the rainbow, from the red of the extreme left – Brecht and Toller – across the whole scale of the Expressionist school to the antimilitarist, antiwar book *Im Westen nichts Neues*, and over to the dark green of aged, moss-grown nativist writers – *Heimatsschriftsteller* – like Richard Skowronnek.

Indeed, the Weimar era on the whole was a high point for German and Berlin literature, with local writers – by now including Kurt Tucholsky, Erich Maria Remarque, Alfred Döblin, Joseph Roth, Vicki Baum, Walter Benjamin, Christopher Isherwood and Franz Hessel – producing not only a slew of avant-garde and commercial works but also *flâneur*-esque feuilletons and other texts that put the city under intensive examination. As Walter Benjamin writes in his posthumously published story collection *Berlin Childhood around 1900* (1950):

> Street names must speak to the urban wanderer like the snapping of dry twigs, and little streets in the heart of the city must reflect the times of day, for him, as clearly as a mountain valley. This art I acquired rather late in life; it fulfilled a dream, of which the first traces were labyrinths on the blotting papers in my school notebooks.

Even as this remarkable cultural and literary landscape proliferated, many of its underlying progressive ideas and aesthetics were being challenged by the increasingly powerful Nazis. Painter George Grosz, in his autobiography *A Small Yes and a Big No* (1946), describes the strange mix of tensions in the capital in the late 1920s:

> The times were certainly out of joint. All moral restraints seemed to have melted away. A flood of vice, pornography and prostitution

swept the entire country [...] Men in white shirts marched up and down, shouting in unison: 'Up with Germany! Down with the Jews!' They were followed by another group, also in disciplined ranks of four, bawling rhythmically in chorus: 'Heil Moscow! Heil Moscow!' Afterwards some of them would be left lying around, heads cracked, legs smashed and the odd bullet in the abdomen [...] The city was dark, cold and full of rumours. The streets were wild ravines haunted by murderers and cocaine peddlers, their emblem a metal bar or a murderous broken-off chair leg.

Upon coming to power, the Nazis closed down or 'Aryanised' Jewish businesses, including publishers like Ullstein (which was renamed Deutscher Verlag in 1937 and published propaganda newspapers and magazines until 1945, when it was returned to its owners) and S. Fischer Verlag. Founded in Berlin in 1886 by another Jewish entrepreneur, Samuel Fischer, S. Fischer Verlag had established itself in the German market as a leading publisher of naturalist and modernist works, releasing books by the likes of Henrik Ibsen, Thomas Mann, Hermann Hesse and Gerhart Hauptmann. In 1890 it also began the *New Observations* (*Neue Rundschau*), which by the Weimar era was a leading German literary magazine publishing regular work by Robert Musil, Arthur Schnitzler and Alfred Döblin, among others, and which is still going strong today, making it one of the oldest cultural publications in Europe.

By the time the Nazis took over, S. Fischer Verlag was being run by Samuel's son-in-law Gottfried Bermann Fischer, who was forced to flee and set up a branch of the company in Vienna. While in exile, Fischer supported the Amsterdam-based German-language publisher Querido, which became the main publisher for exiled authors like Stephan Zweig and Joseph Roth after 1933. S. Fischer Verlag kept its name and, while publishing a more 'Germanised' programme, was led by moderate board member Peter Suhrkamp, who subsequently founded the Suhrkamp Verlag publishing house in 1950. Gottfried Bermann Fischer took over S. Fischer Verlag again after the war.

Jewish writers, who made up a considerable element of the Weimar firmament, were also forced to flee the city, many – such as Joseph Roth, Walter Benjamin, Franz Hessel and Kurt Tucholsky – perishing before the end of the war in 1945. Non-Jewish writers, especially those whose works were burned at Bebelplatz in 1933 (see Chapter 2), also left Berlin, Bertolt Brecht, Vicki Baum, Alfred Döblin and Erich Maria Remarque among them. Only a few, like Brecht, returned to their destroyed and divided city afterwards. During the Nazi regime a few writers such as Hans Fallada and Erich Kästner preferred to take the risk and stay – both survived. Resistance writers like Russian poet Musa Cälil and German diplomat Albrecht Haushofer created their literary legacy while awaiting execution, while Jewish war survivors such as Victor Klemperer, Inge Deutschkron and Marie Jalowicz Simon lived to publish their poignant experiences during the horrors of the Holocaust. In the end, whoever survived had to watch their city turn to rubble around them. As English historian Cornelius Ryan states in his account of the Battle of Berlin in 1945, *The Last Battle*:

> As the smoke drifted slowly across the ruins, Germany's most bombed city stood out in stark, macabre splendor. It was blackened by soot, pockmarked by thousands of craters and laced by the twisting girders of ruined buildings. Whole blocks of apartment houses were gone, and in the very heart of the capital entire neighbourhoods had vanished. In these wastelands what had once been broad roads and streets were now pitted trails that snaked through mountains of rubble. Everywhere, covering acre after acre, gutted windowless, roofless buildings gaped up at the sky.

Following the Nazi era and its heavily censored 'Blood and Soil' propaganda, German literature took an inevitably reflective turn. Nicknames such as *Kahlschlag* (clear-cutting), *Stunde Null* (zero hour) and *Trümmerliteratur* (rubble literature) have been commonly applied to this environment, where writers attempted to find a new collective voice that necessarily avoided any excessive nationalism and tried to come to terms with the immediate past while envisioning what kind of future might emerge from their decimated country. One of the first postwar publications, *The Call* (*Der Ruf*), was founded in a US prisoner-of-war camp in 1945 by Hans Werner Richter and Alfred Andersch. Marked by a tendency to eschew complicity in Nazi crimes, it was banned by American occupation authorities in 1947, but Richter went on to found the influential – and often controversial – Gruppe 47, a literary circle that continued to maintain some distance from the Nazi past through works such as Wolfgang Borchert's play *The Man Outside* (*Draußen vor der Tür*, 1947), Richter's novel *Beyond Defeat* (*Die Geschlagenen*, 1949) and Heinrich Böll's novella *The Train Was on Time* (*Der Zug war pünktlich*, 1949).

The best-known novels, plays and poems of the postwar years were not written in Berlin (Gruppe 47 only met once in the city, in 1962), though local writers such as Gert Ledig penned significant works during this time. Ledig was one of the first to talk openly about the effects of Allied bombing on the civilian population in his novel *Payback* (*Vergeltung*, 1956):

> Next to the mother stood a woman burning like a torch. She was screaming. The mother looked on helpless, then she too was on fire. It raced up her legs, up her thighs, to her body [...] a shock wave exploded along the graveyard wall and in that moment the road burned too. Asphalt, stones, air. That was what happened in the graveyard.

The formal division of Germany by its conquering powers created two separate literary cultures, especially after the Berlin Wall went up in 1961. From that point on, West Berlin increasingly became an isolated West German island in the middle of the Communist German Democratic Republic (GDR); as the only place in Germany where military service was not compulsory, its districts – in particular Kreuzberg, Charlottenburg and Schöneberg – attracted students, draft-evaders and, naturally, underground writers such as Jörg Fauser and Jürgen Ploog. The conditions created an alternative culture that peaked during the student protests of 1968 and with societal experiments such as Kommune 1 – the first political commune in Germany, located in Schöneberg apartments provided by Hans Magnus Enzensberger and Uwe Johnson (see Chapter 6). Teenage drug addict Christiane F. witnessed and chronicled the heroin scene around Bahnhof Zoo in her memoir *Zoo Station* (*Wir Kinder vom Bahnhof Zoo*, 1979), while German mainstream literature found state support in literary institutions such as the Literarisches Colloquium Berlin (established 1963, see Chapter 5) and the Literaturhaus Berlin (opened 1986, see Chapter 4).

The 1960s also saw many violent student protests against the establishment, especially during the visit of the shah of Persia in 1967, which led to the formation of the Red Army Faction, a leftist terrorist group. In his 1981 novel *Raw Material* (*Rohstoff*) – which is set in 1960s West Berlin – Jörg Fauser describes a scene from such protests in Charlottenburg:

Stones were being hurled at America House, but word got round that we were to take the Kurfürstendamm, and so we charged onwards, past Zoo station. Stones were everywhere on the ground; I'd picked up a couple myself – smooth, grey cobbles. I'd soon forgotten the LSD, and Sarah too. I charged with the crowd. There was the Ku'damm, the colourful facades, the onlookers, the massive vehicles with their water cannons. We were coming from all sides, we were storming. There was Cafe Kranzler, temple of the bourgeoisie, there were the police, chains of uniformed men that entangled us. No sooner had the echoes of our war cries died down than the first screams of those being beaten by truncheons resounded in the street. I threw a stone, then turned and saw a policeman charging towards me at full pelt. I dropped the other stone and ducked. The truncheon only hit me as I bent down, a second blow found my arm, and another policeman hauled me off to a patrol car, but let me go when a new troop of assailants broke through and made for Kranzler.

The GDR's cultural landscape in the East was inevitably different to that of West, although it initially attracted many postwar German writers, playwrights and poets. Anna Seghers, Arnold Zweig, Hans Mayer and Bertolt Brecht all chose to move to East Berlin to support the fledgling 'anti-fascist' socialist state. Brecht was given his very own theatre as a reward for his efforts; Zweig was made president of the Academy of the Arts (1950–3) and Mayer became a professor of literary studies and a prominent critic of postwar German literature. The main cultural institution of the GDR was the Kulturbund zur Demokratischen Erneuerung Deutschlands (Cultural Federation for the Democratic Renewal of Germany), founded in 1945 as a state-controlled association for the arts in East Germany, organising exhibitions, talks and also an all-German writers' conference in Berlin in 1947 and in 1950 in East Berlin. It existed until the dissolution of the GDR in 1990, and over the years members of the association included Fritz Erpenbeck, Victor Klemperer, Anna Seghers, Christa Wolf and Arnold Zweig.

As East German society became increasingly oppressive, and literary criticism and thematic diversity repressed in favour of state-approved 'Socialist Realism' narratives, many artists and writers began to distance themselves from the regime, including Brecht and Mayer, the latter of whom resigned his university post in 1963 and subsequently decided to remain in West Germany during a visit. During the 1960s and 1970s, GDR writers and poets contrived that their work got past the censors, usually in the shape of autobiographical novels or poems, via Western publications (often under pseudonyms) or in subtly cryptic formats. Examples include Uwe Johnson's *Speculations about Jacob* (*Mutmassungen über Jakob*, published in 1959 by Suhrkamp), Peter Huchel's poetry collection *Avenues, Avenues* (*Chausseen, Chausseen*, published by Fischer Verlag in 1967) and Christa Wolf's *New Life-Views of a Tomcat* (*Neue Lebensansichten eines Katers*, 1981).

A turning-point came in 1976 with the forced expulsion of songwriter and regime critic Wolf Biermann, who was stripped of his citizenship while on an officially authorised tour of West Germany. The move prompted outrage – and a major petition – by many of his fellow artists, writers and musicians. Many signatories and supporters of the petition who had not already left the country – an increasingly difficult thing to accomplish – were harassed by the East German secret police, the Stasi, thrown into prison for a spell and/or had their works banned.

By the 1980s, a more defiant counterculture emerged in the East Berlin district of Prenzlauer Berg as writers, poets and songwriters such as Sascha Anderson, Lutz Rathenow and Annett Gröschner began to express their dissatisfaction through small, locally produced 'samizdat' publications. Ruth J. Owen states in her book *The Poet's Role: Lyric Responses to German Unification by Poets from the GDR* (2001):

> The new writing broke publishing taboos by existing in a niche outside state jurisdiction in the small print-runs of magazines which the artists published themselves. Adolf Endler has called these magazines 'Heftpublikationen' [booklet publications] over which the poet exclaimed, 'Klein, aber mein!' [Small, but mine!]
>
> The first of the 'samizdat' magazines, issued in 1981, was *Der Kaiser ist nackt* [*The Emperor is Naked*], edited by the young poet Uwe Kolbe. The title recalls the fairytale in which a boy alone dares to speak the obvious truth and mock the king. In the foreword to the anthology of magazine issues which were put together for West German readers, Kolbe wrote 'wir wollten einfach eine eine andere Öffentlichkeit' [we just wanted a different publicity].

By the end of the 1980s, writers had grown bold enough to campaign openly for more freedom of speech in their work as well as in East German society: the 4 November protests at Alexanderplatz (see Chapter 3) drew speeches from authors such as Hein, Wolf, Heym and Müller. Interestingly, after the Wall fell a few days later, Wolf appeared on television to try and persuade her fellow East Germans to stay and continue with the socialist project. In 1990 she also published *What Remains* (*Was bleibt*), a book written in the 1970s that criticised the regime (see Chapter 9), but which in turn received major criticism for appearing too late to be considered a credible critique and playing an overly victimised role. Such criticism intensified following revelations in 1993 that Wolf (as well as Müller and even 'underground' figures like Anderson and Rathenow) had cooperated with the Stasi, though her involvement has since been declared minimal and her reputation restored.

Writing about the city since 1989 has been a decidedly mixed bag. Katharina Gerstenberger, author of 2008's *Writing the New Berlin*, states that no one has quite written *the* reunification novel: rather (she claims), there have been a multifaceted number of takes that form an aptly diverse patchwork of perspectives. German writers from both East and West – Ingo Schulze, Thomas Brussig, Peter Schneider, even Günter Grass – have naturally been inclined to write about the decades of division. Many, like Schneider's *The Wall Jumper*, have been earnest meditations, but others, such as Thomas Brussig's *Heroes Like Us* (*Helden wie wir*, 1996) have used satire as a tool to approach the past (in the book, one of the characters claims the real reason the border guards began allowing people to pass through the Wall was because someone showed them his unusually large genitalia).

Travel writer Jan Morris (born 1926) was one of the international authors who travelled to the city shortly after 1989 (and quite often before), describing her impressions of the reunited city in the collection *A Writer's World* (2003):

> Liberty is in the very air of Berlin now. It is good to be alive here, and to be young must be heaven. Everything is in flux, everything is changing, new horizons open, and nothing demands unqualified

respect or allegiance. Although half of Berlin is the theoretical headquarters of the about-to-be-disbanded and thoroughly discredited People's Republic of East Germany, the city is not really the headquarters of anything much, and this gives it a stimulating sense of irresponsibility. Tokens of fun abound, indeed, and none are more endearing than the preposterous little Trabant cars, like goblin cars, that swarm out of east Berlin for a night out or some shopping in the West, with hilarious clankings and wheezings of their primitive engines, and faces smiling from every window.

The last 25 years have seen yet another huge influx of German and foreign writers into the city, many of whom have used its broader past as a muse and a strategy for exploring the contemporary city: Chloe Aridjis's *Book of Clouds*, Anna Winger's *This Must Be the Place* and Ida Hattemer-Higgins's *History of History* all belong to this category, as do works by German authors such as Uwe Timm (*Midsummer's Night*), Wolfgang Herrndorf (*Why We Took the Car*) and David Wagner (*What Colour Has Berlin?*).

The city's burgeoning multiracial demographic has been reflected in a growing number of immigrant and expat writers based here, ranging from Russian-born Wladimir Kaminer, British writers Priya Basil and Clare Wigfall, American playwright C. J. Hopkins and Jewish poet Admiel Kosman. The large Turkish and Middle Eastern community in Berlin has also produced many writers and artists engaging with the situation of second- and third-generation immigrants in the German capital, Yadé Kara, Emine Özdamar and Dilek Güngör among them.

It is impossible to predict what the future will bring, especially in a city with a history like Berlin's. But right now the island-city on the Spree is host to a prolific independent literary scene in many languages and seems as open to writers, dreamers, immigrants and their ideas as it always has been.

🐻 2 🐻

MITTE: THE ROYAL CITY

The Royal Palace

Anyone visiting central Berlin up until 2018 – and likely much later than that – won't fail to notice the large construction site opposite the historic Lustgarten. Covering a vast swathe of ground on what is today known as the Museum Island, the agglomeration of grey concrete, abundant scaffolding and swooping cranes represents the controversial rebuilding of the city's Royal Palace, which stood in this location for over five centuries.

The palace, perhaps more than any other local building, provides a portal into Berlin's broader history. Its foundations were laid in 1443 by Frederick II, a.k.a. 'Irontooth', on what was then the modest

1   *Berlin's historic Altes Museum and Lustgarten*

island-city of Cölln. Frederick II, prince-elector of the margraviate of Brandenburg and a member of the house of Hohenzollern, moved into the palace when it was completed in 1451, ostensibly to control the trade routes passing through the city and to impose some authority on a community of merchants and peasants that already had a reputation for being 'troublesome'.

Many of the palace's owners – who have ranged from Brandenburg electors and Prussian kings to German emperors – have adapted or extended the building. Two restructurings have been particularly significant: in the early sixteenth century, Margrave Joachim II ordered the demolition of the original structure and commissioned Caspar Theiss to rebuild it in a grander Italian Renaissance style; and in the early eighteenth century it underwent another thorough rebuilding courtesy of royal architect Andreas Schlüter, who created the Protestant baroque version between 1699 and 1705 – the design on which the new replica is based. One of the earliest reports of a visit to the palace dates back to December 1785, and was printed – anonymously – in an edition of the *Edinburgh Magazine of Literary Miscellany*: 'The Royal Palace, old as it is, has no bad appearance; its court, however, is not to be entered; and it is very ill-judged to leave that side to the Spree to stand as it does, it is not presenting an object considerable enough for the great open view of it from the water.'

This visit came at the end of the reign of Prussia's most famous and enlightened ruler, King Frederick II of Prussia, otherwise known as Frederick the Great, the 'Philosopher King' or, more casually, 'Alter Fritz' (Old Fritz). A notoriously multifaceted personality, he played the flute, loved the arts and had a long-term friendship with French philosopher Voltaire, but also possessed a fearsome military prowess that won many victories and greatly enhanced Prussia's standing in Europe. Although he mostly resided in his Potsdam palace at Sanssouci, it was also Frederick who laid out the plan for the Friedrichsstadt and created the Forum Fridericianum (see below).

Half a century or so later, in March 1848, crowds gathered outside the palace to demand certain civil liberties, including a constitution, liberal reform and German unification. In an attempt to avoid carnage of the kind that had recently occurred in Paris and Vienna, Frederick William IV came out to appease the crowds with conciliatory proclamations, which seemed to work, until shots were fired in the air; the ensuing panic prompted palace troops to charge the crowd. The subsequent revolution lasted a couple of days, until – on 21 March – the king grudgingly accepted some of the demands of the revolutionaries, including allowing Prussia to become part of a unified German nation, and appointing a new ministry. His address, issued on the evening of the same day and called 'To My People and to the German Nation', included the words:

> Germany is in ferment within, and exposed from without to danger from more than one side. Deliverance from this danger can come only from the most intimate union of the German princes and people under a single leadership [...] I have taken this leadership upon me for the hour of peril [...] I have today assumed the old German colours, and placed Myself and My people under the venerable banner of the German Empire. Prussia henceforth is merged into Germany.

By the end of 1848 the wily monarch had dissolved the new parliament, used his army to crush any remaining insurgents and reversed pretty much all of the revolutionaries' advances. By 1851 even the Basic Rights for the German People, which proclaimed equal rights for all citizens before the law, had been mostly abolished; many of the so-called '48ers who hadn't been executed or thrown into prison left for America.

It wasn't until 1871 that Germany was finally unified by King William I and Otto von Bismarck. The King was accordingly elevated to emperor (Kaiser), Bismarck became Germany's first chancellor, and Berlin's population swelled from around 800,000 in the 1860s to 2 million by the early 1900s. The capital threw itself into its new role as head of the empire, fuelled by major advances in industry, science and culture. Kaiser William II, who reigned throughout much of this period (1888–1918) was devoted to making Berlin into a *Weltstadt* – one that would be 'recognised as the most beautiful in the world' – though his staunchly conservative taste generated mostly ultra-conservative buildings and pompous Prussian monuments.

Despite the construction of the Reichstag (German parliament) in 1894, the Stadtschloss (City Palace) remained the key symbol of the German Empire for some time, as well as a popular tourist attraction. In her 1911 guidebook *Peeps at Great Cities: Berlin*, English travel writer and cookbook author Edith Siepen describes her visit:

> At the end of the Unter den Linden is the Emperor's Castle, the Schloss, an imposing building where, during the Berlin season, all the Court functions are held. The Schloss stands boldly out upon the street. There is no garden to speak of; the only place that could be called by that name extends along the side of the river, which is the most ancient part of the building. The Schloss contains over 700 rooms altogether. The floors of the rooms being all highly polished, walking boots would scratch them, and therefore all visitors are compelled to don huge felt slippers. It is great fun shuffling across the big rooms, and, of course, when the guide is not looking, everyone yields to a temptation to slide.

By 9 November of that year, tensions between the European powers had grown to the extent that the cofounder of the Social Democratic Party, August Bebel, felt compelled to issue his starkly prescient warning in the Reichstag. 'There will be a catastrophe. Sixteen to 18 million men, the flower of different nations, will march against each other, equipped with lethal weapons [...] I am convinced that this great march will be followed by the great collapse.' To the subsequent roars of laughter, he responded: 'All right, you have laughed about it, but it will come. What will be the result? After this war, we will have mass bankruptcy, mass misery, mass unemployment and great famine.' As if to prove Bebel right, just three years later – on 31 July 1914 – the Kaiser was out on the Royal Balcony of the palace, declaring war:

A momentous hour has struck for Germany. Envious rivals everywhere force us to legitimate defence. The sword has been forced into our hands. I hope that in the event that my efforts to the very last moment do not succeed in bringing our opponents to reason and in preserving peace, we may use the sword, with the help of God, so that we may sheathe it again with honor. War will demand enormous sacrifices by the German people, but we shall show the enemy what it means to attack Germany. And so I commend you to God. Go forth into the churches, kneel down before God, and implore his help for our brave army.

Four years and approximately 37 million military and civic casualties later, a defeated Germany was seeking an armistice. Calls for Kaiser William II to abdicate grew in intensity until the decision was announced on his behalf by Chancellor Prince Max von Baden. On that day in 1918 – again on 9 November, historically a fateful day for Germany often referred to as Schicksalstag, Day of Fate – diplomat, writer and art patron Count Harry Kessler noted the event in his diaries (*Berlin in Lights, 1918–1937*, 1971):

The Emperor has abdicated. Revolution has won the day in Berlin. On the strength of my new papers, I passed the barrier on the Potsdamer Platz and walked in the direction of the Palace, from which the sound of isolated shots still came. Leipziger Strasse was deserted, Friedrichstrasse fairly full of its usual *habitués*, Unter den Linden opposite the Opera in darkness. The Schinkel Guard Room was brilliantly lit, with clouds of smoke and lots of soldiers. The white stone figures of naked warriors and victory goddesses had the Schlossbrücke to themselves. Lights burned brightly but desultory in one or another part of the Palace; everything was quiet. Patrols all around; they challenged and let me through. In front of the Imperial Stables a good deal of splintered masonry. A sentry told me that 'young rascals' are still hidden in the Palace and the Stables. Slowly I made my way home. So closes this first day of revolution which has witnessed in a few hours the downfall of the Hohenzollerns, the dissolution of the German Army, and the end of the old order of society in Germany. One of the most memorable and dreadful days in German history.

As is clear from the entry above, the Kaiser's abdication led to immediate and general chaos. In the subsequent scramble for power, leader of the Social Democratic Party (SPD) Philipp Scheidemann spontaneously announced a new German republic from the Reichstag; he did so due to an insider tip-off about Spartacist leader Karl Liebknecht's plan – executed a couple of hours later from the palace's Royal Balcony – to declare a Free Socialist Republic (Freie Sozialistische Republik). Fighting broke out between left-wing groups and troops supporting the new republic, and in December 1918 the palace briefly served as a makeshift headquarters for Communist troops, before being cleared by republican soldiers.

Between 30 December 1918 and 1 January 1919 the left-wing parties, led by Rosa Luxemburg, Liebknecht and others, formed the KPD (Kommunistische Partei Deutschlands or German Communist Party), which was committed to an armed revolution. Their resultant uprising in January 1919 was again crushed by the SPD government of Friedrich Ebert, again with the help of the remnants of the Imperial German Army and militias (Freikorps), and this time Liebknecht and Luxemburg were interrogated, tortured and murdered (see later in this chapter), prompting an incensed statement from none other than V. I. Lenin on 21 January:

> Today the bourgeoisie and the social-traitors are jubilating in Berlin – they have succeeded in murdering Karl Liebknecht and

Rosa Luxemburg. Ebert and Scheidemann, who for four years led the workers to the slaughter for the sake of depredation, have now assumed the role of butchers of the proletarian leaders. The example of the German revolution proves that 'democracy' is only a camouflage for bourgeois robbery and the most savage violence. Death to the butchers!

The Weimar Republic – memorably summed up by historian Peter Gay as an era 'born in defeat, lived in turmoil, and died in disaster' – nonetheless continued. Following the appointment of Ebert as leader, its constitution was ratified in the eponymous city – where the poets Goethe and Schiller had once lived – establishing a federal republic of 19 states. Since there was little use for the palace without a royal Kaiser or king, it was used by subsequent regimes, including the Nazis and the GDR, for a variety of other uses: receptions and state functions but also for exhibitions and other cultural purposes.

In 1950 Walter Ulbricht, then head of state of the Socialist Unity Party of Germany (Sozialistische Einheitspartei Deutschlands, or SED), ordered the structure to be demolished on the grounds that it represented an awkward, ugly and ultimately unwanted reminder of Prussian militarism. The only preserved section was the balcony from which Liebknecht had given his speech, which was incorporated into the Staatsratsgebäude (Council of State building) that initially took the palace's place; the balcony can today be found embedded in the European School of Management and Technology, just behind the current palace building site.

The war-damaged Stadtschloss was eventually replaced in the mid-1970s by the GDR's own version of a palace: the box-shaped, glass-and-steel Palast der Republik (Palace of the Republic), commissioned by Ulbricht's successor Erich Honecker. The polar opposite of what the Stadtschloss had symbolised, the Palast der Republik housed the East German parliament and also served as a cultural centre and featured a surprisingly lavish, high-tech interior:

marble floors in the foyer, an assortment of restaurants, a theatre and a *Jugendtreff* (youth club) were all a part of the multifaceted structure – though the building's most famous aspect were arguably its 10,000 or so lights, which earned the palace the sarcastic nickname Erichs Lampenladen (Erich's Lamp Shop). Ironically, one of the Palast der Republik's last major events was the moment, in August 1990, when the GDR accepted the West German constitution; the palace's in-house studios were even used to film and record the occasion.

After the fall of the Wall and the demise of the GDR, the question of what to do with the building began to take shape. A large number of Berliners – from East and West, including several high-profile German theatre and film directors – campaigned to keep the structure, though many others felt it was not only a sore reminder of a defunct regime but also a good opportunity to avenge the GDR's destruction of the Royal Palace. In the end, the discovery of between 5,500 and 7,700 tonnes of carcinogenic asbestos provided a strong enough argument for its demolition.

Before it was fully demolished, the Palast became a site for experiments and ideas by the local creative community. Frank Castorf, the *enfant terrible* of Berlin's theatre scene, staged a production of Döblin's *Berlin Alexanderplatz* (see Chapter 3) inside it in 2005. The year before, another art group created a performance called *The Façade Republic*, which involved flooding the building's ground floor with 300,000 litres of water that visitors could drift through in white inflatable boats; guests were even provided with fishing rods that they used to catch floating trays of sushi.

The Palast der Republik was ordered to be fully destroyed in January 2006, though since the asbestos made it too dangerous to demolish quickly it wasn't completely torn down until 2008. In her award-winning 2003 book *Stasiland* (see Chapter 10), for which she interviewed citizens of the GDR and ex-Stasi men, Australian author Anna Funder describes how the Communist relic looked:

It is brown and plastic-looking, full of asbestos, and all shut up. It is not clear whether the fence around it is to protect it from people who would like to express what they thought of the regime, or to protect the people from the Palast, for health reasons. The structure is one long rectangular metal frame, made up of smaller rectangles of brown-tinted mirror glass. When you look at it you can't see in. Instead, the outside world and everything in it is reflected in a bent and brown way.

The subsequent decision to rebuild the Stadtschloss (or part of it), though approved by the Berlin Senate, did not originally stem from official sources. Rather, it was the idea of a tractor salesman from Pomerania, Wilhelm von Boddien, who visited East Berlin in 1961 and was disconcerted to see the dilapidated state of the former Prussian capital. As he told the *Daily Telegraph* in 2013, he had been 'expecting to see a great capital, but I found myself in a demolished city. The whole city was gone, there were ruins everywhere. They had destroyed it to make a pure socialist city. I saw a pile of rubble and asked the people what used to be there. And they told me that was the palace.'

Von Boddien became increasingly obsessed with the idea of rebuilding the Hohenzollern palace. Following years of personal research, he met a group of scholars at the end of the 1970s who were compiling extensive documentation about the Schloss. His plans gathered new momentum and were eventually picked up by the media and became a mainstream topic that more or less split Berlin officials and the general public alike. According to Berlin author Peter Schneider, a turning-point came when von Boddien managed to raise funds – several million euros, by all accounts – for an enormous painted façade of the old palace to be mounted on scaffolding at its former site, which showed the public how such a grandiose project might look. As Schneider recalls in his 2014 non-fiction book *Berlin Now*:

The effect of the faux facade was especially powerful and romantic at night, in the light of the half-moon, billowing outward or curving inward, depending on the direction of the wind [...] even notorious Prussian-haters had to admit: the Schloss was not quite as ugly as they had imagined during the long period of its absence. In any event, its western facade looked significantly better than a great deal of what modern architects had built between Potsdamer Platz and the city centre after German reunification.

In the end, a compromise of sorts has been reached in that only three sides of the original palace façade are being rebuilt. Inside, a modern interior will host a mix of academic and art institutions provided by the Prussian Cultural Heritage Foundation, the Humboldt University of Berlin and the Federal State of Berlin, with the unifying theme of Germany's relationship to the rest of the world. The question of who will foot the remaining costs of the 590 million euro project, however, remains unanswered.

Just across from the palace site is the outsized Berliner Dom (Berlin Cathedral), which actually began as a much smaller Catholic chapel within the palace. The current baroque building, built in 1905 on the site of several earlier buildings (including the St Erasmus Chapel and an earlier Neoclassical design by Karl Friedrich Schinkel), was designed by Julius Raschdorff as a Protestant counterpart to St Peter's Basilica in Rome. The cathedral's imposing dome offers an impressive collection of intricate mosaics (as well as stellar views), while the basement hosts 90 sarcophagi from the Hohenzollern family crypt.

Next to the Dom is the equally historic Lustgarten (Pleasure Garden). Created in 1573 as a fruit and herb garden belonging to the palace, 'Great Elector' Frederick William turned it into an ornate pleasure garden for his wife Luise in the seventeenth century. It was transformed into a military parade ground by Frederick William I (the 'Soldier King') before being turned back into a garden and park at the end of the eighteenth century by Frederick William II. After the establishment of a museum built by Karl Friedrich Schinkel (now known as the Altes Museum), the Lustgarten was renovated yet again by landscape architect Peter Joseph Lenné. Throughout the twentieth century, the area was used both for various recreational and political purposes, from May Day gatherings to the mass rallies of the Nazis, where crowds of over a million were addressed by the likes of minister for propaganda and district administrator (*Gauleiter*) Joseph Goebbels.

But the Lustgarten was a site of Nazi resistance too. Not only were some of the last mass protests against the Nazis held here in 1933, but in 1942 an underground Jewish resistance group led by Herbert Baum launched an arson attack on a Nazi propaganda exhibition here. The act was only partially successful, however, and over 30 young men and women were subsequently rounded up; most were guillotined at Plötzensee prison, though Baum was tortured to death in Moabit prison (see Chapter 7). A granite block designed by Jürgen Raue and erected in 1981 in the southeastern corner of the Lustgarten memorialises Baum and the event. A more general protest against war also took place here in 2010 when Chilean art collective Casagrande, in collaboration with Literaturwerkstatt Berlin, organised a helicopter to drop 100,000 poems over the garden. The performance was called *Poetry Rain* (*Regen der Gedichte*).

The Lustgarten today serves as an entry to the five museums collectively known as the UNESCO-heritage Museum Island. The first of these museums, the Schinkel-built Altes Museum mentioned above, is located directly opposite the palace and frames the Lustgarten. Known initially as the Royal Museum, it was commissioned in 1810 by King Frederick William III to showcase Prussian art treasures to the public – the first of its kind in Germany. The Neues Museum (New Museum), which housed Egyptian and prehistoric collections, followed in 1859; the Alte Nationalgalerie (Old National Gallery), for nineteenth-century German and European paintings, in 1876; the baroque Bode

Museum, renowned for its sculpture collection and Byzantine art, in 1904; and Alfred Mussel's Pergamon Museum, built to house artefacts from the nineteenth-century excavations in Pergamon and Asia Minor, finalised the ensemble in 1930.

German artist Käthe Kollwitz (see Chapter 10) recorded a 1911 visit to a couple of the museums in her diary, published as *The Diary and Letters of Käthe Kollwitz* in 1988:

> Incidentally, I went to the Old Museum yesterday. The depressing amount of half-good stuff, even in sculpture, was such a letdown that I told myself I'd run over to the National Gallery and see something really good for a change. And it was really very nice. Since the lower rooms are being redone they have pretty much assembled the elite in the big hall upstairs with its overhead light. Menzel, Boecklin, Feuerbach, Truebner, Thomas, Liebermann. Then I went up to the French artists, and in the very first room – which holds the famous Rodin bust – I began to regret my having signed Vinnen's protest. For here I saw French art once more represented in really good works and I said to myself that come what may, German art needs the fructifying Romance element.

Nearly 70 per cent of the Museum Island buildings were destroyed during the Second World War. After the war, the collections were split between East and West Berlin before being brought back together again after reunification, when the whole museum complex was redesigned. One of the main crowd-pullers today is the monumental Pergamon Museum, which contains Greek, Roman and Babylonian antiquities, including the Ishtar Gate of Babylon, the market gate of Miletus and the jaw-droppingly enormous Pergamon Altar. Irish writer Hugo Hamilton describes a visit to the Pergamon Museum in his 2014 novel *Every Single Minute* (see Chapter 4):

> The Pergamon Altar is great. I know the Nazis loved it, she says, let's not forget that. But that doesn't stop you admiring the sheer

size of it, like a city inside a huge room. It makes you feel small and powerless. The altar with the wide marble steps and the temple at the top is only a tiny fragment of the city, you can check that on the scale model. And around the walls are these marble carvings showing what people were up to in those days. Figures of semi-naked men and women. Some peaceful scenes, women bathing, children playing, men carrying fruit. And war, plenty of war. Arms and legs missing, never found or reattached by archaeologists. Horses with missing heads. Chariots. People in rage. People in agony. A lion biting into the leg of a man, that sort of thing.

Unter den Linden and Brandenburger Tor

Berlin's most famous boulevard, Unter den Linden, was laid out between the Royal Palace and Tiergarten park in 1647, originally as a bridle path for 'Soldier King' Frederick William. Named for

2 *One of the city's biggest icons, the Brandenburger Tor (Brandenburg Gate)*

the *Linden* (lime) trees that line it on both sides, the street today is largely a postwar facsimile of the original, intended to recall its nineteenth-century heyday – though the endless throngs of traffic, tourists and construction sites along its 1.6-kilometre length tend to diminish the grandeur of the reconstructed Neoclassical buildings somewhat.

One of the first literary reports on the boulevard and surroundings was written in 1764, by Scottish lawyer, diarist and author James Boswell:

> I was struck with the Beauty of Berlin. The Houses are handsome and the streets wide long and strait. The Palace is grand. The Palaces of some of the Royal family are very genteel. The Opera-House is an elegant Building with this Inscription: Fridericus Rex Apollini et Musis. At night we sauntered in a sweet walk under a grove of Chestnut-trees by the side of a beautiful Canal.

The Opera House in question was built as the Royal Opera between 1741 and 1743 according to a design by Georg Wenceslaus von Knobelsdorff. Part of the annex to the Forum Fridericianum, it was the first free-standing opera house in Germany as well as the largest in Europe. After it burned down in 1843, it was redesigned by Carl Ferdinand Langhans – the architect behind the Brandenburg Gate – only to be levelled again during the Second World War. Rebuilt by the GDR in the 1950s (according to the Knobelsdorff design), it was renovated again in the 1980s and is undergoing yet more refurbishments currently, with an anticipated reopening date of 2018 (official tours of the site are possible in the meantime).

Over its long existence, the venue has been graced by a veritable who's who of world-famous personalities, from Berliners like Giacomo Meyerbeer, Wilhelm Furtwängler and Felix Mendelssohn Bartholdy to Richard Strauss, Otto Klemperer and Herbert von Karajan. On 19 October 1777, diplomat Nathaniel Wraxall also waxed lyrical about the Opera House, as well as the Royal Palace and other stately buildings in the area. His feelings about Unter den Linden overall, though, were decidedly mixed:

> In the centre of Berlin, a stranger finds himself completely surrounded by a groupe [*sic.*] of palaces or public buildings, of the most striking kind. Several owe their construction to the present King; and on the front of the Opera House, which he built at the beginning of his reign, we read the short and classic inscription affixed by himself, 'Fredericus Rex, Apollini, et Musis.' His universal and creative genius has however been constantly intent on maintaining the spirit of military enthusiasm, in the midst of peace, and among all the display of architecture, taste, or magnificence. We never cease to recollect that we are in a country, where from the sovereign to the peasant every man is born a soldier. But it is in the Garrison Church, that those feelings are peculiarly awakened, animated, and called into action. If, however, Berlin strikes by its regularity and the magnificence of its public buildings, it impresses not less forcibly with a sentiment of melancholy. It is neither enriched by commerce, enlivened by the general residence of the Sovereign, nor animated by industry, business, and freedom. An air of silence and dejection reigns in the streets, where at noon-day scarcely any passengers are seen except soldiers. The population, much as it has augmented during the present reign, is still very unequal to the extent and magnitude of the city. Ostentation and vanity, more than utility or necessity, seem to have impelled Frederic to enlarge and embellish his capital. The splendid fronts of the finest houses frequently conceal poverty and wretchedness.

As Hamburg-based author Brian Melican notes in his 2014 book *Germany: Beyond the Enchanted Forest: A Literary Anthology* (from which the above quote is taken), 'despite Berlin's growing political and economic importance, without a magnetic figure like Frederick and without a unified German state, German cultural life remained elsewhere: in Weimar, in Dresden, on the Rhine. Writers like William Makepeace Thackeray, Herman Melville, and Elisabeth Gaskell all headed for the country's older destinations.' Indeed, it wasn't until 1854 that another international author felt compelled to write about the royal boulevard. Britain's George Eliot recorded the following in her memoirs (published as *The Journals of George Eliot* in 1999):

> We used often to turn out for a little walk in the evening, when it was not too cold, to refresh ourselves by a little pure air as a change from the stove-heated room. Our favourite walk was along the Linden, in the broad road between the trees. We used to pace to old Fritz's monument, which loomed up dark and mysterious against the sky. Once or twice we went along the gas-lighted walk towards Kroll's. One evening in our last week, we went on to the bridge leading to the Friedrichstadt, and there by moon and gas light saw the only bit of picturesqueness Berlin afforded us. The outline of the Schloss towards the water is very varied, and a light in one of the windows near the top of a tower was a happy accident. The row of houses on the other side of the water was shrouded in indistinctness, and no ugly object marred the scene. The next day, under the light of the sun, it was perfectly prosaic.

Although the best-known 'residents' of Unter den Linden have always been the various kings and kaisers that occupied the Royal Palace, several other luminaries – including writers – have lived on or close to the famous street over the centuries. Heinrich von Kleist (see Chapter 5) lived at Mauerstrasse 53 and, from 1850, Swiss writer Gottfried Keller lived for a few years at Mohrenstrasse 6. In the winter of 1891–2, Mark Twain (real name Samuel Langhorne Clemens) took up residence with his family at Unter den Linden's Hotel Royal – an establishment so upscale it deemed beer 'too vulgar' a drink to serve to its guests.

According to Andreas Austilat in *A Tramp in Berlin* (2013), the Clemens family stayed in an 'eight-suite room […] six bedchambers, one dining room and one parlor, where the family arrived on December 31, at 1:30pm.' The room allegedly offered a fabulous view of Unter den Linden, the Brandenburg Gate, and the palaces, fountains and gardens on Pariser Platz. Austilat notes that Twain was already well known in Berlin, to the extent that ordinary Berliners would occasionally greet him on the street. While in the city, Twain mingled in celebrity circles, met the Kaiser and became close friends with local writer Rudolf Lindau, a diplomat of Jewish-German descent who wrote more than a dozen novels in German, as well as several in French and English.

In his story 'Berlin, the Chicago of Europe' – in which he enthuses about the city's many attractive qualities – Twain mentions Unter den Linden while discussing its vast amount of open space – an aspect of the city that residents and visitors still often remark on today:

> There is no other city, in any other country, whose streets are so generally wide. Berlin is not merely a city of wide streets, it is the city of wide streets. As a wide-street city it has never had its equal, in any age of the world. Unter den Linden is three streets in one; the Potsdamer Strasse is bordered on both sides by sidewalks which are themselves wider than some of the historic thoroughfares of the old European capitals.

Twain referred to this middle strip, where only the Kaiser was allowed to ride, as the 'Holy Land', writing in his notes that 'all the horses seem to be of a fine breed; though I am not an expert in horses & do not speak with assurance. I can always tell which is the front end of a horse, but beyond that my art is not above the ordinary.' Twain's wife, Clara Clemens, wrote in her biography that she felt 'perfectly happy' in her new home. She would often 'stand at the window and watch the emperor, Kaiser Wilhelm II, and his entourage leave every morning from the castle, ride along the Linden and then exit through the Brandenburger Gate into the Tiergarten'.

But if Twain was decidedly impressed by Berlin overall, English writer Jerome K. Jerome, who visited in the 1890s, was relatively unmoved – even by the Opera House:

[I]ts centre is overcrowded, its outlying parts lifeless, its one famous street, Unter den Linden, an attempt to combine Oxford Street with the Champs Elysée, singularly unimposing, being much too wide for its size; its theatres dainty and charming, where acting is considered of more importance than scenery or dress, where long runs are unknown, successful pieces being played again and again, but never consecutively, so that for a week running you may go to the same Berlin theatre and see a fresh play every night; its opera house unworthy of it; its two music halls, with an unnecessary suggestion of vulgarity and commonness about them, ill-arranged and much too large for comfort.

By the end of the First World War, the glamour of the monarchy had come to an end and Unter den Linden – and the city in general – took on an entirely different aura. Colin Storer, in his *Britain and the Weimar Republic: The History of a Cultural Relationship* (2010), recounts English poet, novelist and essayist Sir Stephen Harold Spender as saying that prostitution was so common among young girls throughout the city during these years that 'one of the stone lions placed outside the palace roared every time a virgin walked by.' He added that the Berlin visitor should remain wary, however, because 'at nights along the Unter den Linden it was never possible to know whether it was a woman or a man in women's clothes that accosted one.'

It wasn't long before the clacking heels of the prostitutes were replaced with the leather jackboots of the Nazis, who staged one of their first high-profile spectacles – the so-called 'burning of the books' on 10 May 1933. The event took place on what is now Bebelplatz but was then was known colloquially as Opernplatz, a reference to the aforementioned Opera House, which still sits on the square. The burnings were actually initiated by the German Student Association and had got underway a few days before with the emptying of the library of the Institut für Sexualwissenschaft, a non-profit gay rights organisation, into the square. The 10 May burnings, attended by many of the Nazi faithful including the Nazi security forces, the SA and SS, and Hitler Youth, were preceded by a speech by Goebbels. The works of many notable German and Berlin writers went up in smoke, including Erich Maria Remarque, Heinrich Heine and Joseph Roth (see Chapter 4).

Today the site is marked by an installation by Israeli sculptor Micha Ullman, which consists of an underground library – viewed via a thick glass plate set into the square's cobbles – full of empty bookshelves that could hold the approximately 20,000 books that were burned here. Nearby lies another prescient quotation by Heinrich Heine, taken from his 1821 play *Almansor*: 'Das war ein Vorspiel nur. Dort, wo man Bücher verbrennt, verbrennt man am Ende auch Menschen' ('That was mere foreplay. Where they have burned books, they will end in burning human beings').

The 'last of the Romantics', poet and writer Heinrich Heine (1797–1856), came to Berlin in 1821 to study under the philosopher Hegel. His Berlin lodgings were at Taubenstrasse 32, not far from Bebelplatz and close to the Gendarmenmarkt. Heine also wrote his play *William Ratcliff* 'under the limes at Berlin in the last three days of January 1821, when the sun was shining with a certain lukewarm kindliness upon the snow-covered roofs, and the sad leafless trees'. Though Berlin did not feature much in his work, his *Letters from Berlin* (*Briefe aus Berlin*, 1822) serve as a literary testimony to his time here:

Berlin is in truth not a town. Berlin is merely a place whither a crowd of men – and many of them men of intellect – foregather, to whom the place is a matter of indifference: these men make the spiritual Berlin. The stranger, passing through, sees only the terraces of houses, one like unto another, and the long wide streets which are built in regular order, and for the most part to suit the caprice of one man, and give no sort of indication of the disposition of the masses. Only a Sunday's child gazing at the long rows of houses can guess the private feelings of the inhabitants, and the houses try to keep each other at a distance, glaring at each other in mutual distrust. Only once on a moon-light night, as I was returning late from Luther and Wegner, did I see that hard temper resolve itself into gentleness and tender melancholy, and the houses standing opposite each other so inimically, look at each other in true Christian fashion, touched by their dilapidation, and try to throw themselves into each other's arms in reconciliation: so that I, poor man, walked in the middle of the street, fearing to be squashed. There are many who will laugh at this fear of mine, and indeed I laughed at it myself when I walked through the same street the next morning and saw it in the cold light of day, and the houses gaping at each other again so stupidly.

During his relatively short time in Berlin (he left the city in 1823 again to continue studying in Göttingen), Heine was a frequent visitor to the salon of Rahel Antonie Friederike Varnhagen (née Levin), one of the primary meeting points at the time – along with the similar salons of Bettina von Armin and Henriette Herz (see Chapter 1) – for creative intellectuals. Varnhagen's salon took place in the attic space of Jägerstrasse 54–5, whose ground floor now hosts Michelin-starred restaurant Vau. It drew notable Berlin writers such as Adelbert von Chamisso, Baron Fouqué, Ludwig Tieck and Kleist, as well as scientists, philosophers and intellectuals such as Hegel and the Humboldt brothers.

Austrian poet and dramatist Franz Grillparzer recalls a visit to one of Rahel's salons in 1826 and hails her hostess qualities in his *Autobiography* (1853):

[T]hen the aging woman, who had perhaps never been pretty and was now bent over by illness, who resembled a fairy, if not a witch, began to speak and I was enchanted. My tiredness disappeared or rather, gave way to intoxication. She spoke and spoke almost until midnight, and I no longer know whether they chased me away or I left on my own. Never in my life have I heard anyone speak more interestingly or better.

Unter den Linden became one of the main locations for spectacles and marches as the Nazi grip tightened over the city.

When Harry Flannery visited the street during wartime (1941) for his *Assignment to Berlin*, he found a very different scenario:

Crowds milled up and down Unter den Linden, stopped to look in the store windows, and slowly wandered on their way. Almost every Sunday there were men and women on the streets rattling their little red boxes in collections for Winter Relief – a fund for the needy in a country where, with no unemployed, it did not seem logical that there should be anyone who required State aid. It was whispered that most of the money was used to pay the costs of the war. In any case, the Winter Relief collections were made for three days a week beginning Friday about every other week.

As I walked down Unter den Linden on this Sunday, German bands played on the island spaces between the two roadways, and figures in character, including comic cows and horses, danced to the music. Even hot wieners were offered for sale, if you surrendered fifty grams of meat marks to the women attending the temporary booths. People dressed in old-time costumes rode by in carriages and stopped at street corners to collect. Along the Linden, as I went by, the collectors were tall men dressed in tall hats and tight-fitting black clothes, carrying brooms to represent the German good-luck character, the chimney-sweep.

Although the Nazis did not use the Royal Palace much, they did make use of Unter den Linden's Kronprinzpalais (Crown

Prince Palace). Located opposite the Neue Wache, a Neoclassical, Schinkel-designed guardhouse for the Crown Prince's troops built in 1816, and overlooking the Schlossbrücke, the palace was built in 1663. Initially used as a private residence, it was acquired by the Hohenzollerns in the 1700s, who used it for the family's crown princes until their accession to the throne; Kaiser William II was born on its top floor (his father, Frederick William, was still crown prince at the time).

Following the fall of the German monarchy the palace was renamed the Galerie der Lebenden (Gallery of the Living), and used to display works by living contemporary artists. One of the first such museums in the world, it is reckoned to have inspired the New York Museum of Modern Art. In 1938 the building was used by the Nazis to host their infamous Degenerate Art exhibition. Featuring 650 works of art – all confiscated from German museums – the exhibition, which started out in Munich and drew over a million viewers in its first few weeks, declaimed such modernist artworks as facile, decadent and insulting to the idea of German nationality. One of the few 'normal' eyewitness reports of the exhibition was recorded by Berliner Franz Göll, whose memoirs were posthumously transformed into a book – *The Turbulent World of Franz Göll* – by author Peter Fritzsche and published in 2011. 'Standing in front of Otto Dix's famous triptych on war,' writes Fritzsche, Göll made an extraordinary declaration that turned the aim of the exhibit on its head: 'The picture is not a bloody-minded depiction of the degenerate, war is.'

In the 1960s, the façade of the partially destroyed palace was rebuilt and the interior remodelled in the GDR's Socialist Realist style. Used as a guesthouse for visiting GDR dignitaries before the Wall fell, it hosted the signing of the Reunification Treaty between the two Germanies on 31 August 1990. Today the building is used again for cultural events.

After the war, Unter den Linden wound up in the Soviet sector, and was therefore not visited by too many international writers. Nor was it particularly appealing to GDR writers, although East German author Christa Wolf did write a story entitled *Unter den Linden* (1969), in which her (dreaming) narrator takes a *flâneur*-esque stroll along the street. In the story, she meets various characters from East Berlin's intellectual milieu as she ruminates on grand themes such as love and betrayal:

> It has never bothered me that the street is famous, not during my waking hours and most certainly not in my dreams. I am aware that it has suffered the misfortune on account of its location: East–West axis. This street and the one appearing in my dreams have nothing in common. The one is abused by newspaper pictures and tourists' photographs in my absence.

Wolf (1929–2011) was one of the most important writers of the GDR and a controversial key protagonist of Socialist Realist writing. Born in Landsberg an der Warthe (Gorzów Wielkopolski in Poland today), she studied in Jena and Magdeburg. A staunch supporter of Socialism throughout her life, Wolf joined the GDR Socialist Unity Party in 1949 (which she only left in 1989, six months before the Wall fell) and also worked as an informant for the GDR Stasi from 1959 to 1961. Establishing herself as a writer early on, in 1963 with the publication of *Divided Heaven* (*Der geteilte Himmel*), she moved to Berlin in 1976. Wolf was also allowed to visit the USA in the early 1970s, and in 1977 was one of the signatories of a letter protesting the expulsion of political songwriter Wolf Biermann from the GDR, resulting in her own exclusion from the GDR writers' association and herself being watched by the Stasi.

Her subsequent works included autobiographical works such as *The Quest for Christa T.* (*Nachdenken über Christa T.*, 1968), *Patterns of Childhood* (*Kindheitsmuster*, 1976), *No Space. Nowhere* (*Kein Ort. Nirgends*, 1979) and works addressing wider topics like trust and betrayal based on Greek mythology like *Kassandra* (1983) and *Medea* (1996).

At the western end of Unter den Linden the Berlin Wall, which was constructed in 1961, ran right past one of Berlin's most iconic structures: the Brandenburg Gate. Commissioned by Frederick William II, the gate was erected between 1788 and 1791 according to designs by Carl Gotthard Langhans, partly inspired by the Acropolis in Athens. The bronze quadriga – a four-horse chariot – driven by the winged goddess of peace that crowns the gate was created a little later, in 1793, by Johann Gottfried Schadow; it was carried to Paris by victorious French troops in 1806 but returned after Napoleon's defeat at the Battle of Waterloo, at which point an iron cross and eagle were added to the laurel wreath to celebrate victory.

It was after the occupation of Paris in 1814 that the square in front of the Brandenburg Gate was renamed Pariser Platz, which today is still lined with several notable buildings from previous eras. The townhouse at Pariser Platz 7 was the birthplace and family home of German-Jewish Impressionist painter Max Liebermann (see Chapter 5), who painted a host of Berlin luminaries here, including Theodor Fontane (see Chapter 8). It was from this house – owned by Liebermann's banker father – that the painter reportedly watched the Nazis celebrate their 1933 election victory by marching through the Brandenburg Gate and uttered his now-famous quote: 'Ich kann gar nicht soviel fressen, wie ich kotzen möchte' ('I cannot eat as much, as I would like to puke').

The townhouse was rebuilt after being destroyed in the war and now serves as a museum, archive and event space. On his fiftieth birthday, Liebermann was given a solo exhibition at the Prussian Academy of Arts in Berlin, which lies on the other side of the square and is now the Akademie der Künste (Academy of Arts). The academy was founded in 1696 by Crown Prince Frederick III of Brandenburg (later King Frederick I of Prussia) as an 'Academy of Painterly, Sculptural and Architectural Art', making it one of the oldest cultural institutions in Europe.

Today the glass-fronted venue is funded by the federal government, with an annual budget of around 18 million euros. Its current members include Bob Dylan, Ai WeiWei and Wim Wenders, and it continues to host an array of events and exhibitions, including concerts, lectures, readings and performances. The academy's archives include a 550,000-volume library and art collection that spans some 70,000 works and 1,200 artists' estates, including those of Bertolt Brecht, Günter Grass and Christa Wolf. It also awards prizes and scholarships, including several literary prizes such as the Heinrich Mann Award (for essay writing), the Alfred Döblin Prize, donated by Günter Grass in 1979, for unpublished literary works of an epic character, and an Alfred Döblin Scholarship.

The academy, along with the gate, were the only two structures still standing, albeit damaged, on Pariser Platz when the war ended. Though the gate was badly damaged, it was repaired in the 1950s by East Berlin, with West Berlin funding the reconstruction of the destroyed quadriga, whose iron cross and eagle were removed by the Communist regime as offensive Prussian symbols (they were added again after reunification). Up until the Wall was built, vehicles and pedestrians could travel freely through the gate, but after 1961 East Berliners and East Germans needed a hard-to-obtain exit visa in order to cross. During the Wall years, visitors to West Berlin came to climb the observation platform to get a glimpse of the world behind the Iron Curtain, and the gate continued to hold symbolic resonance for the city.

Many significant Cold War events took place here, from a mass demonstration by West Berliners just after the Wall went up (joined by West Berlin's governing mayor Willy Brandt), to Ronald Reagan demanding that Mikhail Gorbachov 'tear down this wall' in 1987. Two years later the Wall did indeed fall, though how much impact Reagan's speech had is moot; only around 45,000 Berliners turned out for Reagan's speech, compared to the 450,000 people who attended John F. Kennedy's 'Ich bin ein Berliner' speech in 1963. Nowadays the Pariser Platz and Brandenburg Gate are fully restored. Ignored by most locals, they are one of the top sights for many of the 11 million-plus tourists who descend on the city each year.

The Reichstag

Just beyond the Brandenburg Gate lies the Regierungsviertel, a cluster of government buildings including the Reichstag, that stretch along the Spree. It is apt that the Reichstag sits right at the opposite end of Unter den Linden from the Royal Palace, since it symbolised direct competition with the monarchy. To say Kaiser William II was opposed to a new building for the federal parliament is an understatement: he once said he would like to have all parliamentarian heads shrunk and displayed on poles.

Today's Reichstag actually rests on one of the city's more unlikely literary sites: that of the former Palais Raczynski, a city palace belonging to Polish nobleman Atanazy Raczyński, a Prussian envoy to Copenhagen, Lisbon and Madrid. The palace housed Raczyński's extensive art collection, which was sold to the German government along with the palace in 1882 by Raczyński's son. Raczyński was the author of a three-volume work called

3   *View across the Spree to the Reichstag and parts of the modernist Government Quarter (Regierungsviertel)*

History of the Newer German Art (*Geschichte der neueren deutschen Kunst*, 1836–41) and rented the upper floor of his palace to writer and salon-hostess Bettina von Armin.

The sister of Romantic poet Clemens Brentano and the wife of German poet and novelist Achim von Armin, Bettina von Arnim became chiefly famous for her correspondence with German author and poet Johann Wolfgang von Goethe, as well as her text *This Book Belongs to the King* (*Dies Buch gehört dem König*, 1843) – one of the first publications describing the human suffering brought about by Prussian industrialisation. From 1811 to 1848, von Armin hosted an important literary salon in a different home in Tiergarten, which was co-organised in later years by her daughter Maximiliane Marie Catharine; Bettina also acted as carer for her terminally ill literary friend Rahel Varnhagen.

The original Reichstag, whose 24-million-mark price tag was covered by French war reparations following the Franco-Prussian War (1870–1), was designed by Paul Wallot and dedicated in 1894, from which point on it became constantly caught up in the city's increasingly tumultuous political life. The inscription on the front of the building – 'Dem Deutschen Volke' ('To the German People') – was added in 1916. Despite being far too democratic a statement for the Kaiser, it was nonetheless allowed as a way of garnering popular support for the war effort underway at the time. As that war moving inexorably towards defeat for Germany, events in the Reichstag grew increasingly chaotic, exacerbated by an unusually deadly influenza pandemic in 1918, which infected some 500 million people across the world. Theodor Plievier, in his book *Berlin* (1969), describes a scene from the Reichstag in October 1918:

> A damp and cold day. Berlin was starving. There was no oil left for the lamps; the trams were clattering noisily and car tyres were worn smooth. You couldn't get anything – no soap, no tobacco, very little bread. Everything creaked, rattled, coughed and was on its last leg.

A war was drawing to its close.

The Kaiser's Empire was drawing to its close.

The twenty-year-old medical soldier looked from the visitors' gallery into the hall across the rows of Reichstag members – bent and shivering figures, many of them coughing; Berlin was in the grip of influenza. The new chancellor, who was making his opening speech, was almost inaudible. He, too, had the flu and could hardly speak. He was Prince Max von Baden.

One after the other stood at the Speaker's table. Hardly anybody listened. The representatives of the people were reading newspapers. Only once a gust of wind seemed to sweep through their rows. They jumped up from their seats and talked all at the same time, to neighbours and also across the rows. Only much later, from the published minutes, had Wustmann learned what that was all about. The collapse at the front, the desperate call for help from General Headquarters, and Wilson's Fourteen Points had been on the agenda. The speaker was Haase, an Independent, followed by representatives of the national minorities – Alsatians, Lotharingians, Poles and Danes.

Following the abdication of Kaiser William II a month later, SPD politician Philipp Scheidemann used the balcony of the Reichstag to proclaim a new German republic and deliver a largely improvised speech that ended with the immortal words: 'The old and rotten, the monarchy has collapsed. The new may live. Long live the German Republic!' The Reichstag subsequently became a battleground for the competing political parties, each of which had completely different visions for a future Germany. As the nobleman and scholar Erik von Kuehnelt-Leddihn wrote in 1943:

Catholic Centrists wanted to create conditions in Germany which would make it easier for the individuals to save their souls; Socialists denied the existence of souls and divided people into classes; the German Nationalists were interested in language and culture; while the National Socialists put the main stress on race. Whereas some looked at pocketbooks, others at the pigmentation of the skin or the index of the skull, fruitful discussions became impossible. When the speaker of one party indulged in his oratory, the others walked out. It was not worth while to listen to somebody's opinion when you knew that his premises were all wrong. The grim determination to silence the unconvincible enemy by execution or imprisonment already existed prior to 1933 in many parties.'

In its 15 years of existence, Weimar Germany elected and re-elected some 23 governments. In the 1928 election, the Nazi Party won just 12 seats, the smallest of the nine parties, but four years later the Nazis and the Communist Party, both of which openly hated the parliamentary system, held an absolute majority. Soon after the Nazis took power, on 27 February 1933, the Reichstag caught fire. To this day nobody knows the truth behind the event, but whether it was a genuine or manufactured attack – or even perhaps an accident – the Nazis were quick to invoke emergency powers and gain near-total authority. The day after the fire, the aristocrat, diplomat and author Count Kessler noted in his diaries:

Göring has immediately declared the entire Communist Party guilty of the crime and the SPD as being at least suspect. He has seized this heaven-sent, uniquely favourable opportunity to have the whole Communist Reichstag party membership as well as hundreds or even thousands of Communists all over Germany arrested and to prohibit publication of the entire Communist press for four weeks and of the Social Democratic Press for a fortnight. There appear to be no limits set to the continuation of arrests, prohibitions, house searches, and closure of Party offices. The operation proceeds to the tune of blood-thirsty speeches by Göring, which savour strongly of 'Stop, thief!'.

At the start of a four-year visit to Berlin, in July 1933, journalist Martha Dodd – whose father was a historian and US ambassador to Berlin – was shown the burned-out Reichstag and gained some first-hand insights into the early Third Reich milieu (she would later meet Adolf Hitler). She recounted the occasion in *My Years in Germany* (1940):

> I was put into a car with a young man who, I soon learned, was our Protocol secretary. I finally got the definition. He was pointing out the sights of Berlin to me. We drove around the Reichstag building, which he duly named. I exclaimed: 'Oh, I thought it was burned down! It looks all right to me. Tell me what happened.' He leaned over to me, after several such natural but indiscreet questions, and said, 'Shssh! Young lady, you must learn to be seen and not heard. You mustn't say so much and ask so many questions. This isn't America and you can't say all the things you think.' I was astonished, but subdued for the time being. This was my first contact with the reality of Germany under a dictatorship and it took me a long time to take his advice seriously. Long habits of life are hard to change overnight.

Mostly ignored throughout most of the Nazi era (when only some of the rooms of the building were used, as exhibition spaces or makeshift hospitals), the Reichstag was decimated during the Battle of Berlin by Soviet troops. Stalin had given specific orders to capture the building by 1 May (International Workers' Day); that battle alone claimed the lives of over 2,000 Soviet soldiers and even more Germans, but the photograph of a Red Army soldier hoisting the hammer-and-sickle flag on what was left of the Reichstag's dome instantly became an iconic symbol of German defeat and the end of the Second World War.

While the Brandenburg Gate ended up in East Berlin following the war, the ruins of the Reichstag lay in the West, with the Berlin Wall running between them from 1961 onwards. The capital of West Germany was moved to Bonn and the Reichstag more or less languished in its no-man's land, though occasional events were held on the Platz der Republik in front of the building. A memorable concert occurred on the 7 June 1987, a couple of months before Ronald Reagan's visit, when David Bowie played his song 'Heroes', which he had written on his three-year stay in Berlin during the 1970s. During the song he addressed, in German, the large crowd of East Germans who had gathered just a few metres away on the other side of the hated divide: 'We send our wishes to all our friends who are on the other side of the Wall.'

Following reunification, the decision was made to re-establish Berlin as the German capital and the Reichstag as the nation's parliamentary building. For the requisite overhaul, British architect Sir Norman Foster created a new glass dome whose transparency was intended as a symbol for the new German democracy. Visitors touring the building today can not only look right down onto the German parliament (Bundestag) and witness the war-era damage and Russian graffiti that Foster preserved in his renovations but also enjoy comprehensive views across the city and even *Kaffee und Kuchen* or a meal in the rooftop café-restaurant.

Tiergarten

Behind the imposing columns of the Brandenburg Gate lies Berlin's most extravagant and best-known green area: the Tiergarten. Spanning 2.5 square kilometres, it is one of the largest city parks in Germany – and offers 23 kilometres of pathways for strolling, jogging, cycling and roller-skating. Many of the Tiergarten's trees and gardens were cut down for firewood and food by freezing, hungry Berliners during the extreme postwar winters of 1946 and 1947, which were savage enough to kill over 1,000 people (and all remaining animals in the zoo). In 1955, the West Berlin government began to replant the Tiergarten, and it is those trees, shrubs and plants that visitors enjoy today.

The park was originally created as a private hunting ground for the electors of Brandenburg in 1530 and opened to the general public in 1742 thanks to Frederick the Great and the roads and throughways designed by George Wenzeslaus von Knobelsdorff. In 1818, in keeping with the vogue for English landscaped gardens, architect Peter Joseph Lenné was commissioned to landscape the park, and his designs still mostly shape the park today.

During the nineteenth century the park became a popular meeting place and muse for many writers. The Brothers Grimm (see Chapter 3) enjoyed long strolls beneath its lime, chestnut and oak trees, and the Romantic poet and playwright Emanuel Geibel (who coined the famous statement 'Am deutschen Wesen soll die Welt genesen' ('The German spirit shall heal the world'), which was misused by the Nazis), lived on its eastern side from 1836 to 1842, on what is Wilhelmstrasse today. In a letter written in 1837 he rhapsodised over his view of the park:

[T]o the west the Tiergarten with its countless treetops, which autumn had clad in the most colourful of garbs, to the south the castle of Prince Albrecht illuminated in dark gold by the morning sun between trees and wine tendrils; to the east and north there was nothing but wide Berlin preponderated by a white sea of fog with only the churches and towers rising from it like dark island fortresses.

The Tiergarten remained one of the most popular destinations for Berliners over subsequent decades, as testified by Robert Walser, whose 1911 story 'Tiergarten' was posthumously published in English in the *Berlin Stories* essay collection in 2012:

Ah, Berlin and its Tiergarten are so lovely just now. The park is overrun with people. The people are dark moving spots in the delicate, fleeting sun-shimmer. Up above is the pale-blue sky that touches, dreamlike, the green that lies below. The people walk softly and indolently, as if they feared they might otherwise slip into a marching step and act coarsely. There are said to be people to whom it would never occur – or who might be too prim – to sit on a bench in the Tiergarten on a Sunday. Such people are robbing themselves of the most enchanting pleasure. I myself find the crowd on a Sunday in all its obvious, harmless Sunday pleasure-seeking more significant than any journey to Cairo or the Riviera. Hardness becomes obliging, rigidity dulcet, and all lines, all commonplaces blur dreamily together. A universal strolling like this is ineffably tender. The walkers lose themselves – now one by one, now in graceful, tightly knit clusters and groups – among the trees whose high branches are still breezily bare, and between the low bushes that constitute a breath of young, sweet green. The soft air trembles and quivers with buds that seem to sing, to dance, to hover. The image of the Tiergarten as a whole is like a painted picture, then like a dream, then like a circuitous, agreeable kiss.

Walser (1878–1956), a man called 'the most unattached of all solitary poets' by unrelated namesake and contemporary German author Martin Walser, was a quiet and somewhat tragic figure. Born in Switzerland into an artistic family as one of eight children, after a bank apprenticeship and a few years working as clerk, he moved to Berlin to live with his brother Karl in 1906. His aim was to work as freelance writer, and indeed Berlin was where he found some success and recognition. Here he finished his novels *The Assistant* (*Der Gehülfe*, 1908) and *Jakob von Gunten* (1909), all issued by the Cassirer publishing house – where fellow author and poet Christian Morgenstern worked as editor – and also wrote numerous short stories for the *Weltbühne* newspaper where Kurt Tucholsky also published. Tucholsky became an admirer and acquaintance of Walser, and other German-language colleagues like Hermann Hesse and Franz Kafka mention him as being among their favourite contemporary writers. Selections of his short stories were later published in *Essays* (*Aufsätze*, 1913) and *Stories* (*Geschichten*, 1914).

Walser moved back to Switzerland in 1913 to live with his sister, and was drafted into the army in 1914, the same year that his father died. Two of his brothers, Ernst and Herrman, also died in the next two years, and Robert was increasingly isolated from his artistic friends in Berlin by the war. He kept publishing in Switzerland after moving to Bern in 1919, but could never repeat the meagre literary successes of his Berlin years; instead he slipped more and more into obscurity. Suffering a nervous breakdown in 1929, he spent the remainder of his life in various sanatoriums, passing his time by going on long walks and occasionally publishing stories and articles. In 1955 *The Walk* (*Der Spaziergang*) was translated into English by Christopher Middleton, the only translation that would appear during Walser's lifetime. It was on one of his walks that Robert Walser died of a heart attack, on Christmas Day in 1956.

The Tiergarten was not spared the upheavals and tragedies of the twentieth century. In 1919, two of Germany's most famous Communist leaders, Rosa Luxemburg and Karl Liebknecht, were brutally murdered by members of the Freikorps on behalf of the new SDP government. Details of their actual demise are murky: some reports say they were shot in a car on the way to prison, others say Luxemburg was hit on the head with the butt of a rifle, then dragged into a car half-dead. It is known, however, that Luxemburg's body was thrown into the Landwehr Canal near the Lichtensteinbrücke in the Tiergarten, as her corpse was pulled from the canal a number of months later. A cast-iron memorial bearing her name in raised capital letters commemorates her death at the site.

The story goes that Liebknecht was also last seen being driven into the Tiergarten. No one ever found his body, but the park's Grosser Weg bears a commemorative brick pillar that reads:

On the evening of 15 January 1919, Dr Karl Liebknecht and Dr Rosa Luxemburg were maltreated and murdered by officers and soldiers of the Guards-Cavalry-Division. Rosa Luxemburg, mortally wounded or dead, was thrown into the Landwehrkanal near the Lichtensteinbrücke by her murderers. Karl Liebknecht was shot here, close to this memorial.

In the fight against suppression, militarism and war the convinced socialist Karl Liebknecht died as the victim of treacherous political murder.

The disregard of life and the brutality against the human enable us to see the human capacity for inhumanity. It cannot and must not be used as a means to resolving any kind of conflict.

Not far from these memorials lies the 35-hectare Zoological Garden, the oldest and largest in Germany, with almost 20,500 animals. Its main entrance, an Asian-style gate flanked by two large sandstone elephant sculptures, lies near the Breitscheidplatz to the south of Tiergarten (see Chapter 4). Roger Moorhouse, in *Berlin at War* (2010), relates an insightful wartime scenario at the entrance in 1940:

A scene recorded by a journalist on the morning of the invasion was perhaps typical of the low-key reaction of the Berlin public. He watched as a man walking his dog through Berlin Zoo approached the barrier, where his entry ticket was clipped: 'Morgen,' said the doorman,

'See we invaded Norway this morning?'

'Ja,' said the visitor, removing his cigar from his mouth, 'and Denmark too.'

'Ja,' said the ticket-taker handing back the punched ticket.

'Auf Wiedersehen.'

'Wiedersehen.'

The zoo was created by geographer and naturalist Alexander von Humboldt, African explorer Lichtenstein Martin Hinrich and landscape architect Peter Joseph Lenné, and its first animals were donated by King Frederick William IV from his own menagerie and the pheasant house in Tiergarten. The establishment was an immediate hit with Berliners, who have always enjoyed giving nicknames to the animals, such as the famous hippo Knautschke who survived the Battle of Berlin with shrapnel embedded in his thick skin, and the world-famous polar bear Knut who perished in 2011 after drowning in his enclosure's pool while suffering from encephalitis.

By the end of the Second World War, the zoo was fortified with the Zoo Tower, an immense concrete flak tower that became one of the last bastions of German resistance against the Red Army during the Battle of Berlin. As a result, the zoo was completely destroyed during the war; only 91 of the 3,715 animals survived, including Knautschke, two hyenas, an Asian bull elephant, a chimpanzee and a black stork. Cornelius Ryan records the macabre scenario in *The Last Battle*:

> Below the tower lay the wasteland of the zoo. The slaughter among the animals had been horrible. Birds flew in all directions every time a shell landed. The lions had been shot. Rosa the hippo had been killed in her pool by a shell. Schwarz the bird-keeper was in despair; somehow the Abu Markub, the rare stork which had been in his bathroom, had escaped. And now director Lutz Heck had been ordered by the flak tower commandant to destroy the baboon; the animal's cage had been damaged and there was some danger that the beast might escape.

Over the course of time, the zoo and its facilities were expanded and rebuilt, and today the zoo is again one of Berlin's most popular attractions, drawing more than 3 million visitors in 2014. North of the zoo lies the broad Strasse des 17. Juni (17th of June Street), which bisects the Tiergarten and represents one of the few visible traces of Germania, Hitler's plan for a new German capital. The road was to be the central avenue between the east and west axis and was accordingly widened from 27 metres to 53 metres, the width of the current street.

The Siegessäule (Victory Column), formerly located in front of the Reichstag, was also moved to the Grosser Stern (Great Star), the central square and main roundabout of the street and park. The 67-metre-high red granite column is today one of the most visible symbols of Tiergarten and the new west of Berlin. Crowned with a statue of a glittering golden goddess that is known locally as Goldelse (Golden Lizzy), it was built in the late nineteenth century to commemorate the Prussian victory in the Prusso-Danish war of 1864 and played a central role in Wim Wenders's classic 1987 Berlin movie *Wings of Desire*. In his *Trip Around the Victory Column*, Joseph Roth surveys the column – and its admirers – when it was still located near the Reichstag in 1921:

> The Victory Column soars up into the azure, naked and slender, as though sunbathing. Following the law that governs the popularity of all outstanding personalities, it has now, […] attained the level of popularity that only failed assassinations may confer. For many years it was neglected and lonely. Street photographers with long-legged flamingoesque equipment liked to use it as a free backdrop for the vacant smiles of their human subjects. It was a little knicknack of German history, something that appeared on picture postcards for tourists, a nice destination for school outings. No grown-ups or locals would dream of going up it.

Nearby, tucked slightly into the park itself, is the Bismarck-Nationaldenkmal – a memorial that since 1901 has honoured the Prussian chancellor who unified the German states into an empire in 1871. Consisting of a statue of Bismarck himself on a pedestal of red granite, surrounded by four allegorical figures representing Germany's world power, its military might, the suppression of rebellion and history, it was also originally erected in front of the Reichstag in 1901 and moved to its current location – like the Siegessäule – in 1938.

Between the column and the Brandenburg Gate stands the Red Army Memorial, which commemorates the Soviet soldiers who died in the Battle of Berlin. Built shortly after the fall of Berlin in 1945, the memorial was allegedly constructed using marble taken from Hitler's Reich Chancellery and consists of a white colonnade flanked by two T-34 tanks and a massive column featuring a statue of a Soviet soldier. North of this memorial is a modern, decidedly non-Soviet building whose low, wide form and distinctive curved roof have earned it the local nickname Die schwangere Auster (the Pregnant Oyster). Properly known as the Haus der Kulturen der Welt, this was built in 1957 as the US entry for Interbau 57, an architecture exhibition held that year in Berlin. Today it is one of Germany's key venues for the presentation of international arts, and it hosts art exhibitions and theatre performances as well as concerts, and acts as one of the venues of the annual Berlin Literature Festival, the ilb (internationales literaturfestival berlin).

Other notable buildings and structures located in or around the park include the central railway station (Hauptbahnhof, see Chapter 7) to the north and, on the south-eastern border, a trio of Holocaust memorials. One of the most recently built (2012) is the Memorial to the Sinti and Roma Victims of National Socialism, which consists of a circular pool of water with a triangular stone in the centre. The shape of the stone is in reference to the badges worn by concentration camp prisoners, and a fresh flower is placed upon it daily. Set in bronze letters around the pool is the poem 'Auschwitz' by Roma poet Santino Spinelli:

> Gaunt face
> dead eyes
> cold lips
> quiet
> a broken heart
> out of breath
> without words
> no tears

In the south-east corner of the park is the Memorial to Homosexuals Persecuted Under Nazism (installed in 2008), which takes the shape of a slanted concrete column in a sandpit that plays a looped video of – alternately – men and women kissing. Both these memorials were built following protests about the larger and controversial memorial just across from the Tiergarten and south of the Brandenburg Gate. The Denkmal für die ermordeten Juden Europas (Memorial to the Murdered Jews of Europe) – informally known as the Holocaust Memorial – consists of 2,711 concrete pillars, or stelae, of varying heights set on 19,000 square metres of prime Berlin real estate. The grid-like structure, created by architect Peter Eisenmann in 2004, is intended to evoke an atmosphere of uneasiness and claustrophobia. The memorial has invited criticism more or less since its conception, summed up by London-based Mexican writer Chloe Aridjis in her *Book of Clouds* (2009), the story of a young expatriate lady adrift in modern-day Berlin:

> I had yet to visit the place but had read about the controversy surrounding it, some people saying it was too vulnerable and exposed, others complaining it was only dedicated to the murdered Jews and not to other victims of the Nazis, other criticizing the barrenness of the place and its lack of so-called aesthetic principles, and yet others said it was too aesthetic and didactic. Each time there was a new memorial voices of all tenor would start clamoring, always in disagreement, even about whether these monuments were necessary in the first place.

It didn't help said controversies that the company used to clear the memorial of its initial graffiti attacks was connected to one that had manufactured Zyklon B, the very gas used in the concentration camps. Nonetheless, the memorial remains one of the prime tourist sites in Berlin, with around 400,000 visitors each year. Below the memorial lies an underground information centre, where visitors can learn about the victims of the Holocaust and which holds the names of all known Jewish Holocaust victims, obtained from the Israeli museum Yad Vashem.

Potsdamer Platz and Friedrichstrasse

The district of Tiergarten takes its name from the park, but extends to the government and diplomatic area to the north as well as Potsdamer Platz and the Kulturforum to the south. Connected to the Brandenburg Gate via Ebertstrasse, Potsdamer Platz is simultaneously a famous historical square and a visible incarnation of the 'New Berlin' thanks to its shining ensemble of glass and chrome skyscrapers (including the headquarters of Deutsche Bahn (German Rail), the Bahntower, the Sony Centre with its impressive cupola, the Beisheim Centre and the brown-brick Kollhoff Tower).

4 The modern skyscrapers that characterise today's Potsdamer Platz

The square's unapologetically modern look was created in 1999 in a concerted effort to rebrand the reunified city as a significant commercial entity on a par with other world centres such as New York and London. The offices of both Daimler AG and PriceWaterhouseCoopers are located here, and the large multiplex cinema inside the Sony Centre is the principal venue for the Berlinale International Film Festival. In *Berlin Now: The Rise of the City and the Fall of the Wall* (2014), Peter Schneider recalls how the city managed to transform Daimler's construction project into a cultural spectacle by commissioning Daniel Barenboim, musical director of the Deutsche Oper, to conduct a 'building site opera' in 1996 – an event that involved him 'conducting' the site's plethora of cranes:

> Daniel Barenboim conducted the 'Ode to Joy' from Beethoven's Ninth Symphony. Waving his left hand in the direction of the first and second violinists – the nearby cranes – then his right toward the steel monsters farther away – the horns and percussionists – he called everyone up for the tutti. The crane operators did their best to follow the director's vigorous gestures, which they could barely make out from the enormous height of their operating cabins. The Golden Gospel Singers, who had been flown in for the event, belted out the all-too-familiar repertory piece in the vastness of the construction site, independent of the maestro's cues and oblivious to the iron arms that swayed about high above them.

The square marks the point where the old merchant road between Berlin and Potsdam entered the city wall at the Potsdam Gate during the Middle Ages. Over the centuries, it developed from an intersection of rural roads into a busy public transport hub, thanks initially to the opening of Potsdamer Bahnhof in 1838 (the terminus of Prussia's very first railway line, which ran between Berlin and Potsdam), and then with the U-Bahn (built in 1902) and the S-Bahn in 1939.

It was around the start of the twentieth century, and especially during the Weimar era, that the square became known as one of the city's most dynamic cultural and entertainment hubs. Ringed by flashy department stores and pavement cafés and constantly thronged by motor cars, trams and buses, it became synonymous with the glitz and glamour of 'modern Berlin', a place of conspicuous consumerism and a meeting point for artists and intellectuals. A piece by Joseph Roth, 'The Resurrection' from *What I Saw,* captures something of the square's intensity by recounting the experiences of a man who revisits Potsdamer Platz in 1923 following a 50-year prison sentence:

> Then, all at once, B. climbed out of the S-Bahn, and stood in the middle of the twentieth century. Was it the twentieth? Not the fortieth? It had to be at least the fortieth. With the speed of arrows shot from a bow, like human projectiles, young fellows with newspapers darted here and there on flying bicycles made of shiny steel! Black and brown, imposing and tiny little vehicles slipped noiselessly down the street. A man sat in the middle and turned a wheel, as if he were captain of a ship. And sounds – threatening, deep and shrill, plaintive and warning, squeaking, angry, hoarse, hate-filled sounds – emanated from the throats of these vehicles. What were they shouting? What were these voices? What were they telling the pedestrians? Everyone seemed to understand, everyone except B. The world had a completely new language, a means of communication as universal as German – and yet it was composed of anguished, shattering primal sounds, as from the first days of mankind, from the deceased jungles of the Tertiary period. One man stopped, and another sprinted, arms across his chest, cradling his life, right across the Damm. Potsdamer Platz was no longer the end, but Mitte.

One of the square's most iconic turn-of-the-century buildings was Haus Vaterland on nearby Stresemannstrasse. Designed by architect

Franz Heinrich Schwechten, who also built the Anhalter Bahnhof and the Kaiser Wilhelm Memorial Church, the vast sandstone building was erected in 1912 and featured a striking 35-metre-high cupola, the 2,500-seat Café Piccadilly, a 1,200-seat theatre and numerous offices (including the headquarters of UFA, Germany's biggest film company). In 1928, the establishment was redesigned by architect Carl Stahl-Urach, who expanded the movie theatre to 1,400 seats – making it the largest in Berlin – and added a large number of internationally themed restaurants including Löwenbräu (a Bavarian beer restaurant), Grinzing (a Viennese café and wine bar), Csarda (Hungarian), a Wild West Bar, plus a Turkish café and Japanese tearoom. Up to eight orchestras and dance bands could perform in different parts of the building, as well as a host of singers, dancers and other entertainers. Philip Kerr's detective Bernie Gunther (see Chapter 5) visits Haus Vaterland in *March Violets* (1989), set in 1936:

> After leaving Pschorr Haus, I went into the Haus Vaterland, which as well as housing a cinema where I was to meet Bruno Stahlecker, is also home to an almost infinite number of bars and cafes. The place is popular with the tourists, but it's too old-fashioned to suit my taste: the great ugly halls, the silver paint, the bars with their miniature rainstorms and moving trains; it all belongs to a quaint old European world of mechanical toys and music-hall, leotarded strong-men and trained canaries. The other thing that makes it unusual is that it's the only bar in Germany that charges for admission.

Opposite Haus Vaterland sat the elegant Belle Epoque Hotel Esplanade with its neo-rococo Kaisersaal (Emperor's Hall), where Kaiser William II regularly invited his friends for games of cards and political chats. Rivalling the artists' cafés on Kurfürstendamm was Café Josty, local hangout of writers like Erich Kästner and poet Paul Boldt, who immortalised it in his poem 'On the Terrace of Café Josty' (1912):

> Potsdamer Platz in an endless roar
> Glaciates all resounding avalanches
> The street complex: trams on rails,
> Automobiles and the refuse of mankind.
> People trickle over the asphalt,
> Ant-like in their diligence, nimble as lizards.
> Foreheads and hands, flashing with thoughts,
> Swim like sunlight through the dark forest.

The celebrated Wertheim store on nearby Leipziger Strasse was another famous place of the day, as were the large cafés nearby that drew local writers and artists such as George Grosz. The store was constructed in 1896, featured 83 elevators and a glass-roofed atrium, and with 70,000 square metres of retail space was one of the largest department stores in the German capital. As George Grosz writes in his autobiography *A Small Yes and A Big No*:

> Then there were the big department stores, especially Wertheim's in Leipziger Strasse. Here I bought my drawing materials, ties, soaps and groceries; here I was a member of the lending library and took out all the latest publications that smaller lending libraries were much slower to provide, and here I would meet my girlfriend for tea [...] Yes, Wertheim's was a whole world of its own.

All that was left of Potsdamer Platz after the war was an ensemble of bombed-out husks. From 1961 the Berlin Wall ran right through the middle of the square, transforming it into a deserted wasteland. In 1976 Haus Vaterland was demolished, after which only two main buildings remained: the steel skeleton of the Weinhaus Huth (known as the 'last house on Potsdamer Platz'), which was integrated into the DaimlerChrysler building in 1990; and remnants of the former Hotel Esplanade, including the Kaisersaal. The U-Bahn at Potsdamer Platz closed entirely, while the S-Bahn station became one of several *Geisterbahnhöfe* (ghost stations) through which Western trains ran without stopping, its previously bustling platforms literally sealed off and patrolled by armed GDR border guards.

During its 28 years in limbo, the divided square held a strange fascination for tourists and locals alike. Just as at the nearby Brandenburg Gate, an observation platform was erected on the Western side, used by military personnel and members of the public to gaze over the Wall at the Eastern wilderness beyond. North of Potsdamer Platz also lay the so-called Lenné-Dreieck, a triangular piece of GDR territory which had ended up outside the Berlin Wall when the border was closed in 1961. In 1988 a group of leftist protesters briefly occupied this patch of no-man's land to protect the plants and trees that had grown there over the years. As West Berlin police had no jurisdiction here the protesters were left in peace for a few weeks and only evicted forcefully after the West Berlin Senate agreed to an exchange of territory (and a payment of 76 million Deutschmarks) with the GDR in July 1988.

One of the most memorable visual representations of these times comes from a scene in Wim Wenders's 1987 movie *Wings of Desire*, during which an old man, played by Curt Bois, searches in vain for the square he once knew. But, like the protagonist in Roth's piece, he does not recognise the area any more and wanders, lost, amongst the weeds and graffiti.

Potsdamer Platz became one of the key gathering points on the night the Wall fell, as recorded by journalist and eyewitness John Simpson in his 1998 memoir *Strange Places, Questionable People*:

> The reunification was going on all along the Wall. There was the sound of hammering on both sides. People were beating at the Wall with pick-axes and hammers and chisels. The candles they worked by cast a golden light on the Wall itself, and threw shadows of their picks onto the bushes, onto other faces, onto the Wall itself. This was a very sweet revenge indeed. They worked away at the joins between the slabs of concrete, making little loopholes which were

slowly getting bigger; when the crowds parted you could sometimes get a glimpse through to the no man's landscape beyond.

Following the collapse of the Wall and the GDR regime, architects and politicians swooped quickly on the newly accessible square, which suddenly represented not only a large swathe of prime real estate but also a chance to rebrand the city anew. The publicly sponsored Potsdamer and Leipziger Platz Competition for Urban Design Ideas in 1991 initiated a passionate debate about the future of the square, and was won by 'starchitects' Renzo Piano and Helmut Jahn. Günter Grass, in his post-Wall novel *Too Far Afield* (1995, tr. 2000), describes the square's attraction as a site of capitalist speculation, one where history is sacrificed to a bright and shiny future of corporations and commerce: '[A] strip that for many decades had been a barren no-man's land and was now a vacant lot, panting for developers; already the first projects were underway, each striving to outdo the others; already the building boom was breaking out; already land prices were on the rise.'

Indeed, the only elements to remind one of Potsdamer Platz's previous incarnations are a replica of its famous traffic tower – the first one in the city, built in 1924 – the restored 1906 Kaisersaal from the former Hotel Esplanade (which was moved to its current location with the help of air cushions during the refurbishment of the area in 1996) and a few original sections of the Berlin Wall. For the most part, though, visitors tend to breeze past these curiosities on their way to the recently (2014) opened Mall of Berlin or the Sony Centre.

To the west of Potsdamer Platz lies the Kulturforum, a conglomeration of cultural buildings commissioned by the West Berlin authorities in the 1960s to house their share of the city's divided public art collection and provide a counterpoint to the Museum Island, which had wound up in East Berlin. The main art galleries here are the Neue Nationalgalerie (New National Gallery, 1968), a modernist glass-and-steel pavilion designed by Bauhaus maestro Ludwig Mies van der Rohe that houses twentieth-century European paintings and sculptures from the nineteenth century to the 1960s, and the recently refurbished Gemäldegalerie (Portrait Gallery, 1998), which showcases mostly classical European paintings and Old Masters. Also prominent architecturally and culturally is the yellow tent-like Philharmonie (Philharmonic Theatre), designed by Hans Scharoun and built in 1963, and the Kammermusiksaal (Chamber Music Hall), which was realised by architect Edgar Wisniewski in 1987 following Hans Scharoun's unfinished plans.

Connecting Potsdamer Platz with Friedrichstrasse are Stresemannstrasse and Niederkirchner Strasse, where the ominously sounding Topography of Terror is located. Until 1951 Niederkirchner Strasse was known as Prinz Albrecht Strasse and it was here, between 1933 and 1945, that the Gestapo (Secret State Police Office), the SS, the SS Security Service (SD) and the Reichssicherheitshauptamt (Main Office for State Security) had their headquarters. Needless to say, the street was one of the most feared in the entire Third Reich, as Philip Kerr describes in *If the Dead Rise Not* (2009), which is set in 1934:

> With its marble balustrades, high vaulted ceilings, and a stair as wide as a railway track, Gestapo House was more like a museum than a building owned by the secret police; or perhaps a monastery – just as long as the order of monks was one that wore black and enjoyed hurting people in order to make them confess their sins.

Most of the street and surrounding area was destroyed during the war and ended up abutting the eastern side of the Berlin Wall after 1961 (the western side was used as a scrap yard and dumping ground). In 1978 architecture critic Dieter Hoffmann-Axthelm realised the significance of the area and pushed for its preservation as a museum or memorial. In 1987 the cellar of the Gestapo headquarters was excavated and an exhibition installed, and after German reunification a foundation was established to look after the site. Today, an open-air exhibition on the site displays both remnants of the Wall and the Gestapo torture cells discovered underneath, while a documentation centre, constructed in 2010, outlines the structure and history of the institutions of Nazi terror and hosts specially themed exhibitions each year.

Circling back to Unter den Linden from Potsdamer Platz leads to another of Berlin's historical boulevards: Friedrichstrasse. This 3.5-kilometre street – one of the longest in Berlin – is known today for the upscale shops, restaurants and offices built here shortly after the Wall fell, but it has been at the centre of many of the city's key epochs. Named after Frederick I of Prussia, it was laid out in 1674 as the main thoroughfare of the then-new Dorotheenstadt district and extended in 1830 to connect with the city gates at the circular drill ground known as the Rondell (now Hallesches Tor) and Oranienburger Tor.

The street was broad as well as long, which made it ideal for marching Prussian armies, and it was lined with noble and official residences (poet and author Adelbert von Chamisso lived in a garden villa at No. 235), military barracks and commercial beer halls. In 1848 the street was one of the main battlegrounds during the March Revolution. H. W. Koch describes a battle here in *A History of Prussia* (1978):

> The locksmith journeymen Glaswaldt and Zinna defended a barricade on Berlin's Jägerstrasse. When a platoon of infantry approached from the direction of Friedrichstrasse, Glaswaldt fought them with an ancient rifle until he was hit by a bullet. Then Zinna, armed only with a rusty sabre, attacked the platoon alone, injured its officer, and then used paving stones against the soldiers until he was hit. He subsequently died of his wounds.

After unification in 1871 the street's northern section developed into a bustling commercial and cultural area, its lively bars, cinemas, theatres and cabarets exemplifying the modern city's cosmopolitan *joie de vivre* and the famous Parisian-style Kaiser-Passage – which contained restaurants, stores and a wax museum – showcasing both the city's royal and consumer prowess.

In his short story 'Friedrichstrasse', Robert Walser paid the street homage in 1907:

Never in all the time this street has existed has life stopped circulating here. This is the very heart, the ceaselessly respiring breast of metropolitan life. It is a place of deep inhalations and mighty exhalations, as if life itself felt disagreeably constricted by its own pace and course. Here is the wellspring, the brook, the stream, the river, and the sea of motion. Never do the movement and commotion here fully die out, and just as life is about to cease at the upper end of the street, it starts up again at the bottom. Work and pleasure, vices and wholesome drives, striving and idleness, nobility and malice, love and hate, ardent and scornful natures, the colorful and the simple, poverty and wealth all shimmer, glisten, dally, daydream, rush, and stumble here frenetically and yet also helplessly. It's wonderful how ceaseless and incessant the twofold stream of people on the sidewalks is, like a viscous, shimmering, profoundly meaningful body of water, and how splendid it is the way torments are overcome here, wounds concealed, dreams fettered, carnal appetites reined in, joys suppressed, and desires chastened, since all are compelled to be considerate, considerate, and once more lovingly and respectfully considerate. Where a human being finds himself in such proximity to human beings, the concept neighbor takes on a genuinely practical, comprehensible, and swiftly grasped meaning, and no one should have the gall to laugh too loudly, devote himself too assiduously to his personal difficulties or insist on concluding business matters too hastily, and yet: what a ravishing, beguiling haste can be seen in all this ostensible packed-in-ness and sober-mindedness.

By the end of the First World War the street's glamour had come to an end, with the *Berliner Illustrierte Zeitung* claiming in 1919 that 'her glitter has gone [...] the only things that remain are the side streets, at the corner of which street vendors stand peddling chocolate, shoe wax, pancakes, shoelaces, cigarettes, sandwiches, an endless chain along the building fronts from Belle-Alliance Platz to Weidendammer Bridge.'

By the Nazi era the street had been more or less completely tamed. In 1944's *Escape from Berlin*, a memoir by Jewish war survivor Catherine Klein, the author describes a scene on the street in 1939:

I cannot bear this room any longer. I'll have to go for a walk. The lady next door warns me: 'I shouldn't go out if I were you, the whole town is in an uproar, they're all mad with enthusiasm.' That is just what interests me. I remember my father telling us about the mass hysteria in the streets of Berlin in August, 1914.

I take a bus into town. There is hardly anyone about. Unter den Linden you wouldn't notice anything unusual. Just a few people trotting peacefully up and down, dreaming in front of shop windows. 'I suppose there will be a lot of noise in the Friedrichstraße,' I think and so I walk in that direction.

When I get there it is as quiet as ever. No flags, no soldiers, no songs, no military bands, no torchlight processions; nothing but the sluggish peace of a warm Sunday afternoon in early autumn.

Two men are talking to each other. I try to catch what they are saying. The moment they notice me, they stop and look into space aimlessly. The same everywhere else. They all seem to have lost the capacity for speech. The subdued atmosphere in what used to be such a noisy town, pulsing with life and good humour, is quite uncanny to behold. One of Goebbel's victories. After seven years of terror politics, he has at last achieved the impossible: he has curbed the tongues of the Berlin people.

During the war the street's historical train station, Bahnhof Friedrichstrasse – which was built at the Spree end of the street in

1882 and retains its dark-tiled clinker façade to this day – was the point of origin for the so-called Kindertransporte, the transport programme organised by the Central British Fund for German Jewry to bring local Jewish children to safety following the 1938 Kristallnacht pogroms. Today a sculpture entitled *Trains to Life, Trains to Death* can be found near the station's side entrance. This double memorial, which mirrors a memorial at the destination station, London's Liverpool Street, serves as a reminder that Bahnhof Friedrichstrasse Station was also one of the starting points of the later transports to the death camps.

Around the corner from the memorial, a discreet plaque commemorates a related wartime event, that of two young but nameless deserters who were caught and hanged by the SS from the railway tracks that cross above Friedrichstrasse. This event took place during the last throes of the war, during which Friedrichstrasse became one of the main axes for the Soviet attack on the Reichstag. The street fared badly during this fighting as one might expect. Theodor Plievier, in *Berlin*, set during the Battle of Berlin, describes it:

> Ruins and debris and not a single human being. Only shadows, human fragments – who had said that, surely somebody had written it. But he who had not seen the shadows on the walls, the fragments in the dust, the upright shells of what had been human figures in the doorways and shops and snack bars; he had not seen Friedrichstrasse, not like this.

During the Cold War, Bahnhof Friedrichstrasse remained a key location, providing the main link for mainline, suburban and underground trains and a connecting point between the divided East and West. Although technically in East Berlin, it was the only GDR station where passengers from the West were allowed to transfer to the other West Berlin S-Bahn and underground lines that intersected here. The state-run Intershop at the station became a popular place for *Wessis* – Westerners – to trade their desirable Westmarks for cheap Eastern cigarettes and vodka. Peter Schneider recounts such an experience in his autobiographical book *The Wall Jumper*:

> No sooner has the train stopped at Friedrichstrasse train station than a line for schnapps and cigarettes forms at the Intershop kiosk. Even before I reach the steps, I see a fellow passenger holding a plastic bag take a seat on the return train. The border official compares the picture in my passport several times over with the living specimen. He looks me in the face at inexplicable length, focusing not on my eyes but on a spot to one side of my nose. Then he demands to see my ear – not the right ear but the left. As I hold my hair up off my ear, I have a vision of Paul Getty Jr., pulling a severed ear from his jacket pocket and turning it over to the official in an envelope.

West Germans with the right papers could also enter East Berlin at Friedrichstrasse Station, passing through a customs hall that – due to the many sad adieus visiting Westerners were forced to bid to their family and friends here – became known as Tränenpalast (the Palace of Tears). The concrete pavilion, which still stands in its original location at the northern side of the main station, is today a museum. Christa Wolf, who lived close to the station for a time, at Friedrichstrasse 133, meditates about the 'palace' in *What Remains*, written during the 1970s:

> Not thinking anything I walked the few steps past the low stone balustrade, which is interrupted by the confluence of the way to the door of that glass pavilion – vernacularly called 'bunker of tears' – where the metamorphosis of citizens of various states, also of mine, into transitioners, tourists, immigrants and emigrants is executed, under the light from small windows up very high reflected by greenish tiled walls and where assistants of the city's ruling master dressed as policeman or border guards exercised the right to bind

or to release. This structure must be standing there like a monster, should its outer form reflect its function, and not like a normal building made of stone, glass and iron cross beams, surrounded by tidy lawns which are of course forbidden to walk on. The distrust for these neat objects I had had to learn, had to understand that they all belonged to the master undisputedly ruling my city: the ruthless advantage of the moment.

A more famous GDR landmark on Friedrichstrasse is Checkpoint Charlie, which became globally famous in 1961 when American and Soviet tanks – both packed with live ammunition and orders to return fire if fired at – faced each other down for a tense day or two. From 1961 to 1990 the checkpoint here was mainly used by Allied forces personnel, Western diplomats and journalists who were not allowed to use the civil border crossing at nearby Bahnhof Friedrichstrasse. On the Eastern side of the checkpoint stood the GDR border fortifications, complete with watchtower, guard dogs, barbed wire and an inspection point for cars. On the Western side, the Allies erected only a small wooden shed to process border traffic, as the inner Berlin sector boundary was not considered an international border.

A large sign was also set up on the Western side, stating YOU ARE NOW LEAVING THE AMERICAN SECTOR in English, Russian, French and German. Today the site is a major tourist destination, complete with fake border guards who charge tourists for fake East German passport stamps and an associated private museum – the Haus am Checkpoint Charlie – dedicated to showcasing the various Wall-related escapes made by East Berliners over the decades.

A character in Len Deighton's spy novel *Berlin Game* (1983) visits the checkpoint in the early 1980s:

> This side of Checkpoint Charlie had not changed. There never was much there; just one small hut and some signs warning you about

leaving the Western Sector. But the East German side had grown far more elaborate. Walls and fences, gates and barriers, endless white lines to mark out the traffic lanes. Most recently they'd built a huge walled compound where the tourist buses were searched and tapped, and scrutinized by gloomy men who pushed wheeled mirrors under every vehicle lest one of their fellow-countrymen was clinging there.

The checkpoint is never silent. The great concentration of lights that illuminate the East German side produces a steady hum like a field of insects on a hot summer's day. Werner raised his head from his arms and shifted his weight. We both had sponge-rubber cushions under us; that was one thing we'd learned in a quarter of a century. That and taping the door switch so that the interior light didn't come on every time the car door opened.

One of the most famous – and fatal – crossing attempts took place just along the road from the checkpoint, on Zimmerstrasse, when 18-year-old bricklayer Peter Fechter tried to flee to the West in August 1962. Shot by GDR border guards while crossing the no-man's land between the Eastern and Western side of the Wall, he died after lying in no-man's land for an hour, in full view of both sides. A memorial on Friedrichstrasse bears the inscription: '… he just wanted freedom.'

❧ 3 ❧

ALEXANDERPLATZ, THE
SCHEUNENVIERTEL AND
THE SPANDAUER VORSTADT

Alexanderplatz

Alexanderplatz – or Alex as it's more colloquially known – is one of Berlin's oldest, bleakest and best-known squares. Dominated by Communist high-rises and modern malls, and towered over by the needle-like spire of the Fernsehturm (TV Tower), it is today considered at best a convenient meeting point and shopping location and at worst a charmless transport hub.

Named in honour of a visit from Russian Tsar Alexander I in 1805, the square began life outside the city walls as a wool and livestock market known as the Oxen Market. Gradually growing in importance as one of the city's main entry and exit points for trade goods, by the late nineteenth century it had a *Stadtbahn* (train station), hosted the city's main *Markthalle* (covered market hall) and – by the early twentieth century – had even gone upscale with a major department store (Tietz) and other commercial establishments.

By the 1920s, Alexanderplatz was successful and lively enough to rival Potsdamer Platz. In order to promote the square as an eastern counterpoint to the then-burgeoning Kurfürstendamm, municipal planner Martin Wagner was commissioned to transform the square into a modern, traffic-friendly *Weltplatz* (world square) in 1928. Famous architects such as Mies van der Rohe and Peter

5 *A socialist memorial appears to be grabbing the famous TV Tower (Fernsehturm) in Berlin-Mitte*

Behrens presented plans for the scheme, but only two buildings – Alexanderhaus and Berolinahaus – by Behrens were ever completed, and no matter what glamorous pretensions the square may have had, it could never quite shake off its rough-and-ready image. Peter Jelavich, in his non-fiction book *Berlin Alexanderplatz: Radio, Film and the Death of Weimar Republic* (2006), describes the slightly schizophrenic nature of the square around this time:

> Berlin's Alexanderplatz had a reputation for impermanence, insta-bility, criminality, even insurrection – all of the values, in short, that stood opposed to those embodied in the royal palace located a few hundred meters away [...] on the one hand, it represented the modernity of Berlin, with its department stores, cinemas, hectic traffic, and constant construction [...] on the other hand, the Alexanderplatz signified poorer sectors of the population:

proletarians, part-time workers, unemployed, criminals, prostitutes, Jewish immigrants. If both aspects of the square implied instability, it was because they were related: the processes of modernization brought with them massive social and economic change, which offered employment to some but made other jobs redundant.

This characterful melting pot inevitably attracted many of the Weimar era's artists, writers and filmmakers. The square features in Walter Ruttmann's movie *Berlin: Symphony of a Great City*, (*Berlin: Die Sinfonie der Großstadt*, 1927), and also in Ernst Haffner's novel *Blood Brothers* – originally titled *Youth on the Country Road Berlin* (*Jugend auf der Landstrasse Berlin*, 1932) – which does a remarkable job of eschewing the usual 'Golden Twenties' mythologies to capture instead the underbelly of the capital. The book briefly garnered critical acclaim when it was published, before being banned by the Nazis a year later. Haffner, a social worker, journalist and novelist, disappeared during the course of the Second World War and no professional or personal records have ever been found. But the novel – his only one – was recently rediscovered and reissued in 2013 by small German publishing house Metrolit Verlag as *Blutsbrüder*. The debut English edition (*Blood Brothers*) was translated by Michael Hofmann and published by Other Press (New York) in 2015.

It tells the story of an eponymous street gang made up of teenage runaways and juvenile delinquents who struggle for survival and integrity amid the prostitution, gang warfare and petty crime of the capital while constantly dodging police and the youth welfare office. Alexanderplatz is repeatedly criss-crossed by the various gangs even as they try to avoid being taken into the square's large police station:

Alexanderplatz in the hours between 9 p.m. and midnight. Where to start in the confusion of humanity? Prostitution in every form. From the fifteen-year-old-girl, just slipped out of welfare, to the sixty-year-old dreadnought, everyone is feverishly on the make.

Male prostitutes, flocks of them, outside the toilets, in bus and tram stops, outside the big bars. Homeless of both sexes sniff around. Loiter, move off. Aimlessly. Sit on a pile of planks for the new underground station. 'Move along now!' Police patrol. Move along, sure, where to? It's almost tempting, the looming bulk of the police HQ on Alexanderplatz. There you can get something to eat and drink and a bed for the night. But only if the desperate fellow has hurled a brick through a shop window. Pimping, with its specific grimness, is everywhere. Hundreds on Alexanderplatz alone. They own the street, and they certainly own the working girls. They stick to the punters like glue; yes, they animate flagging interest by talking up the girls. Human beings are touted and appraised like lame nags in a horse market.

The police station (*Polizeipräsidium*) mentioned in the passage above was taken over by the Nazis and used as a prison during the war. The Hampels were brought here for questioning in Fallada's *Alone in Berlin* (see Chapter 7).

The literary work most associated with Alexanderplatz, though, is Alfred Döblin's 1929 masterpiece *Berlin Alexanderplatz: The Story of Franz Biberkopf* (*Berlin Alexanderplatz: Die Geschichte vom Franz Biberkopf*). A Jew from a lower-middle-class mercantile family, Döblin (1878–1956) spent several years completing his medical degree at the University of Freiburg in 1905 before setting up a practice and a home in Friedrichshain. He established himself on the Berlin literary scene with contributions to the journal *Sturm* – one of the central organs of German Expressionism – and early stories like *The Murder of a Buttercup* (*Die Ermordung einer Butterblume*, 1912), followed by the epic historical novels *The Three Leaps of Wang Lun* (*Die drei Sprünge des Wang-lun*, 1916), *Wallenstein* (1920) and the science-fiction novel *Mountain Seas and Giants* (*Berge Meere und Giganten*, 1924).

Emigrating first to France and then to the USA in 1933, he returned to West Germany in 1945, where he published a tetralogy of novels about the German Revolution of 1918, on which he had worked during his exile. His last novel, *Hamlet, or Tales of a Long Night* (*Hamlet oder Die lange Nacht nimmt ein Ende*) was published in 1956, one year before his death. *Berlin Alexanderplatz*, an immediate bestseller, was Döblin's main commercial success. The story revolves around the life and inner thoughts of Franz Biberkopf, a small-time criminal fresh out of prison, who is drawn immediately back into the underworld. Set on and around Alex, the book employs a dizzying variety of modernist techniques – from juggling multiple perspectives and stream-of-consciousness thoughts to splicing in elements from contemporary newspaper articles, songs, speeches and even other books:

> He is no longer alone on Alexanderplatz. There are people to the right, and people to the left of him, some walk in front of him, others behind him.
>
> Much unhappiness comes from walking alone. When there are several, it's somewhat different. I must get the habit of listening to others, for what the others say concerns me, too. Then I learn who I am, and what I can undertake. Everywhere about me my battle is being fought, and I must beware, before I know it, I'm in the thick of it.
>
> He is assistant gatekeeper in a factory. What is fate anyway? One is stronger than I. If there are two of us, it grows harder to be stronger than I. If there are ten of us, it's harder still. And if there are a thousand of us and a million, then it's very hard, indeed.

Despite the challenging narrative style of the book, it was adapted twice for the screen: first as a 1931 movie directed by Piel Jutzi, which Döblin also worked on; and second as a German television series in 1980. The latter, written and directed by Rainer Werner Fassbinder, runs for 15½ hours; when it was released in New York, ticket holders were required to come to the theatre for three consecutive nights to see the entire film.

Jewish journalist, historian and critic Arthur Eloesser (1870–1938) was born close to Alexanderplatz, at Prenzlauer Strasse 26, a street that no longer exists. Spending almost all his life in the city, Eloesser gained renown as a critic and literary historian, working for a variety of newspapers and magazines before and after the First World War. In 1919 Eloesser published a small collection of memories and sketches of life in Berlin titled *The Street of my Youth: Berlin Sketches* (*Die Strasse meiner Jugend: Berlin Skizzen*), which was hailed by contemporaries like Kurt Tucholsky (see Chapter 7).

Eloesser also published a biography of Thomas Mann (1925) but his magnum opus was a 1,300-page history of German literature, *German Literature from Baroque to Present* (*Die deutsche Literatur vom Barock bis zur Gegenwart*, 1930–1). After the Nazis seized power he was forced to find work at the Jewish weekly *Jüdischer Rundschau*, and helped initiate the *Jüdischer Kulturbund*, set up to help Jewish artists and writers, for which he also wrote features and essays. One of his last works was *From Ghetto to Europe: Judaism in the Spiritual Life of the Nineteenth Century* (*Vom Ghetto nach Europa: Das Judentum im geistigen Leben des 19. Jahrhunderts*, 1936). Forced to emigrate to Palestine in 1934, he nevertheless returned to his hometown in 1937, dying there of natural causes one year later, and thus spared the horrors to come. Two essays from *Die Strasse meiner Jugend* have been published in English by Berlin independent publishing house Readux in 2014 as *Cities and City People*. Today, the Margarete-und-Arthur-Eloesser-Park in Charlottenburg is named after him and his wife, who perished in a concentration camp in 1942.

After the square was destroyed during the Second World War, redevelopment of Alexanderplatz under the new socialist powers proved slow. The two Behrens buildings were rebuilt after 1945, but the rest of the square was not restructured until the 1960s and 1970s. Redesigned to reflect the socialist ideals of the GDR, one of most iconic buildings erected here was the Fernsehturm, built between 1965 and 1969, and the 1970 skyscraper Interhotel Stadt Berlin, which was used to house visiting foreign dignitaries and has today been remodelled as the Park Inn. Other distinctive buildings around the square that still stand today are Hermann Henselmann's Haus des Lehrers (House of the Teacher, 1964), with its famous mosaic mural by Walter Womacka; the Haus des Reisens (House of Travel, 1971), now famous for hosting the techno nightclub Weekend; and the abandoned Haus der Statistik (House of Statistics, 1970).

The GDR also added decorative elements on the square itself, such as the World Time Clock, a rotating installation that shows times across the globe, and the Brunnen der Völkerfreundschaft (Fountain of Friendship between Peoples), both of which remain common meeting places on the square. East German author Monika Maron (born 1941), mostly known for her debut novel *Flight of Ashes* (*Flugasche*, 1981), the first critical analysis of environmental pollution in the GDR, recalls growing up in the East and the 'old Alexanderplatz' in her 2003 collection of autobiographical essays *Place of Birth, Berlin* (*Geburtsort Berlin*):

> It's an effort to remember the old Alexanderplatz, even when I see it on postcards. It was once a proper square, criss-crossed by innumerable dangerous trams. There, where the old market hall used to stand, right by the entrance, I meet myself holding my Aunt Maria's hand, she is buying me a bag of red crayfish, five pfennigs each. I don't want to eat the crayfish, I want to play with them. It's summer, shortly after the war. (That came back to me thirty years later when I had to buy my son a pig's foot which *he* wanted to play with).

Though a popular public square throughout GDR times, Alexanderplatz became one of the main sites of protest during the regime's final dissolution. On 4 November 1989, hundreds of thousands of East Germans flooded the square to call for the abolition of one-party rule and for fuller democratic rights. It was one of the largest demonstrations in East German history:

17 speakers offered their perspectives, ranging from party officials and church leaders, actors and dissidents and writers like Stefan Heym and Christa Wolf. While most of the party officials were jeered at, Wolf's speech was eloquent and impressive:

> Dear Citizens. Revolutions liberate language. Words that were once so hard to say suddenly tumble from our lips. We marvel as our beliefs, held for so long, now fill the streets as people shout it out loud at the tops of their voices. Democracy, now or never. We have in mind a country ruled by the people. Let us look back through history and remember the many efforts that came to a standstill or were brutally suppressed. A great opportunity, one that awakens a power in us that can achieve so much resides at the heart of this crisis. We must not sleep through it again. Revolutions begin at the roots. Top and bottom switch places in the value system. This shift will turn our socialist society upside down. Powerful social movements are gathering pace. Never have we talked so much as in these past few weeks. Never have our conversations been so passionate, so full of fury and grief and so alive with hope. If this demonstration stays peaceful until the end we will learn a lot about what we can achieve, and we will accept nothing less. May I suggest that on May 1st, our leaders march in honour of the people.

The Wall fell five days later. After reunification, the city's planning authorities, which by then were mostly composed of West Germans, opted to rid Alexanderplatz of its socialist aesthetic. Plots of land were sold as early as 1991 to West German investors, prompting artist mock-ups of gleaming skyscrapers and commercial offices that aimed to make the square a desirable and globally relevant place to live and work.

But, with the exception of a couple of new department stores and a 39-storey Frank Gehry residential tower block slated for completion in 2018, most of these plans – including the comprehensive overhaul proposed by architect Hans Kolhoff in 1993 – have remained unrealised. So long has been the delay that official and public sentiment has swung the other way and the Senate recently designated the GDR architecture on and around the square as a listed heritage site. Peter Schneider discusses the controversial preservation decision in his 2014 book *Berlin Now: The Rise of the City and the Fall of the Wall*:

> Berlin is facing a new battle between the defenders of long-standing eyesores and the advocates of new architecture. No one would deny that the *Plattenbau* towers near Alexanderplatz deserve several illustrated pages in a scholarly piece on Berlin's building history. But do they really need to stand there full-size and in full view of future generations – as a historical lesson for the construction sins of their forefathers? Imagining a future flaneur's stroll through the city, the Berlin journalist and city expert Peter von Becker muses 'What begins as a center of the capital at Unter den Linden would thus end in Pyongyang for an eternity.'

For many, the architecture on and around Alexanderplatz remains not only a quintessential part of the city's history but a familiar aspect – however bleak – of the contemporary cityscape. The TV Tower, meanwhile, has become an iconic symbol of Berlin, on a par with the Brandenburg Gate, and the most recognisable aspect of its skyline. As such it often makes an appearance in Berlin novels such as Chloe Aridjis's *Book of Clouds*:

> On afternoons when the sky was especially clear the television tower's metallic sphere would catch the sun's rays and hover like a spacecraft over Alexanderplatz. At times like these the tower exuded an air of otherworldliness, more extraterrestrial than mystical. It wasn't the eye of God beaming down; if anyone were going to descend from its heights, it would be a cement-trunked alien with a brass ball for a head rather than a robed creature with a halo.

The Scheunenviertel

The area roughly between Alexanderplatz and what is today Rosa-Luxemburg-Platz to the north of the square was once known as the Scheunenviertel, or Barn Quarter. The name references the barns built around these streets to store the hay used for the cattle market that once occupied Alex. It was in this section of the city that King Frederick William I of Prussia allowed Berlin Jews to settle from 1737 onwards.

The Scheunenviertel slowly became synonymous with Jewish life and culture, especially during the nineteenth century as large influxes of Jewish immigrants flowed into the city from Galicia and other parts of Eastern Europe to escape persecution and revolution. Many planned to pass through Berlin on the way to port cities like Bremen and Hamburg and, ultimately, to the USA, but a lack of funds and visas meant that many wound up stuck in the city. By the turn of the twentieth century around a third of the Scheunenviertel comprised impoverished orthodox Jewish immigrants. Joseph Roth's 'Refugees from the East' (1920) describes a typical boarding house on Grenadierstrasse (now Almstadtstrasse):

That boarding house is currently home to 120 Jewish refugees from the East. Many of the men arrived straight from Russian POW camps. Their garments were a weird and wonderful hodgepodge of uniforms. In their eyes I saw millennial sorrow. There were women there too. They carried their children on their backs like bundles of dirty washing. Other children, who went scrabbling through a rickety world on crooked legs, gnawed on dry crusts. They were refugees. We know them as the 'peril from the East'. Fear of pogroms has welded them together like a landslip of unhappiness and grime that, slowly gathering volume, has come rolling across Germany from the East. A few clumps of them have come to rest for the time being in the East End of Berlin.

Many of the neighbourhood's main streets, including Grenadier-strasse, were lined with Jewish prayer rooms, bookshops selling Yiddish books, kosher grocery shops and other businesses that mixed German and *Ostjuden* culture – and many of the Jewish inhabitants pop up in the local literature of the time. It is Scheunenviertel Jews, for example, who help look after an overwhelmed and disoriented Franz Biberkopf following his release from prison, while Adolf Sommerfeld's 1923 novel *The Ghetto of Berlin* (*Das Ghetto von Berlin*) describes the neighbourhood as a place where Jews and Christians, workers and crooks live in peaceful coexistence, united against police and Nazis.

Martin Beradt's *Little Eternity Street* (*Die Strasse der kleinen Ewigkeit*, posthumously published in 1965) is set entirely in the Scheunenviertel and also references the multi-ethnic makeup of the district during the Weimar period:

> Many such ordinary people inhabit the street, the majority of them poor foreign Jews, but dispersed among them also other worn out and inconspicuous creatures. This minority, Christian, consists of coachmen, glaziers, retirees, side-show directors, scribes, messengers, a policeman, an undertaker's assistant […] In the street live also a number of old-established Jews, truly poor, half poor, wealthy, who cannot separate themselves from the world in which their immigrant parents lived […] And among all these people in the street live, finally – and they are the ones who make it disreputable – habitual criminals, highly *questionable* riff-raff with its unavoidable female entourage, in which Jews only play an insignificant role, and Jewish women absolutely none at all. Despite these contrasts there is quiet in the street, people get along.

The Spandauer Vorstadt

Inevitably, Jewish life extended outside these few streets, spilling into the broader Spandauer Vorstadt (Spandau Quarter), especially the area east of Alexanderplatz around Friedrichstrasse, Torstrasse, Karl-Liebknecht-Strasse and Oranienburger Strasse. The city's most splendorous synagogue, the Moorish-style Neue Synagoge (New Synagogue), was built at Oranienburger Strasse 29–31 between 1859 and 1866. Consecrated on Rosh Hashanah in 1866, in its prime it could house over 3,000 worshippers.

Despite being vandalised during Kristallnacht, bombed by Allied planes in 1945 and demolished by the GDR in the 1950s, the synagogue was partly rebuilt in the 1990s, and its golden dome is today one of the most striking sights in the area. Although it wasn't possible to restore the entire synagogue, nor its interior, the majestic façade is enough to show how significant the building was. The synagogue continues to hold Jewish services and also serves as a museum of sorts by displaying original elements from the building – carvings, entrance vestibules and anterooms – as well as exhibitions that mostly highlight Jewish life in Berlin.

Interestingly, the reason the synagogue survived the Kristallnacht pogroms (where many others did not) was due to a spontaneous act of resistance. As a mob of brownshirts set about smashing and torching the interior, a policeman named Lieutenant Otto Bellgardt drew his pistol and demanded the crowd disperse due to the historical status of the building. Surprisingly, the thugs did as they were told and the fire brigade managed to put out the fire that had been started. Bellgardt's superior subsequently covered up for him so he did not even get into trouble.

The Spandauer Vorstadt was a natural target for the anti-Semitic policies of the Nazis; as early as April 1933 they were carrying out 'special raids' through the Scheunenviertel, often in broad daylight. But it also became an area connected with acts of resistance such as that described above. Around the corner from Oranienburger Strasse, at Rosenthaler Strasse 39, close to the commercial hubbub that marks the renovated Hackescher Markt shopping area, lies the Haus Schwarzenberg, a scruffy, unrefurbished building with a brown, pockmarked façade and a heavily graffitied inner courtyard.

This artist-run enterprise contains several alternative venues – a street art shop, a dimly lit DJ bar, a low-key cinema – as well as three museums dedicated to acts of wartime resistance. The Anne-Frank-Zentrum is a modern and engaging exhibition that expands on the life story of the well-known Jewish girl who went into hiding with her family in Amsterdam, while the Gedenkstatte Stille Helden (Silent Heroes Memorial) honours and commemorates local inhabitants who risked their lives to hide, help and rescue persecuted Jews.

Among those heroes is Otto Weidt, a blind German entrepreneur who helped save a number of his employees, most of whom were also blind, from his workshop next door. Now called the Museum Blindenwerkstatt Otto Weidt, the workshop has been kept in its original postwar state and features photographs and personal mementos of Weidt's life as well as stories and documents relating to his workers. The original false room where Weidt hid Jewish families when the Gestapo came knocking (he offered the officers bribes of luxury goods) has also been retained. Hidden behind a backless wardrobe, it is a hauntingly claustrophobic reminder of the horrors of the era.

One of the people Weidt saved was his sighted secretary, Inge Deutschkron. She was one of the approximately 1,700 Jews who managed to survive illegally in Berlin, along with her mother, throughout the entire war. In 1978, Deutschkron – who had in fact grown up a socialist and not a religious Jew at all – wrote an autobiography about her experiences called *I Wore the Yellow Star (Ich trug den gelben Stern)*. The memoir not only highlights the terror of the regime but also mentions many instances where ordinary Germans risked their lives to help, whether it was by offers of rooms for a few days, police officers tipping Jewish people off about impending arrests, or help in obtaining forged documents. Although only published in German, a passage from Deutschkron's book appeared in the *Berlin (City-Lit Series)* anthology courtesy of Berlin-based translator Katy Derbyshire:

It must have been around 25 February when Hans called me in the shop. 'For God's sake don't go to Weidt's tomorrow!'

I wanted to know why but he refused to answer my questions. I promised not to leave the house.

The next morning, we saw police vans speeding through the streets of Berlin. Every time they stopped outside a building, officers in plain clothes and uniforms stormed out, ran inside and marched someone off, put him in the van and drove quickly onto the next building. They were collecting the last Jews left in Berlin. They dragged them out of their homes and out of their factories, wherever they found them. And they took them with them just as they were – in pyjamas, in their work clothes, without coats. Watching from the window I saw them, I can still see them now – as if frozen by shock – as they were shoved into the vans by policemen, SS Men, plainclothes men.

[…]

The operation lasted several days. Then they were all gone. We hadn't heard a single scream, no protests. On Monday I went back to Weidt's workshop. There was no one left there. My steps echoed through the empty rooms. The blind workers were gone, the bookkeeper Werner Basch, the sighted workers.

Only the few non-Jews were still sitting at their workplaces. Blind Charlotte was crying; she had been with her Jewish workmates for so long.

Fritz, who had had a 'hat business' – as the Berliners called beggars – before he came to Weidt, kept saying 'Oh God, oh God, what'll they do to them?'

In 1988, Deutschkron returned to Berlin for the stage adaptation of her autobiography at the Grips-Theater in Tiergarten's Hansaviertel district. Since 1992 she has lived between Tel Aviv and Berlin and has penned more books about her life and also about Weidt, for children and adults. She also advised on a forthcoming film, *The Blind Hero*, about Weidt's life and work.

Near to the Haus Schwarzenberg, on Rosenstrasse, sits a resistance memorial of a slightly different kind, one commemorating the protests of non-Jewish women against the arrest of their Jewish husbands and relatives for deportation. The 1,800 so-called 'privileged Jewish males' had been collected as part of the same 1943 Fabrikaktion (factory action) referred to above and were housed temporarily at Rosenstrasse 2–4, which at the time was a welfare office for the Jewish community.

Between February and March 1943, the protests gathered force, starting with just a few women in the first days until 600 protesters were gathered in front of the building. For a week the women turned up every morning, protesting loudly until all of the men were released, making it one of the most significant – and successful – instances of public opposition during the entire Nazi regime. The original building was destroyed during Allied bombing but the event is referenced by a rose-coloured column that displays information about the event, as well as a nearby sculpture called Block der Frauen (the Block of Women), created by East German sculptor Ingeborg Hunzinger and erected in 1995.

The protests also formed the basis of the 2003 film *Rosenstrasse*, directed by German actress and director Margarethe von Trotta, one of the key figures of German cinema after the Second World War. Philip Kerr also describes the event in his 2013 noir novel *A Man Without Breath*, which is set in 1943:

'Give us back our men!'

You could hear them three streets away – a large and angry crowd of women – and as we turned the corner of Rosenstrasse I felt my jaw slacken. I hadn't seen anything like this on the streets of Berlin since Hitler came to power. And whoever would have thought that wearing a nice hat and carrying a handbag was the best way to dress when you were opposing the Nazis?

'Release our husbands,' shouted the mob of women as we pushed our way along the street. 'Release our husbands now.'

There were many more of them than I had been expecting – perhaps several hundred. Even Klara Meyer looked surprised, but not as surprised as the cops and SS who were guarding the Jewish Welfare Office. They gripped their machine pistols and rifles and muttered curses and abuse at the women standing nearest to the door and looked horrified to find themselves ignored or even roundly cursed back. This wasn't how it was supposed to be: if you had a gun, then people were supposed to do what they're told. That's page one of how to be a Nazi.

Save for the Neue Synagogue and a smattering of small orthodox cultural centres and cafés, the Scheunenviertel is today all but devoid of traditional Jewish life. There are still vestiges of the pre-war era, though – predominantly in the buildings that survived, such as those around Rosa-Luxemburg-Platz. Technically more a triangle than a square, this well-known public area has undergone many name changes, even by Berlin standards. It was called Babelsberger Platz and Bülowplatz in the early twentieth century, Horst-Wessel-Platz under the Nazis, and then Liebknechtplatz and Luxemburgplatz after the war, before finally becoming Rosa-Luxemburg-Platz in 1969.

Many of the main buildings here remain as they were in the 1920s and in fact serve as a sort of outdoor museum of modernist architecture in a surrounding sea of GDR tower blocks and nineteenth-century tenements. On the southern corner is the curvaceous Kino Babylon, which was built by Hans Poelzig and opened in 1929, as well as the equally distinctive Karl-Liebknecht-Haus; built as a factory in 1912, it served as the main headquarters of the Communist Party of Germany (KPD) – one of the final anti-Communist gatherings of the Nazis before they took power happened right outside – before becoming the East German Institute for Marxism-Leninism after 1950. Today it retains its left-wing reputation by housing the offices of German political party Die Linke (The Left).

Set in the middle of the square is one of the city's most distinctive theatres, the Volksbühne. Built between 1913 and 1914, the theatre was actually part of a plan – thwarted by the outbreak of the First World War – to modernise the entire Scheunenviertel, which had long been regarded as unhygienic and overcrowded, even by Jewish sympathisers. A product of the Freie Volksbühne (Free People's Theatre), a workers' movement that had been gathering pace since the early 1890s, the theatre was deliberately designed for the city's burgeoning working classes.

Its first artistic director was Max Reinhardt, who had made a name for himself as a director of the city's Deutsches Theater, which he had helmed since 1905. As well as hosting well-known plays by Goethe and Schiller, Reinhardt deliberately put on politically provocative works by the likes of Henrik Ibsen and Gerhart Hauptmann. One of Reinhardt's successors was Erwin Piscator (1893–1966), a Communist Party member who insisted on producing only contemporary plays that were relevant to Berlin and its inhabitants; these included works by pacifist journalist and playwright Alfons Paquet, a member of the Prussian Academy of the Arts, and playwright Hans Jose Rehfisch, with whom Piscator ran the Central Theater in Kreuzberg before coming to the Volksbühne. Along with his friend and collaborator Bertolt Brecht, Piscator also developed the concept of 'epic theatre', a new form of theatre that aimed to break down barriers between actors and audience by deliberately eschewing traditional emotive illusions and instead prompting political and social thought.

Reduced to rubble in the war, the Volksbühne was rebuilt between 1950 and 1954 with the addition of two supplementary venues, the Green and Red Salons. Partly thanks to its socialist history, the Volksbühne remained of one the leading theatres in the GDR and staged productions by renowned GDR directors such as Heiner Müller and Fritz Marquardt. In the late 1980s the Volksbühne was active in campaigning for the fall of the Berlin Wall, after which East Berlin director Frank Castorf took over leadership. Castorf has continued the theatre's noble tradition of political provocation, producing works like 2008's *Fuck Off, Amerika* – an adaption of the 1979 novel *It's Me, Eddie* by Russian writer Edward Limonov – for which he placed the show's title atop the theatre building for all to see.

Closely connected to the Volksbühne is Turkish-German writer, director and actress Emine Özdamar (born 1946). In 1991 she became the first Turkish author to win the prestigious Ingeborg Bachmann Prize, and in 2009 she also won Berlin's Fontane Prize for literature, placing her in the company of Günter Grass and Wolf Biermann. Özdamar has also starred in numerous films depicting Turkish Germany, earning herself the title of Mutter aller Filmtürken (Mother of all Turks on film) in Germany.

After working and living in Istanbul during the 1960s, Özdamar returned to Berlin and started working as director's assistant at the Volksbühne, where she worked closely with directors Matthias Langhoff and Heiner Müller. Özdamar's connection to German theatre would continue throughout the 1980s, with a period as director's assistant and actress at the Bochumer Ensemble in West Germany. Some of her experiences are included in her memoir *My Berlin* (2001), which offers a rare immigrant's perspective on life in the East:

> Later I worked at the Volksbühne Theatre on Rosa-Luxemburg-Platz as Benno Besson's assistant. So during the day I lived in the theatre in East Berlin and at night I went back to West Berlin to Kati and Theo. Every time I came out of the underground I was surprised. 'Ah, it snowed in the West too. Ah it rained here too.'
>
> [...]
>
> In the theatre canteen, an actor told stories about getting out. Once a man had tried to flee to the West as a swan. He made himself a swan's head, put it on and swam through the Spree. The real swans came over to him, pecked at his fake swan head, and swam with him to the West.

Connecting the Volksbühne and Rosa-Luxemburg-Platz with the former customs gate at Oranienburger Tor is the 2-kilometre-long Torstrasse. Mostly lined with chic boutiques, bars and restaurants these days, it was built in 1786, forming part of the customs wall, and for the next 200 years marked the border between medieval Mitte and blue-collar Prenzlauer Berg. Number 58/60 houses Kaffee Burger, a bar and club that dates back to 1936. In GDR times it became an artist hangout, frequented by many cultural figures from the nearby Volksbühne and the arts scene in Prenzlauer Berg (see Chapter 10) such as director Heiner Müller, writer Klaus Schlesinger and actress Katharina Thalbach. The venue was closed for a while in 1979 by the authorities, prompting the artists to move on and the owner to renovate the bar. Upon reopening it remained a neighbourhood bar for the next 20 years and was given a new lease of life in 1999 under a new owner, since when it has remained a vibrant cultural and nightlife hotspot. It became particularly well known throughout the 2000s for the bi-weekly Russendisko (Russian disco) initiated by Russian-born German-language writer Wladimir Kaminer.

Kaminer (born 1967) was born in Moscow to Jewish parents. After working in the Moscow underground arts scene, he emigrated to Berlin in 1990 and received a GDR passport just before the two German states were officially reunited in the same year. He started working as a print and radio journalist and from the late 1990s became well known within Berlin's art scene. His Russendisko nights not only introduced Russian pop and rock songs to a German audience, but spawned a global party series, multiple albums and even a German movie of the same name starring Matthias Schweighöfer as Kaminer (2013).

Kaminer's literary output, entirely in German, mostly sketches the cultural situation of first- and second-generation Russian immigrants in Germany since the fall of the Wall. He has published almost 20 German-language novels and continues to DJ at Russendisko nights in Kaffee Burger and elsewhere. His first collection of short stories about his move to Berlin and his experiences in the German capital (published in 2000) was translated as *Russian Disco: Tales of Everyday Lunacy in the Streets of Berlin* by Michael Hulse, and published in English by the Ebury Press in 2002. In the extract below he remembers his entrance into Germany via the refugee processing centre in Marienfelde:

> In Marienfelde and at the Berlin Mitte police headquarters we met like-minded Russians, the vanguard of the fifth wave of emigrants. The first wave was the White Guard during the Revolution and the Civil War; the second wave emigrated between 1941 and 1945; the third consisted of expatriated dissidents in the Sixties; and the fourth wave commenced with Jews who migrated via Vienna in the Seventies.
>
> The Russian Jews of the fifth wave in the early Nineties were indistinguishable from the rest of the German population by their creed or by their appearance. They might be Christians or Muslims or even atheists; they might be blonde, red-heads or dark-haired; their noses might be snub or hooked. Their sole distinguishing feature was that, according to their passports, they were Jews. It was sufficient if a single member of the family was Jewish, or a half or quarter Jewish, and could prove as much in Marienfelde.
>
> As with any game of chance, a good deal of cheating went on. Among the first hundred were people from every walk of life: a surgeon from the Ukraine with his wife and three daughters, an undertaker from Vilnius, an old professor who had done the calculations for the metal casings of the Russian sputniks and told anyone and everyone all about it, an opera singer with a funny voice, a former policeman, and a whole bunch of younger folk, 'students' such as ourselves.

During the 1920s and early 1930s the area around Torstrasse was dominated by petty crime and cheap dives. Ernst Haffner describes a scene from a bar at nearby Linienstrasse in *Blood Brothers*:

The nighttime equivalent to the Rückerklause is Schmidt's on Linienstrasse. Of course it's busy and there's a din of brass band music all day here as well. But, after dark, the bustling little bar becomes a thronging, teeming scene. The beer tap isn't idle for a minute, and every chair is occupied twice over. And whoever hasn't got one at all leans against the stage or just stands anywhere he can, beer glass in hand. The inevitable paper chains, essential for producing a festive atmosphere, are permanently shrouded in thick tobacco fumes, even though a ventilator is doing its best to restore law and order to the air. The band plays energetically and without a break. Generous rounds of beer and shorts sustain them. Sustain them to the point that the alcohol starts to affect the tunefulness of their playing. That's when Schmidt's really comes into its own. Then the whole bar becomes one roaring foot-stamping chorus.

Another literary locale of sorts is Gaststätte Prassnik, an unpretentious corner pub at Torstrasse 65. Just a small tap room with a bar and a few rickety tables, the pub was the preferred watering hole of Wolfgang Herrndorf and his friends. Herrndorf (1965–2013) was a painter, author and amateur footballer (in the German national authors' football team). He studied painting in Nuremberg and moved to Berlin in 1995, publishing his first novel *In Thunderstorms of Plush* (*In Plüschgewittern*) in 2002.

In 2010 Herrndorf was diagnosed with a terminal brain tumour, which spurred an outburst of productivity. He finished and published the novels *Tschick* (2010) and *Sand* (2011) as well as the blog *Work and Structure* (*Arbeit und Struktur*, posthumously published as a print collection in 2013), where he details his sickness and work progress. *Tschick*, a young adult novel which tells the story of a road trip by two 14-year-old boys through the outskirts of Berlin and Brandenburg in a stolen Lada, won multiple awards, such as the Deutschen Jugendliteraturpreis, the Clemens-Brentano-Prize, the Hans-Fallada-Prize and the Rolling Stone German Teen Literature Prize. It was published in English by the Andersen Press in 2014 as *Why We Took the*

Car, translated by Tim Mohr: 'There isn't much you can learn from your mother. But this you can learn from your mother: firstly that you can talk about everything. Secondly that you should not really give a fuck about what people think.' Herrndorf took his own life by shooting himself on the banks of Berlin's Hohenzollern Canal on the 26 August 2013. In his blog he had stated, 'I hope no one suggests a death notice or buys a wreath. Get wasted in Prassnik instead.'

Near the western end of Torstrasse, on Chausseestrasse, are two distinctive Berlin literary destinations: the Dorotheenstadt Cemetery at No. 126 and the adjacent Bertolt Brecht-Literaturforum. The cemetery, officially named the Cemetery of the Dorotheenstadt and Friedrichswerder Parishes, is a Protestant burial ground first used in the late eighteenth century and can be considered as a local version of Père Lachaise in Paris. While not as large as the famous French necropolis, it nevertheless boasts an impressive number of celebrity graves, including those of theologian and resistance fighter Dietrich Bonhoeffer, industrialist August Borsig, philosopher Georg Wilhelm Friedrich Hegel and celebrated nineteenth-century Berlin architect Karl Friedrich Schinkel.

A small area within the cemetery, surrounded by a low hedge, is reserved for members of the Berlin Academy of Arts, such as Lin Jaldati, a Jew who survived three concentration camps to make a successful career as a dancer and singer, and theatre director and author George Tabori. The city of Berlin also maintains a number of honorary graves here, including those of playwright and Volksbühne director Heiner Müller and Johannes Rau, the eighth president of West Germany, who expressly asked to be buried here. Then there are the writers: Wolfgang Herrndorf, Christa Wolf, on whose grave visitors leave colourful pens in a small vase as a token of respect, philosopher and political theorist Herbert Marcuse (whose headstone bears the wonderful inscription 'Weitermachen!' – 'Carry on!') and, last but not least, Bertolt Brecht and his wife Helene Weigel, resting side by side in a small grave with two natural granite headstones carrying only their names in white letters.

Eugen Bertolt Friedrich Brecht (1898–1956) was one of the most important German playwrights and theatre directors of the twentieth century. After studying drama at the University of Munich, he moved to Berlin in 1924 and started working as assistant director at the Deutsches Theater. Brecht soon became one of the key theatre personalities of the emerging New Objectivity movement and also established the Brecht Collective, a shifting arts group that he would remain connected with all his life. Brecht also grew interested in Marxism throughout the 1920s and developed a politicised form of 'epic theatre' with Erwin Piscator (see above). He also worked with composer Kurt Weill, with whom he penned one of the biggest theatre hits in Berlin, *The Threepenny Opera* (*Die Dreigroschenoper*, 1928), which contains the cult songs 'Mack the Knife' and 'Pirate Jenny'.

In 1929 Brecht married his long-time lover and collaborator, Austrian-German actress Helene Weigel (1900–71). The day after the Reichstag burning in 1933 the pair left Berlin; having had their work increasingly targeted by the Nazis, they knew the event did not bode well. Weigel and Brecht then moved around Europe over the following years: first to Paris, then on to Sweden, Denmark and Finland. In *Steffin's Collection* (*Steffnische Sammlung*, 1940), Brecht wrote:

> Fleeing my compatriots
> I now reached Finland. Friends
> that I did not know yesterday, put a few beds together
> in clean rooms. On the radio
> I heard the victory declarations of the scum. Inquisitive
> I looked at the map of the continent. High up in Lapland
> Near the northern Arctic Ocean
> I can make out a small door

In 1941 they finally fled to the USA via Moscow and Vladivostok. Brecht and Weigel settled in Santa Monica in California, working on translations of his works. Returning to Europe in 1947, first to Switzerland (where Brecht's version of Sophocles' *Antigone* premiered in Chur) and then to East Berlin in 1948, Brecht and Weigel dwelled briefly in the reopened Adlon Hotel before relocating to a house in Weissensee. Together they formed the Berliner Ensemble, a new theatre company housed in the Theater am Schiffbauerdamm building in Mitte, which was gifted to them by the GDR authorities.

Here they performed plays like Brecht's 1939 anti-war masterpiece *Mother Courage and her Children* (*Mutter Courage und ihre Kinder*). In 1953 the couple moved to Chausseestrasse 125, a house overlooking the cemetery. Despite living on separate floors and communicating mostly by handwritten notes and invitations, Weigel and Brecht managed to continue working with a large group of friends and collaborators. In 1956, Brecht suffered a fatal heart attack at the age of 58, but his wife continued managing the Berliner Ensemble until her own death in 1971.

Chausseestrasse 125 today houses Brecht's historical working and living room – open to visitors via guided tours – the Brecht Archive and the Literaturforum (Literary Forum). Originally opened as the Brecht-Centre of the GDR in 1978, today the forum organises readings, workshops and exhibitions with the aim of preserving Brecht's idea of critical engagement with society.

❦ 4 ❦

CHARLOTTENBURG

Charlottenburg is often regarded as a something of a separate city from the 'real' Berlin – especially since reunification put the spotlight firmly on the city's hip (read: gentrifying) eastern districts. In fact the district, which has been joined with Wilmersdorf since 2001, *was* a separate city up until 1920, and still carries its own specific, relatively bourgeois aura, one that is tied in with its royal heritage – Charlottenburg Palace is the largest surviving royal palace in Berlin and a tourist highlight – and its propensity for consumerism, not least along the 200-year-old shopping boulevard Kurfürstendamm.

6   *Schloss Charlottenburg, one of the finest extant castles in Berlin*

The old Prussian village of Alt Lietzow at the core of the area makes Charlottenburg one of Berlin's older districts. This village was already populated during the Middle Ages and gifted to Sophia Charlotte of Hanover in 1695 by her husband, Elector Frederick III of Brandenburg, as part of the margraviate of Brandenburg. The summer residence Frederick built here, designed by the architect Johann Arnold Nering between 1695 and 1699 and originally named Lützenburg Castle, was named Schloss Charlottenburg (Charlottenburg Palace) after Sophie Charlotte died in 1705.

Frederick's successor, Frederick the Great, ignored the palace in order to build his own (Sanssouci) in Potsdam, but Frederick William III, who came to the throne in 1797 and reigned with his wife for 43 years, moved the royal court back to Charlottenburg. His queen-consort, Louise of Mecklenburg-Strelitz (1776–1810) became a royal celebrity in her time and remains one of the most popular royal Prussian figures to this day. As Christopher Clark writes of her in *Iron Kingdom: The Rise and Downfall of Prussia, 1600–1947* (2006), Louise was 'a female celebrity who in the mind of the public combined virtue, modesty, and sovereign grace with kindness and sex appeal, and whose early death in 1810 at the age of only thirty-four preserved her youth in the memory of posterity'.

In the years before the Napoleonic Wars engulfed Europe, Louise developed an interest in literature, mostly fuelled by the literary salon of her lady-in-waiting Karoline Friederike von Berg in Tiergarten. Here she met many of the early Romantics, such as German poet and writer Jean Paul and Heinrich von Kleist (see Chapter 5). After entering war with France and following their country's subsequent defeat in 1806, the King and Queen fled to East Prussia, where Louise personally surrendered to Napoleon in the small town of Tilsit. When Napoleon met Tsar Alexander of Russia in the same year he allegedly stated that 'the Queen of Prussia is very charming. One would like to lay a crown at her feet instead of taking it away.'

The French also took over Charlottenburg Palace in 1806 and made an army camp nearby. Following the Napoleonic Wars,

Charlottenburg became part of the new Prussian province of Brandenburg in 1815, after which point the only other royal resident of the palace was Frederick III, who reigned for just 99 days before dying of cancer. After Frederick III's death, the palace was used as a theatre, hospital and seat of the Berlin park management after 1888. Theodor Fontane has his protagonists visit the castle in *Trials and Tribulations*:

> And so they went on their excursion and although the air of Charlottenburg was still less like the breath of God than the Berlin air, yet Katherine was fully determined to stay in the castle park and to give up Hallensee. Westend was so tiresome and Hallensee was half a journey further, almost as far as Schlangenbad. But in the castle park one could see the mausoleum, where the blue lights were always so strangely moving, indeed she might say it was as if a bit of heaven had fallen into one's soul. That produced a thoughtful mood and led to pious reflections. And even if it were not for the mausoleum, still there was the bridge where you could see the carp, the bridge with the bell on it, and if a great big mossy carp came swimming by, it always seemed to her as if it were a crocodile.

Badly damaged by bombs in 1943, the palace park was slated to be demolished but was saved by the efforts of Margarete Kühn, director of the state palaces and gardens, who campaigned for it to be restored to its former condition. (Kühn also rescued an early eighteenth-century statue of Frederick William from the waters of Lake Tegel, where it had been deposited during the war, reinstalling it in front of the castle in 1952.) From 2004 to 2006, Charlottenburg Palace was the seat of the president of Germany whilst Schloss Bellevue in Tiergarten was being renovated.

Today, the palace is a major tourist sight in Berlin, its wings and baroque state rooms displaying a mix of restored ceiling paintings, porcelain cabinets and a collection of eighteenth-century French art. The meticulously landscaped gardens, originally designed in 1697 by Simeon Godeau in the style of the gardens of Versailles, are also a big hit with visitors, not only for their summer blooms and geometric allure but also for containing the mausoleum of Queen Louise and Frederick William III, the Belvedere tea house, Orangerie restaurant and palace theatre. A very popular Christmas market is also held in the palace grounds each year.

South of the castle lies the aspiringly bourgeois shopping street, the 3.5-kilometre-long Kurfürstendamm (Elector's Causeway, also referred to more casually as Ku'damm). As the name suggests, the street has royal origins. It was originally laid out around 1542 as an access road to the Grunewald hunting lodge (see Chapter 5) by order of Hohenzollern elector Joachim II Hector. Its current incarnation – a Parisian-style boulevard – occurred as a personal initiative from Chancellor Otto von Bismarck, who also proposed the building of the Grunewald mansions colony at its western end.

7   West Berlin's most famous boulevard, the Kurfürstendamm (Ku'damm)

Far away from the cramped medieval streets of Mitte and the overcrowded, unsanitary tenement buildings in Wedding and Moabit, the buildings and streets around this new area were mainly planned and erected in the mid-nineteenth century, specifically for the upper-middle classes. As might be imagined, the area was not well received by less wealthy Berliners, nor was it considered especially tasteful, as scholar and author Arthur Eloesser (see Chapter 3) confirms in his essay in *Cities and City People* in 1919:

> And the new West itself is a faceless expanse of flotsam. It may have outer boulevards – very imposing ones in fact, for all the excesses of arriviste taste – but despite greater spaciousness, despite trees, promenades, and bridle paths, they merely reproduce the Berlin prototype of the residential and commercial street; they are not rooted in an autochthonous, half-urban, half-rural way of life.

A growing selection of entertainment and leisure options (theatres, restaurants, cabarets, cafés) helped the Ku'damm's gradual transformation into a vibrant hotspot. By the start of the twentieth century it was generally regarded as the city's Fifth Avenue or Champs Elysée, a place to not only shop but to meet, gossip and generally see and be seen. Its glamour and glitz stood in stark contrast to the tenements and factories of the city's more proletarian eastern districts, as recorded by Ernst Haffner in *Blood Brothers* (see Chapter 2), who explores the boulevard through the eyes of two street urchins in 1932:

> Ludwig and Willi trudge through the crowds and lights of Tauentzienstrasse. They feel they are in a foreign city. What's Berlin? As far as they were concerned, Berlin was Münzstrasse and Schlesischer Bahnhof. It never occurred to them to go to the west of the city. Gray streets with one yard and then another behind and then maybe a third, that was home to them. Here they feel they're somewhere else. In a rich and cheerful abroad, as it would

appear. Everyone is wearing brand-new clothes, as though it were a holiday and not some ordinary Wednesday. The shops are like palaces, in which His Majesty the customer is standing around idly, on the lookout for some precious knick knack or other. And the women – the ladies. Every one, apparently without exception, well dressed, fragrant, lovely. Even the little dogs the ladies press to their furs, or have trotting along beside them, are dressed in cute little blankets and have sparkling collars. And a dog, one little dog, a tiny bundle of fluff, actually wears little patent leather booties on all four feet.

The cafés, restaurants and increasingly louche nightlife on Ku'damm, and the streets around it, became working and gathering places for the city's writers, artists and intelligentsia between the early 1900s and the 1930s, bolstered by the abundant publishers and newspapers offices along nearby Kantstrasse. Local authors like Erich Maria Remarque, Erich Kästner and Joseph Roth mingled here with artists such as Georg Grosz and Otto Dix, theatre directors like Bertolt Brecht and foreign regulars including André Gide, T. S. Eliot and Thomas Wolfe. The most frequented establishments were Schwannecke's, the Café des Westens and the Romanisches Café.

Between 1899 and 1943, the neo-romantic Romanisches Haus with its two distinctive towers and oriel above the main entrance and the Romanisches Café on the ground floor stood on what is today Breitscheidplatz. Originally named Auguste-Viktoria-Platz in honour of German Empress Augusta Viktoria of Schleswig-Holstein, the eastern side of the square is today dominated by the nondescript Europa-Center mall and office building; a Cold War capitalist showpiece built in 1965, it features a giant rotating Mercedes-Benz logo on the roof and an ugly brown fountain in front.

It is hard to contemplate this logo-spattered building today and imagine all the great minds and personalities who passed through the square on a daily basis, mingling with up-and-coming artists trying to get their careers kick-started. Ilya Ehrenburg (1891–1967), a Russian Jewish author who lived in Berlin from 1922 to 1924, summed up the ambiance of the Romanisches Café in a letter to a friend:

> I am writing this letter from the Romanisches Café. This is a very respectable place. It resembles a staff headquarters for fanatical vagabonds, everyday folk, and the educated crooks who have been entirely cured of narrow-minded nationalism [...] I don't know why all these people live in Berlin! Foreign currency, passport visas? [...] Immigrants or thrifty tourists? At any rate, they're all dissatisfied with Berlin and seize every opportunity to get angry at it. Particularly the Russians, who consider it a good style. I don't want you to think I'm attempting to be witty. I'm afraid you won't believe me – it obviously sounds paradoxical: I have grown fond of Berlin.

The Weimar era, with its unbridled consumerism and ever-increasing local population, saw the resurrection of the literary *flâneur*, a concept that originated with Baudelaire in the nineteenth century but was brought to life by two Romanisches Café regulars: Walter Benjamin and Franz Hessel. Benjamin (1892–1940) was a German writer, philosopher and cultural critic born to a wealthy Jewish family near Tiergarten. After marrying in 1917, he moved to Switzerland with his wife and newborn son to avoid being drafted into the German army and in 1919 earned his doctoral degree at the University of Bern.

Later that year, unable to support himself and his family, Benjamin returned to Berlin to live with his parents. In 1926 he began writing for German newspapers, which paid enough to enable him to reside in Paris for a couple of months and continue his research and writing. For the remainder of his life, he continued travelling between these two cities, both of which would shape his writing and worldview. His first trip to Paris was in 1914, during which he began translating the works of Baudelaire (his German translation of Baudelaire's *Tableaux Parisiens* was published in 1923) and, along with his Berlin friend Franz Hessel, also translated the first volumes of Proust's *In Search of Lost Time* (*À la Recherche du Temps Perdu*). It was these experiences that led both Berlin writers to grow obsessed with the idea of the *flâneur*, which Baudelaire defined in his 1863 essay 'The Painter of Modern Life' as follows:

> The crowd is his element, as the air is that of birds and water of fishes. His passion and his profession are to become one flesh with the crowd. For the perfect flâneur, for the passionate spectator, it is an immense joy to set up house in the heart of the multitude, amid the ebb and flow of movement, in the midst of the fugitive and the infinite. To be away from home and yet to feel oneself everywhere at home; to see the world, to be at the centre of the world, and yet to remain hidden from the world – such are a few of the slightest pleasures of those independent, passionate, impartial natures which the tongue can but clumsily define. The spectator is a prince who everywhere rejoices in his incognito. The lover of life makes the whole world his family, just like the lover of the fair sex who builds up his family from all the beautiful women that he has ever found, or that are – or are not – to be found; or the lover of pictures who lives in a magical society of dreams painted on canvas. Thus the lover of universal life enters into the crowd as though it were an immense reservoir of electrical energy. Or we might liken him to a mirror as vast as the crowd itself; or to a kaleidoscope gifted with consciousness, responding to each one of its movements and reproducing the multiplicity of life and the flickering grace of all the elements of life.

Benjamin and Hessel brought Baudelaire's *flâneur* up to date by giving him a more literary persona. Their *flâneur* doesn't stroll simply to 'feel oneself everywhere at home' but also to observe, analyse and – ideally – to produce texts that offer insights and epiphanies into modern society. It was actually mostly Hessel who created these texts, collected together in his 1929 book *Walking in Berlin* (*Spazieren in Berlin*). Snappily subtitled *A Textbook of the Art of Walking Berlin Close to the Magic of the City of which Itself Knows Nothing*, it offers an assortment of perspectives on Weimar Berlin that are written by a native but aim to experience the city as if for the first time.

Two pieces from the book have been published in English by Berlin independent publishing house Readux, as *In Berlin* (2013). In one of them, Hessel discovers the problem of being a *flâneur* in a city with a very different temperament and tempo from nineteenth-century Paris:

> Walking slowly down bustling streets is a particular pleasure. Awash in the haste of others, it's a dip in the surf. But my dear fellow citizens of Berlin don't make it easy, no matter how nimbly you weave out of their way. I always catch wary glances when I try to play the flaneur among the industrious. I believe they take me for a pickpocket.

Born into a wealthy Jewish family, in 1900 Hessel moved to Munich, where he began writing poetry and commenced a *ménage à trois* with fellow student Franziska Gräfin zu Reventlow (who went on to become a writer and illustrator before dying in a 1918 bicycle accident) and his friend Bogdan von Suchocki. Suchocki was replaced in this arrangement in 1907 by French author Henri-Pierre Roché, by which time Hessel had moved to Paris and began working with Benjamin. Roché and Hessel later maintained a similar relationship with German journalist Helen Grund, whom Hessel married in 1913. This particular *ménage* became famous as the centrepiece of Roché's novel, *Jules et Jim* (1953), which in turn formed the basis of Francois Truffaut's film of the same name (1962), with the character of Jules firmly based on Hessel.

Hessel, like many German Jews, volunteered to fight for Germany in the First World War. Afterwards he started working at

Rowohlt Verlag in Berlin as well as writing more novels and essays, and working with Benjamin. Despite being targeted by the Nazis, Hessel and his family did not flee for France until 1938. Two years later, he and his son Ulrich were sent to the internment camp Les Milles, where he suffered a stroke, dying shortly afterwards from long-term complications. Hessel's other son with Grund, Stéphane, fought for the French Resistance and went on to become a diplomat and author of the worldwide bestselling anti-capitalist essay *Time for Outrage!*

Benjamin's uniquely scattered approach to culture (he wrote on everything from ethics to Jewish mysticism, contemporary art to hashish) made him far too radical for any serious academic job at the time, despite being often associated with the Frankfurt School and critical theory via his good friend Theodor Adorno. Alongside his many other writings, Benjamin also explored the idea of the *flâneur*. In 1927, he began his Arcades Project, an enormous and unfinished study of urban strolling related to the famous shopping arcades in Paris.

In 1928 he also published *One-Way Street* (*Einbahnstrasse*), which merged aphorisms, philosophical fragments and associative insights into the conceptual structure of a randomised walk. In 1938 he revised his book *Berlin Childhood around 1900*, which he had begun writing in 1932. Forced to flee Berlin in the same year, he took up residence in Paris and, after the German invasion of France in 1940, fled to Port Bou in northern Spain where, threatened with deportation by the authorities, he committed suicide. In 1950 Adorno finally published *Berlin Childhood* posthumously, a personal homage to the city which contains many *flâneur*-esque asides and insights:

> Not to find one's way around a city does not mean much. But to lose one's way in a city, as one loses one's way in a forest, requires some schooling. Street names must speak to the urban wanderer like the snapping of dry twigs, and little streets in the heart of the

city must reflect the times of day, for him, as clearly as a mountain valley. This art I acquired rather late in life; it fulfilled a dream, of which the first traces were labyrinths on the blotting papers in my school notebooks.

Despite his enormous stature today in academic, literary and cultural circles, the only real public accolade to Benjamin in Berlin is the modest Walter-Benjamin-Platz, located just off Kurfürstendamm. Perhaps this is fitting for a quiet, home-loving man who always preferred the library to the limelight.

Cultural development on and around Auguste-Viktoria-Platz really began again after the First World War. By 1928 the square had become something of a moviegoer's paradise thanks to a cluster of premier cinemas – Ufa-Palast am Zoo, Gloria-Palast (where *The Blue Angel* premièred in 1930), Capitol and Marmorhaus – in addition to a slew of new cafés, theatres and shops. Jewish war survivor Catherine Klein recalls watching a film at the Ufa cinema in 1939:

The Ufa cinema near the Zoo was sold out. We managed to get seats at an exorbitant price from a dealer in the street. It was a story of the Boer war seen from an anti-British angle. The climax which had been described minutely in all the newspapers showed an English concentration camp where Boer families were herded together like sheep and treated abominably.

You could have heard a pin drop, it was so silent in the cinema. The close-up of the face of an old peasant woman being tortured moved all hearts. Waves of pity swept the building.

Suddenly I heard next to me – even now while recalling it I go ice-cold with horror – the voice of my American shouting in disgust: 'Those are phoney! They are authentic photographs of a German concentration camp!'

My pulse raced. Should I jump up and run out of the place? But before I could even move a muscle I heard my own voice shout back at him: 'Aren't you ashamed of yourself? We Germans do not torture women!'

'Well said young woman,' someone near us joined in. All around me I heard excited whispers. Apparently one wasn't quite sure who the culprit was, the search for him in the dark proved difficult.

A reminder of the 1943 air raid that irrevocably changed this part of the city, the neo-Romanesque Gedächtniskirche (Kaiser Wilhelm Memorial Church) – originally built between 1891 and 1895 by architect Franz Schwechten as a symbol of Prussian unity – has also been turned into a highly visible memorial to the destruction of the Second World War, by deliberately not repairing its decapitated tower, which has come to be known locally as the 'chipped tooth'.

Cornelius Ryan, in *The Last Battle*, describes how the church looked to passers-by in the aftermath of the war:

At the top of the battered Kurfürstendamm, Berlin's Fifth Avenue, bulked the deformed skeleton of the once fashionable Kaiser-Wilhelm Memorial Church. The hands on the charred clock face were stopped at exactly 7:30, they had been that way since 1943 when bombs wiped out one thousand acres of the city on a single November evening.

The memorial idea actually came about due to public protests that blocked the West Berlin Senate's plans to demolish the church ruins. A modern parish church and separate belfry were also erected and the new building ensemble consecrated in 1961. The base of the old spire and entrance hall now serves as a memorial hall whose exhibits document the old church through photos and artefacts that survived the bombing.

After 1945 Auguste-Viktoria-Platz became the symbolic centre of West Berlin. Large-scale reconstructions were planned in order to compensate for the loss of the former historical centre around Alexanderplatz and Unter den Linden to East Berlin. In 1947 the square's name was changed to Breitscheidplatz, after Rudolf Breitscheid, a German social democrat killed at Buchenwald concentration camp. The subsequent development included the erection of the Zoo Palast cinema in 1956, the modernist Bikini-Haus office building on the northern side, which was finished in 1957 and houses a 'concept mall' today, and the Schimmelpfeng-Haus office complex, which was built in 1960 on the site of the old Gloria Palast.

After the war, the Kurfürstendamm was rebuilt as West Berlin's retail boulevard par excellence. Several cafés and restaurants were re-established, such as the Café Kranzler (actually just a branch of the now-vanished original on Unter den Linden), and a host of high-end fashion stores moved in, which over subsequent decades have been juxtaposed with high-street shops, electronic shops and fast-food outlets. As well as quickly becoming the leading commercial street of West Berlin during the *Wirtschaftswunder* days of German economic recovery in the 1950s, it was also the site of protests and major demonstrations, mostly by the German student movement.

Ku'damm has long been a draw for foreign writers, not just during its Weimar heyday but also during the Nazi era and afterwards. American author and journalist Thomas Wolfe gives us a description of the street in 1936 via his autobiographical novel *You Can't Go Home Again* (published in 1940), which draws heavily on the author's travels to Berlin:

> It was a grey morning. Below him, save for an occasional motorcar, the quiet thrum of a bicycle, or someone walking briskly to his work with a lean, spare clack of early morning, the Kurfürstendamm was bare and silent. In the centre of the street, above the tram tracks, the fine trees had already lost their summer freshness – that deep and dark intensity of German green which is the greenest green on earth and which has a kind of forest darkness, a legendary sense of coolness and of magic. The leaves looked faded now, and dusty. They were already touched here and there by the yellowing tinge of autumn. A tram, cream-yellow, spotless, shining like a perfect toy,

slid past with a hissing sound upon the rails and at the contacts of the trolley. Except for this, the tram-car made no noise. Like everything the Germans built, the tram and its road-bed were perfect in their function. The rattling and metallic clatter of an American street-car were totally absent. Even the little cobblestones that paved the space between the tracks were as clean and spotless as if each of them had just been gone over thoroughly with a whisk broom, and the strips of grass that bordered the tracks were as green and velvety as Oxford sward.

On both sides of the street, the great restaurants, cafés, and terraces of the Kurfürstendamm had the silent loneliness that such places always have at that hour of the morning. Chairs were racked upon the tables. Everything was clean and bare and empty. Three blocks away, at the head of the street, the clock on the Gedächtnis-kirche belatedly struck seven times. He could see the great, bleak masses of the church, and in the trees a few birds sang.

Sven Regener's Herr Lehmann, the main protagonist of his Kreuzberg slacker novel *Berlin Blues* (published 2001), visits the street in 1989 and is less than impressed:

Herr Lehmann crossed Joachimsthaler Strasse, firmly resolved not to allow his better mood to be spoiled by the sight of the Café Kranzler, which to him symbolised all that made the Kurfürstendamm so intolerable. He strode swiftly along the extreme outer edge of the pavement, where dogshit proliferated and no one else cared to tread, and made for his destination past hotels and motor-showrooms, steakhouses and cafés, souvenir stalls and kitsch shops, thimbleriggers and three-card tricksters.

These days the street has been smartened up to some extent and is more or less constantly thronged with tourists, at least during the daytime; at night it is all but deserted. It also offers several interesting, if less visible, literary sights. One such can be found at No. 15. Today the address houses the franchise of a famous fast-food brand, but the building once housed Mampes Gute Stube, the pub where Joseph Roth wrote his most famous novel, 1932's *The Radetzky March*.

Roth (1894–1939) was an Austrian-Jewish journalist and novelist, and *The Radetzky March* is about the decline and fall of the Austro-Hungarian Empire. Roth moved to Berlin from Vienna in 1920, working mainly as a journalist for a variety of liberal newspapers until he fled the Nazis in 1933. Initially he was not taken with the city, considering it a strange island on the plains where the flotsam and jetsam of Europe had gathered in the wake of the First World War, but he nonetheless made a reputation as an honest and occasionally ruthless chronicler of the city.

His writings are critical dispatches on all aspects of Berlin life. He wrote about the shabby Scheunenviertel (see Chapter 3) where Jewish refugees from Eastern Europe had found a temporary home, he interviewed Czarist army colonels living in homeless shelters and spent weeks in decrepit Kneipen where moneylenders held sway. The cafés and bars around Ku'damm and West Berlin were both office and playground – and sometimes even his living room, since in all his Berlin years he never had a fixed address in the city, preferring to live mostly in hotels and pensions. Besides his journalistic work, Roth also published a series of significant novels, such as *The Spider's Web* (*Das Spinnennetz*, 1923), a novel about the growing influence of the Nazis, *The Rebellion* (*Die Rebellion*, 1924), *The Flight without End* (*Die Flucht ohne Ende*, 1927) and *Job* (*Hiob*, 1930).

One of his temporary Berlin addresses lies a little further along the road at No. 25: the Hotel Zoo. Recently reopened and renovated, the hotel's heyday was during the 1950s and 1960s, when it was the main venue of the Berlinale Film Festival and frequented by many a glamorous film star. Despite such conspicuous accommodations, Roth took a generally dim view of middle- and upper-class Berlin society. *What I Saw*, a collection of his essays, feuilletons and articles, was published as English translation by Michael Hoffmann in 2004, based on the 1996 German collection *Joseph Roth in*

Berlin: A Reading Book for Walkers (*Ein Lesebuch für Spaziergänger*) by Michael Bienert. Roth was not a *flâneur* per se, but nevertheless preferred to get lost in the crowds on Ku'damm from time to time, both for pleasure and inspiration, as confirmed in his essay 'Going for a Walk' (1921, featured in *What I Saw*):

> What I see is the old man with the tin trumpet on the Kurfürstendamm. He is a beggar whose plight draws all the more attention to itself for being inaudible. Sometimes the falsetto of the little tin trumpet is stronger and more powerful than the entire Kurfürstendamm. And the motion of a waiter on the café terrace, swishing at a fly, has more content in it than the lives of all the customers on the café terrace. The fly gets away, and the waiter is disappointed. Why so much hostility to a fly, O waiter?
>
> A cripple who finds a nail file. Someone, a lady, has lost the nail file in the place where he happens to sit down. Of course the beggar starts filing his nails – what else is he to do? The coincidence that has left the nail file in his possession and the trifling movement of filing his nails are enough to lift him about a thousand social classes, symbolically speaking A dog running after a ball, then stopping in front of it, static now and inanimate – unable to grasp how some stupid, brainless rubber thing only a moment ago could have been so lively and spirited – is the hero of a momentary drama. It's only the minutiae of life that are important.

Roth left Berlin for good on 30 January 1933, the day Adolf Hitler was elected chancellor. His books had been burned by the Nazis along with those of his friends Stefan Zweig and Alfred Döblin (see Chapter 3), and he died in Paris in 1939 of exhaustion and the long-term effects of his alcoholism, his collapse without doubt exacerbated by news of the suicide of another of his friends, the playwright Ernst Toller.

His French death certificate lists his occupation as *sans profession*, without profession, a description Roth would no doubt have liked.

Mampes Gute Stube was turned into a stable by Red Army troops in 1945; today only a plaque above the door reminds us of both bar and writer. Though always present in the German literary canon, Roth's work has been increasingly rediscovered by an English-language audience in recent years, with many more collections of his writings being published, such as *Joseph Roth on the End of the World* (Hesperus Press, 2013) and, most recently, *The Hotel Years: Wanderings in Europe between the Wars* (New Directions, 2015).

Roth was not the only writer to combine bars and books on the Kurfürstendamm. At No. 11, another author of the era literally sold his debut novel from a 'book bar' he founded himself in 1912. The writer was Kurt Tucholsky and the book was *Rheinsberg: A Picture Book for Lovers*, a small novella about the romantic outings of a young couple in the town of the title. Whoever bought a copy from the bar received a free schnapps from Tucholsky and the book's illustrator Kurt Szafranski. In the preface to the 1921 edition of the book, he wrote:

> We had opened up the 'Book Bar' on Kurfürstendamm, student nonsense that annoyed people half to death, because the shop had a polyglot sign in all languages, dead or alive – including mumbling – that cheap books were available within. The genteel clientele received schnapps. The press went berserk. *Breslauer Zeitung* was against it, whereas *Vossische Zeitung* endorsed it; Prague and Riga were neutral – we still have the clippings – and the *St. Petersburg Herald* wrote on December 8, 1912, that those who purchased a Wilde received a whisky soda, and those who bought an Ibsen got a Nordic corn. But it wasn't true – we were the ones drinking. And we sold an awful lot of Rheinsbergs.

The book bar closed after a few weeks, probably because they ran out of either books or schnapps – or perhaps both. Just around the corner from the former bar, at Fasanenstrasse 23, an elegant side street lined with art galleries and fashion boutiques, is West Berlin's

Literaturhaus. Set in a handsome nineteenth-century villa, this literary establishment – a major hub for contemporary German literature in Berlin and beyond – is owned by the city but operated by a private association. Built in 1889, the villa was initially used as a residence before becoming a military hospital during the First World War. Throughout the next decades it was used for all manner of purposes – a soup kitchen, a student hostel, a café, even a brothel and a discotheque – but was turned into the Literaturhaus Berlin in 1986.

The literary scene in West Berlin in the 1960s and 1970s was mostly centred on the Literarische Colloquium Berlin (LCB) in Wannsee (see Chapter 5), but in the mid-1980s the Berlin Senate decided that a more central location was needed to engage more specifically with contemporary writing, and the Literaturhaus was established. While the name, suggesting an open house and forum where everyone can engage with literature, did not make sense to Berliners in the beginning, today the name is well established and the house is one of 14 Literaturhäuser in Germany, Austria and Switzerland.

Throughout the year it hosts a range of (mostly German-language) literary events ranging from readings to exhibitions, symposiums and writing workshops. Past guests include Oskar Pastior, Friederike Mayröcker, Paul Auster and Durs Grünbein, and the house also has an associated bookshop on the ground floor that sells German, French and English books, while the top floor café-restaurant is an atmospheric place to enjoy a coffee, brunch or, indeed, a good book.

Roscherstrasse 16, another Kurfürstendamm side street, not far from the Literaturhaus, was once the home of Erich Kästner. An author, poet and screenwriter, Kästner (1899–1974) is best known for his novel *Fabian: The Story of a Moralist*, which was written at this address, as well as for his humorous poems and several children's books – in particular the bestselling *Emil and the Detectives*. Born in Dresden in 1899, Kästner studied in Leipzig and fought in the First World War. He moved to Berlin in 1927, where he worked as a journalist and author, publishing poems, articles and reviews in many of Berlin's important periodicals (*Berliner Tageblatt, Vossische Zeitung* and *Die Weltbühne* among others), where his contemporaries Tucholsky and Roth also published.

Emil and the Detectives, published in 1928, tells the story of a group of young boys who track down and bring to arrest a man who has stolen money from one of them while on a train to Berlin to visit his aunt. Unlike much children's literature of the period, or of any period come to that, the tale avoids sentimental fairytale worlds in favour of a real-life setting in the German capital:

> It had already grown dark. Electric signs flared up everywhere. The elevated railway thundered past. The underground railway rumbled and the noise from the trams and buses and cycles joined together in a wild concert. Dance music was being played in the Café Woerz. The cinemas, in the Nollendorf Square, began their last performance of the evening. And crowds of people pushed their way into them.

Three years later the book was adapted into a film, which was also filmed in Berlin. The book and its sequel, *Emil and the Three Twins*, have since been translated into 59 languages and adapted for the big screen multiple times. Kästner's only major adult novel, *Fabian*, was published in 1931 and has been republished in English as *Going to the Dogs* (Kästner's original title, which was turned down by the publisher) by the *New York Review of Books* in 2012 (translated by Cyrus Brooks). The story revolves around the eponymous protagonist, an unemployed literary expert whose ethics, over time, stand out positively against the general moral decay of the Weimar period. It is a fairly fast-paced book that manages to be both regularly amusing and poignant as well as capturing the bohemian atmosphere of the times:

> In Kurfürstendamm she signalled to a taxi cab, gave an address, climbed in and constrained him to take a seat at her side.
> 'But I've only got two marks left,' he objected.

'That doesn't make much difference,' she replied, and ordered the driver to put out the lights. They were in darkness. The car started and drove off. At the first turn in the road she fell upon him and bit his lower lip. He struck his temple against the frame of the window, caught his head in his hands and said 'Ah.oo! That's a good beginning!'

'Don't be so touchy,' she said, and smothered him with her attentions.

The assault was too sudden for him. He had a pain in his head, and his heart was not in the business.

'I really wanted to write a letter,' he groaned, 'before you throttle me.'

She punched him on the collarbone, laughed up and down the scale with complete self-possession, and went on strangling him. Evidently his attempts to defend himself against the woman were misinterpreted. Every turn of the road led to new entanglements. He asked the gods to spare them further swerves. But the gods were having a day off.

Unlike many other authors critical of the dictatorship, Kästner did not go into exile when the Nazis rose to power, despite being interrogated by the Gestapo several times and the SA burning his books in 1933 – an event Kästner witnessed in person and even wrote about. Denied membership of the Nazi-controlled national writers' guild, the Reichsverband deutscher Schriftsteller, he lived mostly off his royalties until 1942, when he received special exemption to write the screenplay for the *Münchhausen* film under the pseudonym Berthold Bürger. In 1944, Kästner's home in Roscherstrasse was destroyed during a bombing raid, and he lost his library of 3,000 books, his private archive, eight suits and two typewriters. He lived with friends until March 1945, when he left Berlin with counterfeit papers for Tyrol, where friends hid him until the end of the war. For the remainder of his life Kästner lived in Munich, where he died in 1974.

During the 1920s, Charlottenburg was also famous for its Russian immigrant writers and intellectuals. So many had flooded into West Berlin following the 1917 revolution that the district was jokingly referred to as Charlottengrad; Kurfürstendamm became the Nöpski Prospekt and 'German spoken here' signs were not uncommon throughout the area. Berlin was the preferred destination for these émigrés for various reasons: access to the German capital from Russia was easy, life was still relatively affordable and, most important of all, Berlin had the best publishing infrastructure in Europe.

Russian writers and artists such as Sergey Eisenstein and Ilya Ehrenburg frequented the cafés of Breitscheidplatz and Ku'damm. By 1924 there were around 200 Russian-language newspapers, magazines and journals throughout the city, as well as 80 publishing houses and even a Russian high school. Later, like so many others, these refugees were forced to flee again, this time from the Nazis. The fate of two writers especially demonstrates the glory and the drama of the Russians in Berlin: Vladimir Nabokov and Marina Tsvetaeva.

Nabokov (1899–1977), a prolific Russian writer who achieved notoriety for his controversial 1955 novel *Lolita*, was born in St Petersburg as the son of Vladimir Dmitrievich Nabokov, one of the founders of the Constitutional Democratic Party. In 1917 the entire family fled the Russian Revolution to Berlin. Nabokov Sr became editor of the local émigré daily *The Rudder* (*Rul*) until he was murdered by Communist assassins in 1922. Nabokov Jr went to study in England at the University of Cambridge in 1923 before returning to Berlin and scraping a living by publishing short fiction and poetry, participating in literary groups and giving readings. He also published a steady stream of Russian-language novels, from *Mary* (*Mashen'ka*) in 1925 to *The Gift* (*Dar*) in 1938.

From 1932 to 1937 Nabokov, his wife and their son lived at Nestorstrasse 22, in a smart and quiet residential area of Wilmersdorf: 'That flat of ours in one of those newfangled houses built in the modern, boxlike, space-cheating, let-us-have-no-nonsense style,' the protagonist of his novel *Despair* (1936) commented. Despite his tragic family history, Nabokov loved Berlin, and his time there was one of the most productive periods of his life. In 1925 his short story *A Guide to Berlin* was published in the *New Yorker*, a *flâneur*-style, street-level view of the city:

> The horse-drawn tram has vanished, and so will the trolley, and some eccentric Berlin writer in the twenties of the twenty-first century, wishing to portray our time, will go to a museum of technological history and locate a hundred-year-old streetcar, yellow, uncouth, with old-fashioned curved seats, and in a museum of old customs dig up a black, shiny-buttoned conductor's uniform. Then he will go home and compile a description of Berlin streets in bygone days. Everything, every trifle, will be valuable and meaningful: the conductor's purse, the advertisement over the window, that peculiar jolting motion which our great-grandchildren will perhaps imagine – everything will be ennobled and justified by its age.

In 1938, Nabokov and his family fled via Paris to the USA, where Vladimir continued writing and publishing with great success until his death in Switzerland in 1977.

Moscow-born Marina Ivanovna Tsvetaeva (1892–1941) witnessed the Russian Revolution of 1917 and the famine that followed. In an attempt to save her daughter Irina from starvation, she placed her in a state orphanage in 1919, where the child nevertheless died of hunger. Devastated by the experience and forced to flee with her husband Sergei Efron, who had fought with the White Russian forces in the civil war, the couple arrived in Berlin in 1922, renting a room at Trautenaustrasse 9 in Wilmersdorf.

Their stay in Berlin only lasted a couple of months before they moved on to Prague, but Tsvetaeva was feted as a new voice in poetry, and the majority of her poetry collections – *Parting* (1922), *Poems to Blok* and *Psyche* (both 1923) – were published by Russian publishing houses in the German capital. Like Nabokov, in all her letters and poems she describes her time in Berlin as one of the happiest in her life. In 'Berlin' (1922) she wrote:

> Rain hums a lull-a-bye to pain.
> To downpours like quickly descending shutters
> I sleep. Horses' hooves on the quavering
> Asphalt sound like the clapping of hands.
>
> 'Congrats' were said – and died out.
> In gold-dawned having-been-left-ness
> On the most fairy-tale of orphan-hoods
> You, barracks, have taken mercy!

After leaving Berlin, Tsvetaeva and her family lived in increasing poverty in Paris and Prague before returning to Moscow in 1939, but she remained a great admirer of Germany and German artists throughout her life. Her favourite writer was Rainer Maria Rilke, who became a correspondent of hers. When Nazi Germany invaded Prague and a conflict with the Soviet Union was on the horizon, she asked in her poem 'To Germany' (1939):

> In front of Czech farm girls
> You are not lowering your gaze
> But instead mow down
> the rye of their hope with tanks?

Marina and her family suffered greatly in Stalin's Russia. She struggled to find work as a writer, and her husband and daughter Alya were arrested for espionage; Efron was shot in 1941 and Alya served eight years in prison. In 1941, after the German invasion, Marina was evacuated to Yelabuga in the Tartar Autonomous Republic, where she had no means of earning a living. Out of options to support her only remaining son, she hanged herself on

31 August 1941. Today the city that gave her hope remembers her
with a memorial plaque on the house she lived in.

Although it is not as famous – nor as glamorous – Kurfürstendamm has a lesser-known sibling: Kantstrasse, which also has
several interesting literary connections. This grittier boulevard,
built around the same time as Kurfürstendamm, connects
Breitscheidplatz with the trade fair and the radio tower, and instead
of upscale shops and expensive restaurants, it is lined with offices,
discount stores, Asian restaurants and apartment buildings. Jörg
Fauser describes it perfectly in his Berlin crime novel *The Snake
Mouth* (*Das Schlangenmaul*), published in 1985:

> At night, Kantstrasse is the paradise of fleeting dreams. Then the
> lights of the Turkish luncheonettes and the Egyptian snack bars,
> of the Chinese and Spanish restaurants, of the brandy shops and
> neon cafés, the discotheques and striptease-joints offer the right
> illumination for the stories only the city can tell – and only with
> a raspy voice and forked tongue. At night a man believes that in
> this street he will find everything he needs in life; what cannot
> be bought he can imagine, and if he's out for justice he can drink
> up the way to the Charlottenburg district court and wait for the
> blindfold to fall from Lady Justice's eyes. The *Currywurst* at the
> snack bar opposite is supposed to be one of the best in Berlin. I
> don't like *Currywurst*.

Fauser (1944–87) was a prolific novelist, essayist and journalist.
Born in Frankfurt am Main, he broke off his academic studies to
work and travel, living and working in Istanbul and London as a
casual labourer, airport baggage worker and night watchman while
cutting his teeth as a writer. He met Charles Bukowski in Los
Angeles in 1977 to interview him for the German *Playboy*, and the
writers remained pen pals for the rest of Fauser's life. Fauser also
briefly developed a heroin habit and spent much of the rest of his
working life with an alcohol addiction.

Heavily influenced by beat literature and American crime stories, he produced three successful novels, including the hardboiled crime novel *The Snowman* (*Der Schneemann*, 1981) and a plethora of short stories; he also translated works and song lyrics by John Howlett, Joan Baez and the Rolling Stones into German. Acclaimed as the best crime thriller ever written in German, *The Snowman* sold over 200,000 copies and was made into a film starring German rock musician Marius Westernhagen.

Fauser also wrote and recorded music, mostly together with German rock singer Achim Reichel. One of their songs, 'The Player' ('Der Spieler') from the *Blues in Blond* album, made it into the German top ten in 1981. Fauser remained an ardent admirer of the outsiders who had passed through Berlin before him. Of Joseph Roth he wrote that 'in Berlin I know a man, a monster of a drinker, who cut a photo of Roth from a newspaper and pasted it to his door in the backyard, so that he is greeted by a good spirit when he returns from the infamousness of the world.'

Like his contemporary Hunter S. Thompson, Fauser also remained deeply disillusioned by the failure of the ideals of the 1960s and the society he was living in. He moved to Berlin in 1981 and stayed until 1985, working mostly for the city magazine *Tipp*, whose office was located on Kantstrasse. Fauser often wandered down Kantstrasse after work, exploring its numerous bars and brothels. His breakthrough novel *Rohstoff* (1984), describing the journey of his alter ego Harry Gelb through the Europe of the 1960s and 1970s between heroin abuse and alcoholism and between Istanbul and Frankfurt, has been republished in English in 2014 by the Clerkenwell Press as *Raw Material*. On 16 July 1987, Fauser had been out celebrating his forty-third birthday in Munich. At dawn, instead of going back home, he wandered down a stretch of highway where, by chance or by choice, he was struck by a heavy-goods truck and died instantly. On hearing of Fauser's death, Bukowski dedicated a poem to him, called 'Joe'.

The Paris Bar at Kantstrasse 152, opened in 1979, is regarded as a legendary institution in Berlin for both its extravagant list of patrons (Sigmar Polke, Jack Nicholson, Madonna, David Bowie and Iggy Pop have all hung out here) and the art collection on its walls, which includes works by Werner Büttner, Julian Schnabel, Matthias Schaufler, Hubert Kiecol and many more – all of them patrons over the years. The genesis of the art collection was a meeting between owner Michel Würthle, a painter in his own right, and artist Martin Kippenberger in the 1980s, who gave a number of his works to the café on permanent loan, gaining him the status of a special patron who could eat and drink here without the need for cash payments. The bar subsequently became one of the main artist hangouts near the Bahnhof Zoo between the 1970s and the mid-1990s – a sort of successor to the artist cafés of Weimar times. Jörg Fauser sketched the Paris Bar at midnight during that time in *The Snake Mouth*:

> After midnight at Paris-Bar the habitues are squatting. Playwrights from East Berlin on the way to the brothel, lifestyle-journalists looking for an opportunistic fuck or a portion of coke, up-and-coming avantgardists from Swabia or the suburbs of Graz waiting for the connecting flight to New York, fashion designer creating the beggars' look of the Eighties in Kreuzberg backyards, tipsy movie producer wincing at every call: 'If it's Hollywood, I'll call back.'

Kippenberger's work *Paris Bar*, a large colourful oil painting of the inside of the restaurant, decorated the café walls for a long time until the owner sold it to pay off his debts and prevent the bar from being closed (it was auctioned at Christie's for 2.5 million euros). Even though the Paris Bar's reputation has faded a little today, the place is still frequented by the occasional German celebrity or art collector, and the walls and ceilings remain covered in paintings, photographs, collages, installations and sketches.

In 2008 Irish-German writer Hugo Hamilton took his terminally ill friend Nuala O'Faolain, writer, broadcaster and key Irish feminism figure, to Berlin on what would become her last trip

– she died only ten days later. Hamilton retells the trip in his 2014 novel *Every Single Minute*. O'Faolain is named Una in the book; the narrator is called Liam. Together, they are invited for lunch to the Paris Bar, and Liam observes the art on the walls:

> There's a lot of art on the walls at the Paris Bar. Mad paintings, all the way around the restaurant. A light-box attached to the ceiling, illuminated in different colours with the words 'stand still and rot'. I mean, the art is pretty out there, for a restaurant. There is a large black-and-white photo of a man and a woman naked, in their twenties, having sex. The woman has the man's penis in her mouth. And this other couple are having their meal right next to it in silence, paying no attention whatsoever to the man in the photograph looking down with an unhappy expression on his face while the woman is leaning sideways over him with her knees apart. As if it's the most normal thing in the world to have their lunch beside the man and woman having sex, like it's all part of the same thing and you don't have to keep staring at it.
>
> I want to know where they are now, the man and the woman in the photograph. What age are they now and do they still remember. Do they ever come back to the restaurant to look at each other? Do they come back and have dinner together from time to time underneath the photo of themselves having sex? And would people know it was them having sex so close to them having dinner?

Along the road from the Paris Bar is the main S-Bahn station for the area: Bahnhof Zoo. The original station, which no longer exists, was designed in classic Wilhelmian style and opened on 7 February 1882. In 1902 the first Berlin U-Bahn line, the so-called Unterpflasterbahn (today the U2), was opened here. The station was rebuilt with its current design and layout for the 1936 Olympics. After the final closure of the Anhalter Bahnhof in 1952, Bahnhof Zoo remained the only long-distance train station within West Berlin. After reunification the station saw an increase in traffic, especially from the East, but not for long. Despite an outcry from nearby Kurfürstendamm retailers and local politicians, the station dramatically lost its importance following the opening of the new Berlin main station in 2006, which meant long-distance services could now pass through Bahnhof Zoo without stopping.

Today, only a few casual loiterers, beggars and homeless people are there to remind us of the station's past reputation as a dirty and dangerous place. Throughout the 1970s and 1980s, the area was rife with drug addicts and prostitutes, as portrayed in the cult book *Zoo Station* by Christiane F.:

> We went into a café at Bahnhof Zoo that was already open. The whole place was miserable. It gave me the creeps right off the bat. It was the first time I'd been there. It was absolutely disgusting. There were hoboes lying in their own vomit and drunks stumbling around all over the place. I would have never imagined that I'd be spending every afternoon there within just a few months.

Two journalists from the news magazine *Stern* met teenager Christiane Felscherinow (born 1962) in 1978, when she was a court witness against a man who had paid with heroin for sex with underaged girls near Bahnhof Zoo. The journalists wanted to cover the increasing drug problem in West Berlin and arranged a two-hour interview, which was expanded to a two-month research project once Christiane's street smartness and narrative skills were discovered. The collected interviews were published by the Stern publishing house in 1979. The book chronicles Christiane's life from 1975 to 1978, between the ages of 12 and 15, and provides an enthralling yet horrifying look into the Berlin drug scene. The book is written in the first person and interspersed with quotes from Christiane's police reports, statements by her mother and interviews with city authorities.

The English translation of the book was first published by Bantam in 1982 under the title *Christiane F.: Autobiography of a Girl of the*

Streets and Heroin Addict. In 1981 the book was made into a film directed by Uli Edel, released as *Wir Kinder vom Bahnhof Zoo* in Germany and in English-speaking countries as *Christiane F.* The majority of scenes in the movie were either shot around Gropiusstadt where Christiane grew up, or around Bahnhof Zoo. David Bowie, Christiane's favourite singer at the time of the interviews, appears as himself and also produced the movie's soundtrack. Depicted in both the book and the film is The Sound, a famous Berlin nightclub – no longer extant – at Genthiner Strasse 26, near the station, which Christiane and Bowie both used to frequent:

> The next thing I knew, we were finally doing it: we were going into The Sound. As soon as I walked inside, I stopped dead in my tracks. This was nothing like I had imagined. 'Europe's hottest club' was a basement with a low ceiling. It was loud and filthy. On the dance floor, everyone was dancing by themselves, just doing their own thing. Strangely enough, nobody was touching anyone else. There was no physical contact. The air was unbelievably stale and gross. An oscillating fan pushed the nauseating odour lazily around the room.

Christiane moved to the USA for a few years, before returning to Berlin. She was never able to kick her drug habit and continues to be a methadone user to this day, which is also detailed in her follow-up autobiography *My Second Life* (*Mein Zweites Leben*), published in 2013. On the success of her first book and the subsequent move she remarked that the film was an accurate portrayal of her life at the time, but revealed that she does not like it 'that much'. In a December 2013 interview, with *Vice Magazine* she stated that she attended the German premiere of the film with Bowie, who picked her up in a chauffeured limousine: 'I thought David Bowie was going to be the star of my movie, but it was all about me.'

Bahnhof Zoo is being renovated at the time of writing. The façade is to be renewed, and a new restaurant floor looking out over the adjacent zoo will be built as part of the ongoing overhaul of this area. The Beate Uhse sex shop and erotic museum and sports bar Hanne am Zoo, once local landmarks around the corner, have been torn down for a new car park, and swanky hotels like the Bikini 25-hours and the towering five-star Waldorf Astoria are bringing the media and commercial spotlight back to West Berlin. The Zoo Palast cinema and the façade of the Bikini-Haus are the few reminders left of the postwar life in the area, while the only major reference to the creative glories of the Weimar period is the café on the ground floor of the Waldorf Astoria, which has been named the Romanisches Café.

℥ 5 ℥

GRUNEWALD AND
WANNSEE

Grunewald

Grunewald (Green Forest), a locality within the Berlin borough of Charlottenburg-Wilmersdorf, is mostly known for its homonymous forest which – along with Tiergarten – is one of the primary recreational spaces in the city. Also like Tiergarten, the Grunewald served as royal hunting territory for a few centuries, and in fact the name of the area (and forest) derives from the Grunewald hunting lodge of 1543, the oldest preserved palace in Berlin.

The palace was originally reached by a corduroy road (a road made of logs) leading from the Berlin Stadtschloss (see Chapter 2), which would later become the Kurfürstendamm. Daniel James Brown provides a view over the Grunewald in his 2013 novel *The Boys in the Boat*, set in 1936:

> The spot where they emerged from the car was slightly elevated, about a hundred feet higher than the heart of the city. To the west lay the ancient Grunewald forest, where sixteenth-century German princes hunted stags and wild boars and where Berliners of all classes nowadays enjoyed hiking, picnicking, and foraging for mushrooms. To the east, the ancient church spires and peaked rooflines of central Berlin rose above a sea of trees turned red and gold in the crisp autumn air.

*8   S-Bahn Grunewald,
the main gateway to the
Grunewald Forest and also
home to some significant
memorials*

In 1889 four artificial lakes (Dianasee, Koenigssee, Herthasee and Hubertssee) were added to the forest's two natural lakes (Halensee to the north and Hundekehlesee to the south), and Berlin's wealthier residents began building lakeshore villas with large private gardens and parks. Initiated and promoted by Chancellor Otto von Bismarck in the mid-nineteenth century, who helped create a 'mansion colony' at the western end of the Kurfürstendamm, the neighbourhood was incorporated into Greater Berlin in 1920.

The main road through the Grunewald is the historic Koenigsallee, which is lined with many interesting buildings, some of which hold both historical and literary interest. Koenigsallee 65, for example, a beautiful white-and-yellow classicist villa, was once the home of Walther Rathenau (1867–1922), a Berlin-born German-Jewish intellectual and industrialist who in 1914 became director of the Raw Materials Department of the Prussian War Ministry and in 1922 was appointed foreign minister of the Weimar government.

Rathenau displayed his art collection here and entertained many important public figures, including artists, scientists, theatre directors and writers such as Gerhart Hauptmann, Rainer Maria Rilke, Stefan Zweig and Albert Einstein. Rathenau also wrote himself, publishing essays on capitalism and materialism in the weekly German literary magazine *The Future* (*Die Zukunft*) and several books via the S. Fischer publishing house, among them *Criticism of the Times* (*Zur Kritik der Zeit*, 1912) and *On the Mechanism of the Mind* (*Zur Mechanik des Geistes*, 1913). Though he mainly focused on topics of society and progress, he always remained interested in how change expressed itself at street level in his hometown. In 1899 he expresses it in a sarcastic yet warming essay on Berlin called 'The Most Beautiful City in the World':

> As for the Berliners themselves, I am not really sure: do they exist no longer, or do they not yet exist at all? It is not exactly the fertility of the soil that has made the population grow by a factor of ten in the course of three generations. I believe that most Berliners are from Posen and the rest from Breslau. None of this means that our city is unappreciated, however. The Englishman likes our wide, welcoming streets, with their neatly whitewashed buildings; the Frenchman likes the colorful strings of streetcars and the mounted policemen; the Russian loves our knack of converting all public squares into charming little vegetable patches. One man from Chicago took home a sample paving stone and declared Berlin to be a charming summer resort.

Rathenau's commitment to social justice and equality made him a popular figure in Weimar Germany, but he was despised by the Nazis for his liberal politics and his Jewish background (even though he was secular). On 24 June 1922, while driving from his house towards the Foreign Office in Wilhelmstrasse one morning, his car was overtaken and three right-wing members of the ultra-nationalist Organisation Consul opened fire with a submachine gun and threw a grenade at Rathenau. He was killed instantly, and two of the assassins were also killed in a subsequent firefight with the police.

A memorial stone, erected opposite the corner of Wallotstrasse in 1929 marks the scene of the crime and pays tribute to a politician who, according to Stefan Zweig in his 1942 autobiography *The World of Yesterday*, 'had to master the fate of Germany during a most tragic epoch [...] and who was hit by the first murder shot of the National Socialists eleven years before Hitler rose to power'.

Koenigsallee 45, today a green-and-beige apartment block built in the 1980s, was the home of Weimar writer Hedwig 'Vicki' Baum (1888–1960), who lived here between 1926 and 1931. Born in Vienna into a Jewish family, Baum studied harp at the musical academy in Vienna before moving in 1913 to Darmstadt, where she was employed by the local opera house and met the conductor Richard Lert, whom she married in 1916. After the birth of her first son she switched to writing. Her first novel *Early Shadows: The Story of a Childhood* (*Frühe Schatten: Die Geschichte einer Kindheit*) appeared in 1920, followed by *Stage Door* (*Der Eingang zur Bühne*) in the same year, both family novels drawing heavily on her personal experiences in terms of leaving her home and working as a musician.

The latter novel was published by Ullstein Verlag (see Chapter 1), for whom she worked as an editor after moving to Berlin in 1926. Her main work, *Grand Hotel* (*Menschen im Hotel*, 1929), is considered one of the first so-called 'hotel' novels and tells the story of a fading ballerina, a shady nobleman and other colourful characters passing through an elegant Berlin hotel over the course of a weekend. In the passage below, the main protagonist Kringelein enters the hotel lobby:

> He saw the marble pillars with stucco ornament, the illuminated fountain, the easy chairs. He saw men in dress coats and dinner jackets, smart cosmopolitan men. Women with bare arms, in

wonderful clothes, with jewelry and furs, beautiful, well-dressed women. He heard music in the distance. He smelt coffee, cigarettes, scents, whiffs of asparagus from the dining room and the flowers [...] He felt the thick carpet beneath his black leather boots [...] The lounge was brilliantly illuminated and the light was delightfully golden [...] A waiter flitted by carrying a silver tray on which were wide shallow glasses with a little dark-golden cognac in each [...] but why in Berlin's best hotel were the glasses not filled to the brim?

The book first appeared in serial form in the *Berliner Illustrierte* and was also performed as a play. In 1931 it was translated and performed on Broadway as *Grand Hotel*, and Baum spent seven months in New York and Hollywood to work on a screen adaptation, which premiered in 1932 as *Grand Hotel*. Although she briefly returned to Berlin, she emigrated properly to Los Angeles with her family in the same year, and she worked there for ten years as a scriptwriter and journalist. For subsequent novels, such as *Hotel Shanghai* (1939), she returned to Germany even though her books had been banned; in *Hotel Berlin '43* – published in 1944 – she anticipated the downfall of the Third Reich.

A short distance from Vicki Baum's former home is Grunewald S-Bahn train station, one of the best access points to both the Grunewald neighbourhood and the forest. Opened in 1879 and furnished with its 'castle gate' style entrance in 1889, the station was connected to the city's main S-Bahn network in 1928. From 1941, it served as one of the main hubs for the Nazi deportations, with more than 50,000 Berlin Jews transported from here to Litzmannstadt and Warsaw and, from 1942 onwards, directly to Auschwitz and Theresienstadt.

In front of the station building sits one of Berlin's 12 Buchboxen (book boxes), former telephone boxes that have been transformed into informal public libraries where people can leave and exchange books. The Grunewald Buchbox has a whole shelf dedicated to the history and topic of Mahnmal Gleis 17 (Track 17 Memorial). Inaugurated in 1991, the memorial consists of two parts: along the small road leading down to the Grunewald Forest is an 18-metre concrete block with embedded silhouettes of deportees, the official memorial of the city Senate and the Charlottenburg-Wilmersdorf district, created by Polish artist Karol Broniatowski; and the platforms of the remaining track used for the deportations have been embedded (by Deutsche Bahn) with 186 steel plates inscribed with the dates of the transports, the number of deportees as well as the train's route and final destination.

A brick tunnel through the station leads to what Rainer Maria Rilke called 'the magical forest country' – the 32-square-kilometre Grunewald Forest, which is bordered by the Havel river to the west and Wannsee lake to the south. Rilke (1875–1926) was an Austrian poet and novelist. Born in Prague, he studied literature and art history in Prague and Munich and travelled extensively throughout Europe before arriving in Berlin in 1897 with his girlfriend, the writer Lou Andreas-Salomé. From 1898 to 1900 they lived on the border of the Grunewald Forest, at Hundekehlestrasse Schmargendorf 11. It was at this address that Rilke worked on the first draft of his prose poem *The Love and Death of Cornet Christopher Rilke* (published 1912). Breaking up with Andreas-Salomé in 1900, Rilke left for Paris. His relationship with Berlin, where he returned intermittently in the following years, remained a strained one, as can be seen in a 1910 letter he wrote to Countess Manon zu Solms-Laubach:

This is only to catch up, but still you must know how much I enjoyed your kind letter of January 23. It reached me in Berlin, where (you will remember) I never like being; among the things that come together on such rare visits, there are always some that are warm, good, yes, quite indispensable: I don't want to complain. But there are always too many then for me (who am adhering more and more to an aloof and solitary life), and Berlin hasn't the way of feeding one things one after the other; one gets everything thrown into one's house at once, one is supposed to see and accomplish everything without coming to one's senses; it is assumed that one has a freshness, an uninterrupted capability, a prompt presence of mind, which I can muster only occasionally and only way inside for my work [*sic*]. So in Berlin I always fare like a bad schoolboy who is behind in everything and ends by no longer grasping from his place of punishment what is going on at the blackboard.

Yet Berlin is where Rilke met Stefan George and Gerhart Hauptmann, the latter of whom remained a pen pal throughout his life – 'Ah, how good it is to be among people who are reading,' Rilke exclaims in his semi-autobiographical (and only) novel *The Notebooks of Malte Laurids Brigge* (1910). Rilke continued to travel, and during a stay at Duino Castle near Trieste in Italy began writing what would become his most famous poetry collection: *Duino Elegies* (published in 1923). He visited Berlin again in 1916, and from 1919 settled in Switzerland, where he died of leukaemia at the age of 51.

As rapid urbanisation began encroaching on the city's green spaces in the early twentieth century, the city administration pledged to protect the Grunewald. The forest was designated a nature reserve in 1915, and further construction forbidden. But in 1937 Hitler decided that the forest, specifically the area overlooking the Olympic stadium now known as Teufelsberg (easily accessible from the train station today), would need to make way for his megalomania. His court architect Albert Speer began the design and construction of a 'university town' in the northern part of the forest that, together with the Olympic site, would comprise the western gateway to World Capital Germania.

The planned core of this village was the Wehrtechnische Fakultät (Military Technical Faculty) of the Technische Hochschule academy in Charlottenburg (today TU Berlin) where the cadets of the

Wehrmacht would receive the best training and research facilities; its foundation stone was laid by Hitler personally. Construction was halted in 1941 and was never continued due to the war; the shell of the building was blown up after the war and 25 million cubic metres of Berlin rubble piled upon it, inadvertently creating the highest landmark in flat Berlin.

The 115-metre hill was named Teufelsberg (Devil's Mountain) after the small Teufelssee lake it its base. In 1963, the Allies decided to erect a radar listening post here, and Operation Field Station Berlin began: 1,500 Americans and British soldiers and employees listening in on and recording Soviet communications. The life of a Teufelsberg employee was not necessarily as exciting as Cold War spy novels might present it, however. One former worker told Public Radio International: 'They'd [East German officials] be discussing agriculture reports, things like that. They were having a bad crop of potatoes. And if you were on the graveyard shift, or really just after 8 o'clock at night, we just switched over to Radio Luxembourg and listened to rock 'n' roll.' The station ceased to operate in 1991 but the buildings and five large radar domes are still there, albeit decayed, fenced off and slathered in graffiti, and have become a popular urban exploration site. The slopes below the station building are used as a take-off point for hang-gliders as well as for skiing and sledging in snowy weather.

North of Teufelsberg lies the Friedhof Grunewald. Dating back to 1878, it was originally named Friedhof der Namenlosen (Cemetery of the Nameless), and the oldest graves here are indeed unmarked. This is because the cemetery only took in those who died by their own hand, and a Church decree from 1830 stipulated that those who committed suicide could not be buried in a church-yard and that the bodies were to be interred without ceremony. Cemetery records suggest that many graves were those of young chambermaids made pregnant by their employers, the owners of the nearby Grunewald villas. In 1928 a stone wall was built around the

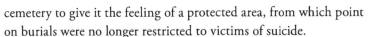

cemetery to give it the feeling of a protected area, from which point on burials were no longer restricted to victims of suicide.

The cemetery is still in use today and its headstones are richly varied, ranging from weeping Victorian stone angels and Orthodox crosses for Russian emigrés, to more contemporary designs. Among those at rest here is Clemens Laar (1906–60), a fiction author popular with the Nazis for works such as *The Bloody Border* (*Die blutige Grenze*, 1937) and *The Ghost U-Boat* (*Das Geister-U-Boot*, 1937). Also buried here is rock singer and actress Nico (Christa Päffgen, 1938–88), the Cologne-born model and singer who also starred in films by Andy Warhol and Federico Fellini and famously sang on the Velvet Underground debut album (1967) that also carries her name: *The Velvet Underground & Nico*. From the age of two Nico lived with her mother, first in the small town of Spreewald in Brandenburg and then, after fleeing Russian occupation in 1946, the American sector in Berlin. Discovered by German fashion photographer Heinz Oestergaard in her teens, Nico started working as a model at the KaDeWE fashion shows as well as in Paris and Rome. Her blonde hair, 1.8 metre height, prominent cheekbones and strangely deep, almost masculine voice made her popular on screen too, hence an appearance alongside Marcello Mastroianni in Fellini's *La Dolce Vita* in 1959.

Moving to New York in 1966, Nico worked with Andy Warhol, who introduced her to the Velvet Underground. After singing on the debut album she was ousted by Lou Reed (with whom she had had a short affair) and began working with Velvet Underground member and producer John Cale, with whom she released a 1968 solo album *The Marble Index*. Nico continued to release a string of albums over the following decades as well as collaborating with major British bands like the Rolling Stones and Siouxsie & the Banshees. A frequent drug user, she died of a heart attack while on vacation on Ibiza. At her funeral, friends played a tape of 'Mütterlein', a song from her solo album *Desertshore* (1970).

West of the cemetery, at the shore of the Havel, sits the Grunewaldturm, a striking 55-metre-high red-brick building designed by architect Franz Heinrich Schwechten and opened in 1898. The monument was erected to mark the hundredth anniversary of the birth of Kaiser William I and to express the gratitude of the people of Brandenburg towards their ruler. The ground floor features a domed hall with a marble statue of the Kaiser, and 204 steps lead up to the top of the monument, offering panoramic views of the region. Next to the tower is a popular restaurant and beer garden with sweeping vistas down to the Wannsee lake.

Further south, almost at the border to Wannsee, lies another idyllic lake: the 5.5-kilometre-long Schlachtensee, a favourite summer spot for Berliners. Alfred Döblin (see Chapter 3) writes about the lake in his science-fiction novel *Mountain Seas and Giants*:

> I walk on the soft, springy ground at the low-lying end of the Schlachtensee. Over there the tables and chairs of the Old Fisherman's Cottage, haze above the water and the reeds. I'm walking on the floor of the air. Enclosed in this moment with myriads of things in this corner of the world. Together we are this world: soft ground, reeds, lake, chairs, tables of the Fisherman's Cottage, carp in the water, gnats above it, birds in the gardens of the villas of Zehlendorf, cuckoo's call, grasses, sand, sunshine, clouds, fishermen, poles, lines, hooks, bait, children singing, warmth, electric tension in the air. How blindingly the sun rages up there. Who is that? What a mass of stars rage beside it; I can't see them.
>
> The dark, rolling, roaring power. You dark, furious, intertwined – you gentle, delightful, unimaginably beautiful, unbearably heavy, unceasing powers. Trembling grasping flickering thousand-foot thousand-spirit thousand-head.

The lake's clear, good-quality water and picturesque contours were a major theme for painter Walter Leistikow (1865–1908). Leistikow travelled to Berlin at the age of 18 to study at the Prussian Academy

9   *The former Cold War spy station known as Teufelsberg (Devil's Mountain)*

of Arts, but was dismissed after two years. He took private classes under landscape painters Hermann Eschke and Hans Gute, going on to work as a freelance painter and art critic. In 1892 he joined the non-academic arts group Die XI, and in 1898 together with fellow painters Max Liebermann (see below) and Franz Skarbian became one of the founders of the Berlin Secession, an independent art movement that rejected the cultural censorship of the Prussian art academies. To support himself financially he also designed furniture, carpets and picture cards (for the Cologne chocolate factory Stollwerck).

In 1894 he married Danish poet Anna Mohr, whom he had met in Berlin, and also befriended modernist Danish painter Edvard Munch, who portrayed the couple after their wedding. Leistikow also tried his hand at writing. In 1893 he published a novella called 'His Cousin' ('Seine Cousine') in the *Freie Bühne* magazine, and in 1896 put out a novel entitled *On the Doorstep* (*Auf der Schwelle*). His literary attempts were not well received by critics, and he remained a landscape painter for the rest of his life.

Wannsee

Located just south of Grunewald, the locality of Wannsee is today an official part of Steglitz-Zehlendorf, the westernmost borough of Berlin. The area is named after the Grosser Wannsee (Greater Wannsee) and the Kleiner Wannsee (Little Wannsee), which – despite their separate names – are actually one lake, both fed by the Havel river and separated by a bridge. The lakefront is peppered with yacht clubs, including the second oldest in Germany, and yachts and excursion boats criss-cross the waters each day of the week. Throughout the centuries the Wannsee has become a primary place of leisure for Berliners – even during the Second World War, as Philip Kerr notes in his 2015 novel *The Lady from Zagreb*, set in 1943:

> The Wannsee looked like an impressionist painting of some idyllic scene on the River Seine at the turn of the century, the kind that looks like the picture is suffering from a severe case of spots. There were canoes and outrigged shells, sailing boats, and sloops, but no boats that required petrol; petrol was even harder to get than pills and booze. There were plenty of young women around, too – which was one of the reasons Nebe liked it here – but no young men; they were all in uniform and probably fighting for their lives in some Russian shell hole.

The Wannsee's most famous leisure spot is Strandbad Wannsee, the lake's famous open-air lido at Wannseebadweg 25. Opened in 1907 the lido offers over 1,275 metres of sandy beach, water slides and a nudist area, and grew so popular throughout the twentieth century that it was immortalised in song by child star Conny Froboess, whose song 'Pack Your Bathing Trunks' ('Pack die Badehose ein') became a cult hit in Germany in 1951. It's also possible to take ferries and pleasure boats across the Wannsee – including an official ferry run by the Berlin public transport system that links Wannsee with the charming village of Kladow – and walk trails along its shores.

Reachable within 30 minutes from the city centre on the S-Bahn, the red-brown expressionist Wannsee S-Bahn station, built in 1928, is the main gateway to the area for many visitors from Berlin. A few minutes south of the station, off a small residential street, is a small park that contains the Kleistgrab (Kleist's grave), a reminder that the banks of the Wannsee were also the place where writer Heinrich von Kleist (1777–1811) shot his beloved Henriette Vogel before killing himself.

Kleist was born in Frankfurt an der Oder in Brandenburg and, after serving in the Prussian army, studied law and philosophy at the Viadrina University in his hometown. After finishing his studies, in 1800 he received a subordinate post in the Prussian Ministry of Finance and moved to Berlin. Always interested in the arts, he travelled extensively in his spare time, managing to meet Goethe and Schiller in Weimar and visiting literary salons in Leipzig and Dresden. In 1803 he procured a leave of absence and settled in Thun in Switzerland, where he wrote his first book, a tragedy entitled *The Schroffenstein Family* (published 1803). In the same year he briefly returned to Berlin before receiving a new posting to Königsberg in East Prussia, where he continued working on plays such as *The Broken Jug* (*Der Zerbrochene Krug*, 1808), *Amphitryon* (1807), *Penthesilea* (1808) and the novellas *Michael Kohlhaas* (1810) and *The Earthquake in Chile* (*Das Erdbeben in Chili*, 1810).

Travelling back to Brandenburg in 1807, Kleist was mistakenly arrested by the French occupation authorities as a spy and incarcerated in a military prison in France. After his release the following year, he moved to Dresden, where he started publishing the journal *Phöbus*, one of Germany's first literary journals. In 1810 he moved back to Berlin to work as the editor of the *Berliner Abendblätter* newspaper, where he published stories and essays by fellow writers such as Achim von Arnim, Clemens Brentano and Adelbert von Chamisso.

It was in the same year, 1810, that he met the married intellectual Henriette Vogel at a Berlin literary salon, and the two began an affair. Always inclined to melancholy, Kleist became increasingly frustrated with what he perceived as a lack of financial success for his literary achievements and academic criticism of his work. The genesis and details of Vogel's and von Kleist's suicide pact are unknown, but it is clear that Vogel was terminally ill with cancer and that Kleist was more disheartened and depressed than ever before.

Vogel wrote to her husband on the day before her death: 'No longer can I endure life, as with iron bands my heart is bound – call it sickness, weakness, whatever you like, I myself cannot name it – I can say only that I look forward to my death as the greatest joy.' On the same day, Kleist wrote to his sister Ulrike von Kleist that 'death may grant you a death that is only half like mine in happiness and inexpressible lightness: that is the most sincere and heartfelt wish I have for you.' On the evening of 21 November 1811, after drinking coffee at a nearby restaurant, Kleist shot Vogel in the heart and then himself in the head. His views on death and consciousness were noted in his essay 'On the Marionette Theatre':

'Now, my excellent friend,' said my companion, 'you are in possession of all you need to follow my argument. We see that in the organic world, as thought grows dimmer and weaker, grace emerges more brilliantly and decisively. But just as a section drawn through two lines suddenly reappears on the other side after passing through infinity, or as the image in a concave mirror turns up again right in front of us after dwindling into the distance, so grace itself returns when knowledge has as it were gone through an infinity. Grace appears most purely in that human form which either has no consciousness or an infinite consciousness. That is, in the puppet or in the god.'

'Does that mean,' I said in some bewilderment, 'that we must eat again of the tree of knowledge in order to return to the state of innocence?'

'Of course,' he said, 'but that's the final chapter in the history of the world.'

Because of the nature of their deaths, Kleist and Vogel were denied a church burial and were instead interred by the lake. An immediate tourist attraction for Romantics, the grave nevertheless soon fell into disrepair and was only refurbished when Kleist was claimed by the Nazis and commemorated with a large headstone for the 1936 Olympic Games. Officials had to redo the stone, however, upon discovering that they had accidentally inscribed it with a quote by Jewish poet Max Ring.

In 2011, the site was completely revamped again: paths were laid through the nearby woodlands, the area was landscaped, and both Kleist and Vogel were given fresh headstones. Hers is new while his is the original, turned 180 degrees and again inscribed with the Ring quote:

> Er lebte, sang und litt
> in trüber, schwerer Zeit.
> Er suchte hier den Tod
> und fand Unsterblichkeit.
>
> He lived, sang and suffered
> in gloomy and difficult times.
> He sought death here
> and found immortality.

In honour of von Kleist's life and work, the Kleist Prize was first awarded in 1912 on the hundredth anniversary of his death and has since become a prestigious award for German literature. It was one of the important literary prizes of the Weimar Republic, awarded to playwrights and writers such as Bertolt Brecht, Carl Zuckmayer and Anna Seghers and – despite being discontinued under the Nazis and during most of the Berlin Wall years – was restarted in 1985. In 2013 it was awarded to contemporary Berlin author Katja Lange-Müller for her life's work.

Near the Kleistgrab, at Sandwerder 5, is a literary meeting point for the living: the LCB. Despite a somewhat hidden location on the shores of the Wannsee, this beautiful red-brick villa and former hotel, which dates from 1885, is one of the main German-language literary hubs in the city. Founded in 1963 by Walter Höllerer, a writer and literature professor, the aim of the LCB was to bring fresh impulses to an ailing West Berlin literary scene. Supported by the Berlin Senate, Höllerer managed to invite many German and international writers to the house for readings and discussions, such as John Dos Passos, Ingeborg Bachmann and, at one point, Gruppe 47 (see Chapter 1).

Today the LCB hosts workshops, readings and conferences, and facilitates collaborations and initiatives such as the literaturport.de online author-encyclopedia, the literary festival European Border-lands for young authors from countries neighbouring the EU, and the Deutsche Übersetzerfonds, a support association for German translators. Last but not least, the LCB also operates as a guest house for speakers and scholarship holders; Slovenian poet Aleš Šteger describes an atmospheric stay in 2010 on the LCB blog:

> Sometimes I left my room late in the evening and went down to the deserted ground floor. The floorboards creaked, and pale silhouettes of the figures on the photos emerged from the walls. I didn't turn the light on. As discreetly as possible, I made my way through the empty room. I always found a chair at the window, and listened to the stories that the throng of writers' ghosts, each of them muttering his unending monologue, tried to fob off on me that night.

There are several more cultural and historical villas worth exploring around the Wannsee. At Colomienstrasse 3, for example, visitors can visit the Liebermann Villa, the former home of impressionist painter Max Liebermann (1847–1935). The famed artist, who also served for a time as president of the Prussian Academy of Arts (see Chapter 1), lived in the house until 1932. The son of a wealthy Jewish fabric manufacturer, Liebermann grew up in a townhouse right next to the Brandenburg Gate and attended the University of Berlin before continuing his studies in Weimar, Paris and the Netherlands. After serving as a medic in the army and living and working as a painter in Munich, Liebermann returned to Berlin in 1884, cofounding the Berlin Secession movement with Walter Leistikow (see above) and Franz Skarbina in 1898 and hiring architect Paul Otto Baumgarten to build the Wannsee villa in 1909 as a place where he could work undisturbed. While refining his personal style, mostly with landscape paintings such as *Landhaus in Hilversum* (1901) and *Das Atelier des Künstlers* (1902), he began his own contemporary art collection and increasingly worked as a portrait painter, depicting the likes of art historian Wilhelm von Bode in 1904.

As president of the Berlin Secessionists, Liebermann also organised many of the movement's exhibitions over the following years, featuring artists such as Arnold Böcklin, Lovis Corinth, Pablo Picasso, Henri Matisse and Georges Braques. After resigning his presidential position in 1913, he continued to work at his city house at Pariser Platz and at Wannsee, commenting at the outbreak of the First World War, 'I'll continue as quiet as possible, as I think this is the best way to serve the public.'

After the war, in 1920, Liebermann was made president of the Berlin Arts Academy. In 1927 he painted an official portrait of President von Hindenburg, which did not sit well with the Nazis, who later forced him to resign his academy presidency and confiscated his villa, which was turned into a secretarial school and later in the war into a hospital. Liebermann returned to his Pariser Platz home, where he died on 8 February 1935.

Another Wannsee villa taken over by the Nazis for more sinister purposes lies close to Liebermann's house. Am Grossen Wannsee 56–8, the expropriated villa of Jewish businessman Ernst Marlier (built 1915), became the house of the Wannsee Conference, where Nazi officials gathered in 1942 to plan the 'Final Solution to the Jewish Question'. The meeting, held on 20 January of that year, was presided over by director of the Reich Main Security Office Reinhard Heydrich and conducted by SS Lieutenant Adolf Eichmann, one of the main planners of the Holocaust. Speaking for an hour before taking questions, Heydrich presented the plan to transport Jewish people from German-occupied territories to labour camps in German-occupied Eastern Europe. After being captured in 1962, Eichmann stated during his trial in Israel that after the meeting, which lasted less than two hours, cognac was served and Heydrich was in excellent spirits. Laurent Binet describes the scene in his novel about Heydrich's subsequent assassination in the Czech Republic, *HHhH* (2010):

> But it was at Wannsee that the genocide was rubber-stamped. No longer need the task be given, more or less on the quiet (if you can really talk of killing millions of people 'on the quiet'), to a few death squads; now the entire political and economic infrastructure of the regime is at their disposal. The meeting lasted barely two hours. Two hours to settle what were essentially legal questions: What should be done with half-Jews? And with quarter-Jews? With Jews who'd been decorated in the First World War? With Jews married to German women? Should these men's Aryan widows be compensated by giving them a pension? As in all meetings, the only decisions that are really made are those decided beforehand. In fact, for Heydrich, it was just a question of informing all the Reich ministries that they were going to have to work together with one objective in mind: the physical elimination of all Europe's Jews.

Philip Kerr's hard-boiled fictional private eye Bernie Gunther pays a visit to the villa in late 1942. Gunther, created by Scottish author Kerr (born 1956) following several trips to the German capital, is a sardonic private eye in the style of Philip Marlowe. By forcing Gunther to work for several Nazi organisations after 1933, Kerr allows the reader a realistic and well-researched glimpse of Berlin during these years. Beginning in Germany in the 1930s with *March*

Violets (published in 1989), the ten Gunther novels cover the Nazi rise to power and the Second World War II, as well the postwar period:

> There was an SS armoured car parked in front of a large set of wrought-iron gates and a guardhouse with a flag, otherwise everything was quiet and respectable as a family of retired honeybees. If there was any trouble around there it certainly wasn't going to come from the villa's moss-backed neighbours. Trouble in Wannsee means your lawn mower has stopped working, or the maid didn't turn up on time. Stationing an armoured car at Am Grosser Wannsee was like insuring a Vienna choirboy to sing Christmas carols. Inside a largish landscaped park was a Greek revival style villa with thirty or forty windows. It wasn't the biggest villa on the lake but the bigger houses had bigger walls and were only ever seen by bank presidents and millionaires.

In 1992, on the fiftieth anniversary of the conference, a memorial was opened in the villa that includes the permanent exhibition Die Wannsee-Konferenz und der Völkermord an den europäischen Juden (The Wannsee Conference and the Genocide of the European Jews). The venue also hosts changing exhibitions related to the subject of the Holocaust as well as a related library that holds all 18 books written by Joseph Wulf (1912–74), a Jewish historian of German-Polish origin.

A survivor of Auschwitz, Wulf moved to Berlin in 1952 to work on a series of books analysing the inner workings of the Nazi regime and the Holocaust, the first of which, *The Third Reich and the Jews* (*Das Dritte Reich und die Juden*), was published in 1955. His research and works were not initially welcome in West Germany, which was still very much in denial about the Holocaust a decade after the war ended, though he did nevertheless obtain academic respect for the thoroughness of his work.

From 1965 onwards, Wulf worked on an initiative to turn the Wannsee villa, by then a holiday hostel for children, into a documentation centre. His initiative was well received in Jewish circles and gained international support by writers such as Ralph Giordano and Golo Mann, and the leader of the Jewish community in Berlin, Heinz Galinski. But the Berlin Senate refused to consider the proposal, even after the World Jewish Congress offered to pay for a new children's home in the villa's grounds. After repeated attempts to convince the Senate over the following years failed, Wulf and his committee gave up all hope of success and disbanded in 1973. A year later, soon after his wife's death, Wulf committed suicide by throwing himself from the window of his Charlottenburg apartment. Shortly before his death, he wrote a letter to his son David: 'I have published 18 books about the Third Reich and they have had no effect. You can document everything to death for the Germans. There is a democratic regime in Bonn. Yet the mass murderers walk around free, live in their little houses, and grow flowers.'

From the villa, visitors can take multiple walking and cycling tracks through the Düppeler Forst, the woodland that covers the north side of the Wannsee neighbourhood, from where regular ferries run to the Pfaueninsel (Peacock Island), whose charming blend of nature and history inspired Theodor Fontane back in 1864: 'An image from my childhood springs to mind like a fairytale: a palace, peacocks sitting up on a high branch or fanning out their tails, fountains, shady lawns, winding paths running in all directions, but leading nowhere in particular.' The island was landscaped and cultivated by Frederick William II in 1794–7, and he also had a small castle built here. His son Frederick William III and Queen Louise (see Chapter 4) used the Pfaueninsel as a romantic retreat, and it quickly became identified with the popular Prussian queen. After Louise's death in 1810, her mausoleum was established at the Charlottenburg Palace and in 1829, when it was replaced by one of red granite, the original sandstone façade was brought to the Pfaueninsel and erected at the edge of the wood as the Luisentempel.

There island also contains the neo-Gothic Kavaliershaus, a folly erected by Frederick William, and the Meierei, a two-storey dairy farm built around the same time as the castle and designed to look like a ruined Gothic church. The Prussian kings also kept an exotic menagerie here that included buffalo, kangaroos and lions, all kept in large enclosures, as well as dozens of exotic birds in the royal aviary. In 1842 Frederick William IV sent the animals ashore, where they formed the beginnings of the Berlin Zoo (see Chapter 4). Only the peacocks that gave the island its name still roam here, and in summer the city of Berlin employs two water buffalo here as natural 'lawnmowers'.

The island was turned into a nature reserve in 1924. In 1936, the Nazi government held the closing celebration of the Olympic Summer Games here, with fireworks and a party organised by the Italian embassy involving over 1,000 guests. During the Cold War, Pfaueninsel ended up right against the West Berlin border, creating a bizarre day-trip and family destination that was closely observed by GDR guard towers and machine guns. Today the fortifications are gone, and the island is an official UNESCO World Heritage site.

South of Pfaueninsel, the large green steel arches of the Glienicke Bridge span the Havel river and connect the Wannsee district with the Brandenburg capital of Potsdam. Although a bridge has been in place here since 1660, the current bridge – named after nearby Glienicke Palace – was completed in 1907. It was reconstructed after the Battle of Berlin in 1945 and renamed the Bridge of Unity in 1949 – a strange choice given that the border between East Germany and West Berlin ran exactly through the middle of the bridge. In 1952 GDR authorities closed the bridge to all civilian traffic, and it was completely closed after the Berlin Wall went up in 1961.

Or almost completely: the Glienicke Bridge is also known as the Bridge of Spies for the agent exchanges that took place here during the Cold War years. The first exchange took place here one year after the closure, when the USA released Soviet spy Colonel Rudolf Abel in exchange for American spy-plane pilot Francis Powers, an event made into a 2015 Steven Spielberg movie aptly named *Bridge of Spies*. There was another exchange in 1964, then a two-decade break before 27 agents were exchanged in 1985. The final spy exchange took place in February 1986, when Soviet dissident Anatoly Shcharansky and three Western agents were exchanged for GDR spy Karl Koecher and four other Eastern agents. The event was hardly clandestine; rather, it was televised.

In John Le Carré's spy novel *Smiley's People* (1979) and the BBC mini-series of the same name (1982), a final confrontation between main protagonist George Smiley and his nemesis, the Soviet spymaster Karla, takes place on Glienicke Bridge:

'I have destroyed him with the weapons I abhorred, and they are his. We have crossed each other's frontiers, we are the no-men of this no-man's land.'

Walking a short way back along the embankment, almost to where the cross stood, Smiley took another look at the bridge, as if to establish whether anything had changed, but clearly it had not, and though the wind appeared a little stronger, the snow was still swirling in all directions.

On the evening of 10 November 1989, the day after the opening of the Berlin Wall, the Glienicke Bridge was reopened for pedestrians and traffic. The intrigue surrounding the Bridge of Spies continues and the bridge remains a popular stop for tourist buses. The bridge itself has stayed largely the same, and, aside from its historical allure, offers scenic views over the Havel and nearby Glienicke Palace.

⅁ 6 ⅁

SCHÖNEBERG

The roots of the former West Berlin district of Schöneberg – which since 2001 has been officially merged with an adjacent borough to form Tempelhof-Schöneberg – date back to the Middle Ages. In the middle of the eighteenth century, Bohemian weavers settled what they called Neu-Schöneberg, which gradually expanded and was incorporated into the nineteenth-century Hobrecht Plan. The main connection to the older parts of Berlin had always been the Hauptstrasse, which became urbanised from the mid-nineteenth century onwards, as many farmers sold their land to developers, who built a string of luxurious mansions.

The large Schöneberg Town Hall was completed in 1914, and Schöneberg was finally incorporated into Greater Berlin in 1920. After the Second World War, the town hall served as the main city hall and administrative seat of West Berlin until 1991. Schöneberg has attracted many artists and writers over the years, such as Else Lasker-Schüler, Christopher Isherwood, Uwe Johnson, David Bowie, Iggy Pop and Jeffrey Eugenides. In the nineteenth century people were attracted by the quietness of the district, but during the Weimar years they flocked here to party with the gay and mixed crowds around Nollendorfplatz. In the 1970s the squatter scene served as a magnet for the alternative culture.

These days, Schöneberg is mostly a quiet, residential area – with a few exceptions. While the squatters have largely disappeared and Potsdamer Strasse (another main drag) is home to an increasing number of trendy bars and galleries, the area around Nollendorfplatz remains a centre of Berlin gay nightlife, and

Kurfürstenstrasse is one of the most notorious areas for street prostitution in Berlin.

One of the earliest writers connected with Schöneberg is Adelbert von Chamisso (1781–1838, see Chapter 8), best known for writing *Peter Schlemihl's Miraculous Story* (*Peter Schlemihls wundersame Geschichte*, 1814), a fable about a man who sold his shadow. Chamisso worked as the main curator of the Botanical Garden close to the elegant Heinrich-von-Kleist-Park. First laid out in 1656 by Elector Frederick William of Brandenburg as a nursery, the garden became the Royal Botanical Garden in 1809 and was moved to Berlin-Lichterfelde in 1899. The Kleistpark, as it is known, today is home to the Schöneberg Office of Art and the Leo Kestenberg Music School, which has housed the exhibition space Haus am Kleistpark since the 1960s.

Not far from here, in the old Berlin St Matthäus cemetery, are the graves of another pair of nineteenth-century literary notables – the Grimm brothers, Jacob and Wilhelm, the men who gave us fairytales such as Cinderella, Hansel and Gretel, and Rumpelstiltskin. Their graves are marked in the cemetery by four dark obelisks that double as headstones. To the left side of the brothers' headstones are the graves of Wilhelm's sons with Henriette Dorothea Wild (1793–1867): Hermann Grimm (1828–1901) and Rudolf Grimm (1830–89). Wilhelm's daughter Auguste Grimm (born 1832) has been buried since 1919 in an urn in her father's grave without a headstone.

Jacob (1785–1863) and Wilhelm (1786–1859) were not only storytellers but respected polymaths: academics, linguists, cultural researchers and lexicographers. Born in the town of Hanau, the brothers attended the University of Marburg, where they developed a curiosity for German folklore. Although often considered Romantics, the brothers never saw themselves as part of the Romantic movement, but more as scholars and researchers investigating the origins and oral traditions of German folk tales. From 1806 on, they started collecting and recording these stories from a variety of sources including

Wilhelm's friend and future wife Henriette Wild and storyteller and market trader Dorothea Viehmann.

The brothers published their first collection, initially intended as an academic research paper, as *Children's and Household Tales* (*Kinder- und Hausmärchen*) in 1812 via Berlin publisher Georg Andreas Reimer. But the collection – the first printed retelling of many of these famous folk tales – proved to be an instant hit with the public. Over the next decades the brothers continued researching and collecting more stories and tales, and constantly revised and updated their collection: the final edition of *Children's and Household Tales* published during their lifetime (1857) contained 200 fairytales, compared to 86 in the first edition. The brothers also translated Thomas Crofton Croker's collection *Fairy Legends and Traditions of the South of Ireland* as *Irische Elfenmärchen* (published 1826), the first work to bring Irish mythology to a German audience, and still in print today.

Prussian King Frederick William called the brothers to Berlin in 1840 and employed them as tutors at the University of Berlin; in addition the Academy of Sciences offered them stipends to continue their research. The brothers, along with Wilhelm's wife Henriette, lived in a series of dwellings around Tiergarten, where they liked to take daily walks. Their first abode was in Lennestrasse (they are remembered by commemorative plaque at Alte Potsdamer Strasse 5 across the street from the original domicile); another home was at Linkstrasse 7, south of Potsdamer Platz.

In 1840, Jacob published his *The History of the German Language* (*Geschichte der deutschen Sprache*, 1840). Wilhelm continued researching folk tales and medieval literature while revising the new editions of *Children's and Household Tales*. After the failed German Revolution of 1848, the brothers grew more distant from the Prussian authorities and resigned their university positions in early 1850. Wilhelm died of an infection in 1859 and Jacob continued work on an unfinished German dictionary – which he had started working on with his brother – until his death in 1863.

The popular folk tales are today available in more than 100 languages. Among the greatest treasures of the Berlin University Library is the private library of the brothers, comprising more than 5,500 volumes. Fittingly, the new central library building off Friedrichstrasse (opened in 2009) bears the name Jacob and Wilhelm Grimm Centre. Since 1961, the city of Berlin has also offered the Brothers Grimm Prize, a 10,000-euro award to promote German-speaking children's and youth theatre.

The Grimms are not the only literary celebrities in the St Matthäus cemetery. In fact, it contains over 50 Ehrengräber (honorary graves), including that of resistance hero Claus Graf Schenk von Stauffenberg (whose body was burned by the SS to leave no trace of the 'traitor') and other resistance fighters. Rudolf Virchow, the 'father of modern pathology', is buried here, as is Rio Reiser, actor and frontman of legendary German-language rock band Ton Steine Scherben.

It was in the twentieth century that Schöneberg really came into its own – more specifically in the Roaring Twenties, when it became one of the most colourful gay and lesbian centres in Weimar Berlin. At its peak, the city offered some 160 gay bars and clubs. The lesbian scene alone was so burgeoning that, as well as a couple of weekly newspapers, two ice-skating leagues and a women-only nudist retreat, an entire guidebook (*Berlin's Lesbische Frauen*) was written in 1928 by Ruth Margarete Roellig to help locals and visitors navigate through the 50 or so lesbian-only bars and clubs that existed. Music and culture critic Alex Ross, reviewing Robert Beachy's *Gay Berlin: Birthplace of a Modern Identity* (2014) in the *New Yorker*, wrote:

> During the golden years of the Weimar Republic [...] gays and lesbians achieved an almost dizzying degree of visibility in popular culture. They could see themselves onscreen in films like 'Mädchen in Uniform' and 'Different from the Others' – a tale of a gay violinist driven to suicide, with Hirschfeld featured in the supporting role of a wise sexologist. Disdainful representations

of gay life were not only lamented but also protested; Beachy points out that when a 1927 Komische Oper revue called 'Strictly Forbidden' mocked gay men as effeminate, a demonstration at the theatre prompted the Komische Oper to remove the offending skit.

In Schöneberg, the heart of this sexually liberated scene was – and still is – around Nollendorfplatz ('Nolli' to locals). Named after Prussian general Graf Kleist von Nollendorf, winner of the 1813 Battle of Kulm, the square is situated at the convergence of four main roads and centred on a large metal U-Bahn viaduct – a replica of the original domed station from 1902. The U-Bahn station bears a memorial to the homosexual victims of the Holocaust in the shape of a triangle – a reminder of the pink triangle badges homosexuals were forced to wear on their concentration camp uniform.

Nollendorf is often associated with the writings of English novelist Christopher Isherwood (1904–86). Between 1928 and 1929, Isherwood had studied medicine in London, but gave up his studies to join his friend W. H. Auden in Berlin, where he wrote and taught English. His first visit was in 1929, at the age of 25; he liked the city so much that he stayed, settling in at Fraulein Thurau's boarding house at Nollendorfstrasse 17. This address was the main base for Isherwood's literary explorations of the area and Berlin in general. His first Berlin novel, *Mr Norris Changes Trains*, was published to great acclaim in 1935 and his seminal *Goodbye to Berlin* followed in 1939. Both books depict the final years of Weimar Berlin and the simultaneous rise of the Nazis by following a string of colourful characters, Germans and expatriates, including the highly memorable Sally Bowles – Bowles being based on flamboyant English singer and writer Jean Ross, who moved into Isherwood's neighbouring room at Nollendorfstrasse. In *Goodbye to Berlin* he writes:

Our street looked quite gay when you turned into it and saw the black-white-red flags hanging motionless from windows against the blue spring sky. On the Nollendorfplatz people were sitting out of doors before the café in their overcoats, reading about the coup d'etat in Bavaria. Goring spoke from the radio horn at the corner. 'Germany is awake', he said. An ice-cream shop was open. Uniformed Nazis strode hither and thither, with serious, set faces, as though on weighty errands. The newspaper readers by the café turned their heads to watch them pass and smiled and seemed pleased.

The two-legged camera, as Isherwood calls himself in the opening paragraph of *Goodbye to Berlin*, left Berlin in April 1933 and taught modern English literature at Los Angeles State College during the 1950s and 1960s. In 1962 Isherwood revisited a fictional Berlin for his collection of short stories, *Down There on a Visit*. In 1964 he published *A Single Man*, a poignant novel depicting a day in the life of a gay English university professor, and in 1976 he published *Christopher and his Kind*, a frank autobiography that focused on his Berlin years but without the self-censorship he had exercised in the novels of those times. His works have provided the inspiration for a plethora of adaptations, most notably the play and 1955 film *I Am a Camera*, both starring Julie Harris, as well as the 1966 Broadway musical and famous 1972 film both titled *Cabaret*.

One of Nollendorfplatz's most famous venues was the Eldorado Night Club, where Isherwood was a regular patron. Today its shell is occupied by a organic supermarket but in the 1920s visitors could buy tokens to exchange for dances with the transvestite hostesses (the painter Otto Dix used Eldorado patrons as subjects for some of his works) and watch performances by local starlets like Marlene Dietrich – who was born and lived in Schöneberg's Rote Insel area until 1930 – and famed cabaret singer Claire Waldoff.

A major Weimar establishment that still exists on Nollendorf is the Neues Schauspielhaus (New Theatre), which started life in 1906 and whose impressive art nouveau façade still dominates Nollendorfplatz. Built originally as a theatre and concert hall, it also included a cinema from 1911 onwards and in 1927 Erwin Piscator and Bertolt Brecht opened the Theater am Nollendorfplatz in the building. The theatre staged critical and avant-garde productions written by left-wing playwrights such as Ernst Toller, Alfred Plaquet and Walter Mehring.

In 1930, the venue drew the attention of Nazi brownshirts for showing the premiere of the American movie *All Quiet on the Western Front* (*Im Westen nichts Neues*). The thugs disrupted the show by releasing hundreds of white mice in the cinema, throwing stink bombs and beating up fleeing punters. One of those beaten was Else Lasker-Schüler (1869–1945), who lived at nearby Motzstrasse 7 between 1924 and 1933.

A German-Jewish poet and playwright born in west Germany, Lasker-Schüller is considered to be one of the first modern German poets. In 1894 she married physician Berthold Lasker and moved to Berlin. Although she lived in comfortable circumstances and took art lessons, it was an unhappy marriage: for example, Else insisted that the father of her son Paul, born in 1899, was an unnamed Greek prince. Her first full volume of poetry, *Styx*, was published in 1902, establishing her in Berlin literary circles, through which she also met composer Georg Levin (who used the pseudonym Herwarth Walden), whom she married after divorcing Berthold Lasker one year later.

Together with Walden she founded the Verein für Kunst (Art Association) in 1904 and organised readings, concerts and dance performances. In 1910 Walden also founded the journal *The Storm* (*Der Sturm*), covering Expressionism, Dada and Surrealism, which became the leading publication for these art movements, thereby establishing Walden as one of the main promoters. *Der Sturm* (which ceased publication in 1932) also published more than 100 poems and prose texts by Lasker-Schüler over the years. A volume of poetry called *My Wonders* (*Meine Wunder*) followed in 1911 and firmly established her as a genuine force within the Expressionist movement.

After her divorce from Walden in 1912, Lasker-Schüler continued to live in Berlin, and in the same year met fellow poet and essayist Gottfried Benn (see below), with whom an intense friendship and (from his side) unrequited romantic relationship developed. Lasker-Schüler also corresponded with painter Franz Marc, who provided her with a frontispiece for *The Malik* (*Der Malik*, 1919), a letter-novel about an Oriental prince fighting and dying in battle, influenced by Franz Marc's own fate – he died in the Battle of Verdun in 1916. Else also designed the covers of a ten-volume edition of her collected works, published by Cassirer Verlag in 1920.

Over the years she had developed a lifestyle that was as flamboyant as her early poems, including wandering the Berlin streets dressed as an Arab prince. In fact, the Orient looms large in her work: in 1923 she published *Theben*, a collection of poems and stories about the oriental realm of Prince Jussuf and the city of Thebes, accompanied by her own pen-and-crayon drawings. A 1913 letter to Franz Marc gives an insight into her somewhat unique thought process:

> My hole in the wall is actually a corridor, a narrow allee without trees. I own roughly 50 birds. True, they live outside, but in the morning they all sit outside my window and wait for me to feed them. Let anyone say anything against the birds! They are the highest beings, they live between God and the air, we live between earth and the grave. My hole in the wall is a long and scary coffin. I am terrified every night to lie down in my coffin. For weeks now I have been taking opium, then the rats become roses, and in the morning the tiny coloured sun motes fly around like angels in my coffin space and dance across the floor, dance over my shroud, painting all kinds of colours.

After her son Paul was diagnosed with tuberculosis in 1926, Lasker-Schüler spent the next years caring for him at her Berlin home and only occasionally published poetry, prose or plays such as *Arthur Aronymus: The Story of my Father* (*Arthur Aronymus: Die Geschichte meines Vaters*, 1932). In 1932 Lasker-Schüler also won the prestigious Kleist Prize for her life's work, though this did not prevent her being harassed and threatened by the Nazis for her Jewish heritage. After emigrating in 1933, she spent time in Switzerland before finally emigrating to her dear Orient, dying of a heart attack in Jerusalem in 1945.

The film that caused so much trouble at the cinema, *All Quiet on the Western Front,* was based on the 1929 novel of the same name by prolific German writer Erich Maria Remarque (1898–1970). Remarque was conscripted into the Kaiser's army and served on the Western Front in Belgium, where in 1917 he was wounded and then spent the rest of the war in an army hospital. After his release from hospital, he worked a in number of different jobs and moved to Berlin in 1925, living initially in a small flat in Hellersdorf and then an apartment in Wilmersdorf, the next district west from Schöneberg.

The book (and film) retell the experience of German soldiers in the trenches of the First World War in a way that – judging by the 2.5 million copies sold in 22 languages in its first 18 months in print – spoke not only to German veterans but to all soldiers who had fought in the war:

> But now, for the first time, I see you are a man like me. I thought of your hand-grenades, of your bayonet, of your rifle; now I see your wife and your face and our fellowship. Forgive me, comrade. We always see it too late. Why do they never tell us that you are poor devils like us, that your mothers are just as anxious as ours, and that we have the same fear of death, and the same dying and the same agony – Forgive me, comrade; how could you be my enemy?

The book immediately established Remarque as one of the most popular writers of his day, helped by his film star looks and penchant for affairs and high-profile relationships with actresses such as Hedy Lamarr, Marlene Dietrich and Greta Garbo. In 1931, after publishing a sequel to his bestseller called *The Road Back*, Remarque bought a villa in Switzerland and left Berlin for good. Like the writings of so many of his contemporaries, his books were burned by the Nazis two years later.

But his connection to the city did not end there. His next novel, *Three Comrades*, set in the Weimar era, can be regarded as an ode to his time in Berlin. Narrated in the first person by a character named Robert Lohkamp, a veteran of the trenches, it describes the era's economic downturn and mass unemployment intertwined with a tragic love story. The novel was first published in Dutch as *Drie kameraden* in 1937, with an English translation by *Western Front*'s translator A. W. Wheen – yet another First World War veteran – in the same year. The first German-language edition was published in 1938 by Querido, Joseph Roth's exile publisher in Amsterdam, but was only properly made available in Germany in 1951. Its descriptions of Berlin, which is never actually named in the book, are unflinching:

> Afterwards we wandered a long time through the city. The streets, though lit, were deserted. Electric signs glowed; lights burned in the shop windows to no purpose. In one were naked wax dummies with painted heads. They looked ghostly and perverted. Next door was a sparkle of jewellery. [...] Pale, half-starved figures were crouched outside a picture house; and alongside, a ham-and-beef-shop spread its splendours: canned fruits piled high into tin towers, peaches bedded in wadding, fat geese strung on a line like so much washing, loaves of brown bread among highly seasoned ham sausages, and, central in it all, gleaming pink and pale yellow, liver patties and sliced salmon.

Another writer connected with the First World War, Ernst Jünger, lived for a time at Lützowstrasse 80, just off Schöneberg's Potsdamer Strasse. A controversial and multifaceted German novelist and essayist, Jünger (1895–1998) is best known for his First World War diary novel *The Storm of Steel* (*In Stahlgewittern*). Like Remarque, Jünger had first-hand experience of the Great War; while serving as an officer on the Western Front he was wounded at least seven times and in 1918 was awarded Germany's highest military decoration, Pour le Mérite, first awarded during the Napoleonic Wars.

The Storm of Steel, published in 1920 while he was still in the army, describes the combat experiences of a young company commander. In contrast to Remarque's anti-war novel, many have accused Jünger's book of glorifying war, mostly due to the dispassionate, matter-of-fact voice in which he narrates the suffering of his fellow soldiers, and his failure to condemn the war and point out its futility:

> These moments of nocturnal prowling leave an indelible impression. Eyes and ears are tensed to the maximum, the rustling approach of strange feet in the tall grass is an unutterably menacing thing. Your breath comes in shallow bursts; you have to force yourself to stifle any panting or wheezing. There is a little mechanical click as the safety-catch of your pistol is taken off; the sound cuts straight through your nerves. Your teeth are grinding on the fuse-pin of the hand-grenade. The encounter will be short and murderous. You tremble with two contradictory impulses: the heightened awareness of the huntsmen, and the terror of the quarry. You are a world to yourself, saturated with the appalling aura of the savage landscape.

Despite the criticisms, the book was a huge commercial success in Germany and beyond. After being discharged from the army in 1923, Jünger went on to study in Leipzig and published more war novels: *The Grove* (*Das Wäldchen*, 1925) and *Fire and Blood* (*Feuer und Blut*, 1925). In 1927 he returned to Berlin, where he rented a flat in Mitte and continued to publish books and articles. Despite his obvious militarism and blood-and-honour ideals, Jünger was never a follower of Hitler and declined to join the Nazi Party. Indeed, in 1939 he wrote a daring allegory on the destruction of a peaceful land in the novel *On the Marble Cliffs* (*Auf den Marmorklippen*), which surprisingly managed to pass the censors. He was dismissed from the army in 1944 after being implicated in the Stauffenberg plot to kill Hitler – though nothing was ever proven, a fact that no doubt saved his life.

After the war, Jünger was banned from publishing in Germany for four years because of his pro-militarist tendencies and service in the Wehrmacht. His public standing was rehabilitated in the 1950s and bolstered when publisher Klett put out a ten-volume collected edition of Jünger's works in 1965. In 1984, he joined German chancellor Helmut Kohl and French president François Mitterrand at a ceremony at the battlefield of Verdun, where he called the ideology of war in Germany before and after the First World War 'a calamitous mistake'. In a fairly surprising departure from his oeuvre, his 1970 book *Approaches* (*Annäherungen*) documented his long-term experiments with drugs such as cocaine, hashish, mescaline and LSD. Clearly these experiments had no major adverse effects on Jünger's health: he died in 1998 at the ripe old age of 102 years, making him the last living bearer of the order of the Pour le Mérite.

Potsdamer Strasse and its side streets also offer several literary sites. At No. 96, for example, is the Wintergarten Variete. Originally located in Mitte, the theatre opened there in 1887; in July 1895 it achieved fame by becoming the venue that showed the world's first-ever movie – a clip by the local Skladanowsky brothers – that preceded the Lumière brothers' Paris screening by almost six months. The Mitte venue was destroyed by bombs in June 1944, and the theatre was reopened on Potsdamer Strasse in 1992, taking over a defunct variety theatre (the Quartier Latin) from the 1930s. Today the theatre continues to showcase burlesque and cabaret productions.

Right opposite, at No. 75, the Joseph-Roth-Diele keeps the memory of the eponymous author (see Chapter 4) alive by serving up hearty and inexpensive meals (schnitzel, pasta, meatballs) to local workers and curious visitors in a theatrical space that features Roth quotes and images on the walls, sells Roth books and hosts occasional literary events. Just up the road, at Potsdamer Strasse 73, were the first and only fixed lodgings that Roth ever lived in: a furnished room he shared with his wife between 1929 and 1930. One of Roth's publishers, the S. Fischer Verlag (see Chapter 1), was founded by Samuel Fischer on nearby Bülowstrasse 80 in 1897.

Schöneberg was bombed fairly mercilessly by both the Allies and the Red Army. Marie Vassiltchikov, a Russian émigré princess whose family fled the Russian Revolution in 1917 and who worked for the German Foreign Office during the Second World War, became a witness to the 1944 Stauffenberg plot to kill Hitler (she was personally acquainted with some of the conspirators). Surviving the war, she published her *Berlin Diaries, 1940–1945* in 1988, detailing events in the capital of Hitler's Germany between 1940 and 1945, which includes several Schöneberg entries from her own perspective, but also conversations she records, like the following from someone called Missy:

Wednesday, 24 November 1944

As I continued down Lützowstraße the devastation grew worse; many buildings were still burning and I had to keep to the middle of the street which was difficult on account of the numerous wrecked trams. On the Lützowplatz all the houses were burned out. I had to climb over mounds of smoking rubble, leaking water pipes and other wreckage to get across. The bridge over the river Spree was undamaged but on the other side all the buildings were destroyed. By now the sight of those endless rows of burntout or still burning buildings had got the better of me and I was beginning to feel panicky. The whole district, many of its houses so familiar to me, had been wiped out in just one night. I started to run and kept on running until a building collapsed as I passed …

One of the most important postwar buildings in the district is the tall sandstone Rathaus Schöneberg (city hall) on John-F.-Kennedy-Platz. Built in 1914, from 1949 until 1993 it served as the seat of the main Senate of West Berlin and until 1991 as the office of the governing mayor. The city hall's associated square, Rudolph-Wilde-Platz, has been a popular site for protests and gatherings over the years, drawing West Berliners to voice their disapproval about everything from the East Berlin Uprising of 1953 (see Chapter 9) to the Hungarian Revolution of 1956. After the construction of the Berlin Wall in 1961, the Rathaus was where US President John F. Kennedy famously declared himself to be a Berliner in a 1963 speech from the balcony:

> Freedom is indivisible, and when one man is enslaved, all are not free. When all are free, then we look – can look forward to that day when this city will be joined as one and this country and this great Continent of Europe in a peaceful and hopeful globe. When that day finally comes, as it will, the people of West Berlin can take sober satisfaction in the fact that they were in the front lines for almost two decades.
>
> All – All free men, wherever they may live, are citizens of Berlin.
>
> And, therefore, as a free man, I take pride in the words 'Ich bin ein Berliner.'

When Kennedy was assassinated in the November of the same year, several thousand Berliners spontaneously regathered at the square, which was officially renamed John-F.-Kennedy-Platz three days later. Today, two memorial plaques on the city hall are dedicated to Kennedy: a larger one commemorating his 1963 speech with a quote from an earlier address to the UN in 1961, and a smaller one by the Ancient and Honorable Artillery Company of Massachusetts (where Kennedy served) attached on the twenty-fifth anniversary of the speech in October 1988. In summer the square is also the site of a large flea market.

Today the city hall also houses the permanent We Were Neighbours exhibition. It is laid out in the style of a library reading room where visitors can browse images, letters and other personal and official mementos that give insights into the Jewish history of Schöneberg and commemorate Jewish neighbours persecuted and murdered between 1933 and 1945. North of the town hall is Bozener Strasse, where physician and poet Gottfried Benn (1886–1956) lived, at No. 20. Born in Brandenburg, Benn joined the Prussian army in 1905 and studied military medicine in Berlin. In 1912 he left the army and began working at the Westend-Klinik am Spandauer Damm in Charlottenburg as assistant pathologist, remaining there for the next two years. His time in the hospital deeply influenced his poetry and outlook on life; in 1912, he published *Morgue and Other Poems* in 1912, a collection of poems about death and decay. 'No. III – Cycle' describes the work of the morgue:

> The lonesome molar of a love-maid,
> who had died unknown,
> wore a gold filling.
> As if by silent agreement the leftovers
> had gone out.
> The mortician knocked out the filling,
> pawned it and went dancing for.
> Because, he said,
> only earth should return to earth.

The collection was well received by critics but caused a minor scandal as many buyers returned the book – they felt betrayed by Benn's hopeless depiction of life. Thus Benn was immediately established in the more progressive literary circles of the capital, through which he met fellow poet Else Lasker-Schüler (see above), with whom he started a brief affair and remained friends with throughout his life.

Never fully identifying himself as a poet, Benn re-enlisted in the army after the outbreak of the First World War in 1914, spending a brief period on the Belgian front and going on to serve as a military doctor in Brussels. Returning to Berlin after the war, he became a dermatologist and venereal disease specialist in Kreuzberg. The misery he saw daily at his practice influenced his subsequent writing: 1922's *Collected Writings* (*Die Gesammelten Schriften*), a collection containing the poem cycle *Sons* (*Söhne*, first published in 1913), the novella *Brains* (*Gehirne*, first published 1916) and a second poetry cycle *Flesh* (*Fleisch*, first published in 1917). This time his poems struck a note with many other authors, readers and veterans who shared a similarly bleak outlook on life as Benn after four years in the trenches.

After publishing another poetry collection in 1927 (*Collected Poems, Gesammelte Gedichte*), Benn was elected to the poetry section of the Prussian Academy of Arts in 1932 – but was forced to leave again a year later by the Nazis, who did not approve of his 'degenerate' poems, and who also banned him from further publication in 1938, even though Benn had joined the Wehrmacht in 1935. In 1937 Benn moved to Bozener Strasse in Schöneberg to work as a military doctor. Posted to Poland after 1940, he continued to write poems in secret. After the war, his work was initially banned by the Allies due to his Wehrmacht service, but he was allowed to publish again in 1949, and, on being awarded the Georg Büchner Prize for his life's work in 1951, re-entered the West German literary mainstream.

Uwe Johnson (1934–84) moved into nearby Niedstrasse 3 in 1959. Another tragic and somewhat rootless literary figure, Johnson was born in Pomerania and in 1945 fled the advancing Red Army with his mother to Berlin (his father had been captured by the Soviets and was declared dead in 1948). Johnson studied German philology in Rostock and Leipzig, but, due to his lack of political support for the Communist regime, was suspended in 1953. In 1956 his mother left for West Berlin, leaving Uwe behind and without a chance of gaining employment. It was around then that he began to translate Herman Melville's *Israel Potter: His Fifty Years of Exile* – published posthumously by Suhrkamp in 1991 – to pass the time. He also wrote the murder mystery *Speculations about Jacob* (*Mutmassungen über Jakob*), which was critical of the GDR and smuggled to West Germany to be published in 1959 – the same year Johnson also fled to West Berlin.

Johnson continued to write and also supported himself as an English–German translator. His 1961 novel *The Third Book about Achim*, about a West German journalist trying to write the biography of an East German cyclist, was well received by critics and hailed for its realistic portrayal of life on both sides of the Iron Curtain. The protagonist crosses the border to visit an unnamed East German city, where he wanders aimlessly while expressing the same estrangement from his former home that Johnson must have felt:

> This language which he knew, which helped him to make himself understood throughout the day, still gave him frequently the illusion of belonging, again he thought that the two countries were comparable, wanted simply to add them up in his mind, since a forgotten sign over a shop, the language, the familiar aspect of public buildings called to mind its counterpart on either side of the border; but then the resemblances did not merge: the last package of cigarettes still advertised in gold and black had been sold here fifteen years ago, a different law was administered in the public buildings, the wording of this law determined the look of the streets, and not the words of the people who were walking about in them, who were looking down from their windows into the cool quiet evening, propped on pillows, chatting: Karsch did not understand the language of the official newspapers.

Johnson remained restless. After expanding his English-language skills he travelled to the USA for the first time in 1961 and in the following year received a scholarship in Rome. In 1965 he won the French Prix International for *Speculations about Jacob* before returning to the USA in the same year. In the meantime, he had sublet his Schöneberg apartment to fellow writer Hans-Magnus Enzensberger (whom he had met during a Gruppe 47 meeting – see Chapter 5), who in turn used it to shelter the Kommune 1, West Berlin's first political commune, which he supported (his ex-wife and brother were members of the group).

The commune was a group of students and artists trying to develop an alternative to the classic 'bourgeois' family structure. While experimenting with free love and shared living, Kommune

1 also engaged in political activities: it was here that the so-called 'pudding assassination' was planned, in which Kommune members attacked visiting US vice president Hubert H. Humphrey with yoghurt and chocolate pudding in 1967. Johnson evicted Enzensberger and the other Kommune members later that year with the help of his friend Günter Grass (who acted as intermediary as Johnson was still in the USA at the time).

During his time in the USA, Johnson began to work on his magnum opus: *Anniversaries* (*Jahrestage*), a series of four novels structured as the fictional diary entries of East German single mother Gesine Cresspahl, living in New York. Returning to West Berlin in 1969, he became a member of the West German International Association of Writers' PEN Centre and of the Berlin Academy of the Arts. In 1970, he published the first *Anniversaries* book and in 1974 he moved to Sheerness on the English Isle of Sheppey, where he continued to work on the final *Anniversaries* volume, published a year before his death, in 1983. Johnson is remembered by a memorial plaque on his former Berlin home which features a quotation from his work: 'There is no: Berlin. Berlin is always two cities.'

Another significant Schöneberg address is Haupstrasse 155, a seven-room apartment where English pop singer David Bowie and his punk rocker friend Iggy Pop (frontman for The Stooges) lived from 1976 to 1979. Both men came to Berlin to kick their drug habits – which patently didn't happen – and work on new material. During their time in Berlin, Bowie helped write and produce *The Idiot* and *Lust for Life* (both 1977), Pop's most acclaimed solo albums. The latter contains the single 'The Passenger', one of Iggy's most popular songs, whose lyrics are influenced by his countless journeys on the Berlin S-Bahn.

Bowie, who had also been tempted to Berlin through the work of Christopher Isherwood, used his time in Berlin to explore the history and cultural heritage of the city (he was a major fan of the Die Brücke painting movement), which he drew on to create his famous 'Berlin trilogy': a trio of experimental and largely ambient albums: *Low*, *Heroes* and *Lodger,* which he released between 1977 and 1979. The albums were mostly recorded at the legendary Hansa Studios – located close to the western side of the Berlin Wall and still operating today – with the input of sonic visionaries such as Brian Eno and Robert Fripp.

Today a dentist's office occupies their former apartment, though between 1999 and 2004 it became home to US writer Jeffrey Eugenides, who worked on the manuscript for his 2002 novel *Middlesex* there. Partially set in the German capital, the book recounts the familial and personal history of Cal Stephanides (initially called 'Callie'), an intersex man working for the US embassy in Berlin The novel's topic of dual identity fits Berlin – and Schöneberg – perfectly:

Like most hermaphrodites, but by no means all, I can't have children. That's one of the reasons why I've never married. It's one of the reasons, aside from shame, why I decided to join the Foreign Service. I've never wanted to stay in one place. After I started living as a male, my mother and I moved away from Michigan and I've been moving ever since. In another year or two I'll leave Berlin, to be posted somewhere else. I'll be sad to go. This once-divided city reminds me of myself. My struggle for unification, for Einheit. Coming from a city still cut in half by racial hatred, I feel hopeful here in Berlin.

Ӿ 7 Ӿ

WEDDING AND MOABIT

Wedding

Extending east of Tegel Airport, north of Tiergarten and west of Prenzlauer Berg, the north Berlin district of Wedding – officially incorporated into Mitte since 2001 – has never been what you could call a beautiful place. This former blue-collar area and 1930s Communist stronghold, which gave it the lasting nickname Red Wedding, remains a sprawling, no-frills area with an abundance of postwar residential estates, fast-food shops and garish casinos interspersed with the occasional trendy bar, restaurant or nightclub.

As the most 'eastern' West Berlin district, it was – like Kreuzberg – surrounded by the Berlin Wall on three sides: along Bernauer Strasse and the Berlin–Spandau shipping canal and intersecting with Chausseestrasse at one of the main East–West border crossings. Also like Kreuzberg, Wedding has preserved something of a 'frontier town' atmosphere that today is intertwined with the immigrant communities – Turkish but also African and Lebanese – that have been settling here since the 1960s. Irish writer and frequent Berlin visitor Kevin Barry paints a vivid description of the district in 'Berlin Arkonaplatz: My Lesbian Summer', as featured in his short-story collection *Dark Lies the Island* (2012):

> Wedding was a raw expanse of towerblocks, tattoo pits, kebab shops. Nogoodniks in mauve-coloured tracksuits decorated every corner. We had a properly respectful air as we passed through. This was how Berlin was supposed to be. We cut down a back way, for

a while, to avoid the main drag, because the sight of the kebab gyros was sickening Silvija's stomach, which was troublesome. The rearsides of the towerblocks loomed either side of a dirt pathway itchy with catkins beneath our sandals, and the word 'proletariat' rolled its glamorous syllables over my tongue.

The district's name comes from the medieval village Weddingcke, which was founded here in 1384. Abandoned a century later, the area remained more or less an urban wilderness that was literally referred to as a 'desert' on old maps. It was even purported to be haunted by Satan: during Berlin's last witch trial in 1728, miller's daughter Miss D. Steffin confessed to having copulated with the devil in Wedding.

Its abundance of cheap, unused land and proximity to the city, however, made it popular with industrialists, and many factories and workshops were built here throughout the nineteenth century, pushing the population from just 150 inhabitants in 1800 to 45,000

10   The Luisenbad Library in Wedding

by 1875. Although much of this infrastructure was destroyed in the Second World War, buildings like the massive Schering chemical works (the Bayer factory today) on Müllerstrasse and the massive Osram light-bulb factory on Seestrasse – which today houses shops, restaurants and a police station – recall the era. Writes Pamela E. Sweet in *Neighbors and Enemies: The Culture of Radicalism in Berlin, 1929–1933* (published 2004):

> North of the city center were the most industrial districts, Prenzlauer Berg and Wedding. As the nineteenth century came to a close, large manufacturing concerns began to seek cheap land beyond the city core. As factories sprang up in Wedding, Prenzlauer Berg and even into Reinickendorf, the workers followed. The biggest factories in these areas, such as AEG electrical, employed tens of thousands of workers each, until the Depression led to massive layoffs at the end of the 1920s and 1930s.

Workers' housing was provided by the five-storey tenements that formed part of the 1862 Hobrecht Plan. As with elsewhere in the city, these overcrowded blocks became hotbeds of poverty and disease by the end of the nineteenth century, their dirty ground-floor bars luring in workers with cheap beer and schnapps to help them forget their days of back-breaking toil. One of the worst examples was the Meyer's Hof on Ackerstrasse, which was demolished in the 1970s. Dagmar Reese describes the conditions in *Growing Up Female in Nazi Germany* (2006):

> A virtual emblem of the slum conditions in Wedding was Meyer's Court (Meyers Hof), praised by William I at its dedication in 1874 as a shining 'example of social policy'. Here, living on an area 40 by 150 meters, there were at times as many as 2,000 persons crowded together, for whom a police officer had to be appointed in order to 'guarantee public safety and order.' In 1889, a chronicler commented:

'How much misery and sorrow, suffering and worry is hidden behind these plain, whitewashed wall, how many imploring prayers for help resound from this wretchedness! When the socialist specter begins to take on flesh and blood, then it will draw an ample nourishment from this Berlin district.'

Some concessions were made by the city towards making the area more inhabitable. In 1885 the Luisenbad Library was constructed on Badstrasse. Originally built as a public pool, the building has also housed a cinema, a dancehall and a restaurant over the years: 'Kaffee Küche' ('Coffee Kitchen') in art deco lettering is still visible to the left side of the entrance. The contemporary library inside is a spacious and bright space thanks to a glass-and-concrete annex added to the original building before the library opened in 1995. Books span fiction, non-fiction and local Wedding and Gesundbrunnen topics as well as a wide array of English-, French- and Turkish-language publications. Some of the old wall structures are still visible inside too, and there is a pleasant reading garden out the back.

The library and the surrounding buildings, including a nearby yard that houses the hip Wilma Bar in a former eighteenth-century stable at Badstrasse 38, are reminders of one of the first heydays of the area. In 1760 a spa (named Luisenbad in 1799, after a visit by Queen Louise of Prussia) opened here, luring visitors in with an iron-rich spring that eventually gave its name to the surrounding Gesundbrunnen (literally 'health-fountain') district. Over the next half-century, Gesundbrunnen evolved into a popular day-trip destination for Berliners, with restaurants and beer gardens lining what is today Badstrasse. This era came to an end with the building of factories and tenement buildings on the surrounding land towards the end of the nineteenth century, which shifted the district's aesthetic away from entertainment and more towards work.

Some leisure spaces remained, though, and some new ones were even added, like the pleasant Schillerpark, which was created in 1909 as one of the area's first public parks. The landscape design of the park – wide avenues, large lawns and a rose garden – also incorporated the sand dunes that already existed, testament to the strong winds that once blew through this open area and powered no fewer than eight windmills between Müllerstrasse and Schäferstrasse in the nineteenth century (the last remaining – and protected – sand dune in Wedding is located in the grounds of a school in Scharnweberstrasse today). The park also features a statue of Friedrich Schiller, which is surrounded by four muses and has always been well regarded by the locals. Joseph Roth (see Chapter 4) visited the park in 1922, as recounted in *What I Saw*:

> Schiller Park opens its portals, quite unexpectedly, in the north of the city, a surprising gem beyond the brewery belt of the various Schultheisses and Patzenhofers: like a park in exile. [...]
>
> Even in Schiller Park the leaves drop from the trees in a timely fashion, in the autumn, but they are not left to lie. In the Tiergarten, for instance, a melancholy walker can positively wade through foliage. This sets up a highly poetic rustling and fills the spirit with mournfullness and a sense of transience. But in Schiller Park, the locals from the working-class district of Wedding gather up the leaves every evening, and dry them, and use them for winter fuel. Rustling is strictly a luxury, as if poetry without central heating were a luxury.

In 1920, Wedding was incorporated into the city proper by the Greater Berlin Act. By that time, the district's population numbered 120,000, the majority of who were workers and their families living in the still-cramped tenements and often threatened by layoffs and ill-health. It was during this time, and especially in response to the rise of the Nazis, that the district gained a reputation as a Communist stronghold.

One of the only monuments to this part of the district's history can be found on the small Walter Röber Bridge, which spans the Panke river. On the bridge sits a large boulder featuring an inscription that translates as 'At the beginning of May 1929, 19 people died here during street battles.' The battles referred to were those that occurred during the traditional workers' May Day parade on 1 May 1929. The parade had been banned by the Berlin Senate but the Communists marched nevertheless and violent street battles erupted between the police and members of the Communist Party of Germany, in particular the latter's militant wing, the Red Combatants' League (RFB).

Parades took place all over the city, but most of the clashes occurred in Wedding and Neukölln, where a state of emergency was declared and 13,000 policemen were deployed with firearms. After three days of bloody civil unrest, 33 people were dead and over 200 injured. This incident, remembered in German as Blutmai (Blood May), caused the SPD-led Prussian government to completely outlaw the RFB a short time later. The riots were captured by author Erich Kästner (see Chapter 4) in his only novel for adults, *Fabian*:

> At Weddingplatz, they closed the Reinickendorfer Straße, up which a crowd of workmen was approaching. Behind the cordon, mounted police were waiting for the word to attack. Uniformed workers, waiting, leather straps beneath their chins, for civilian workers. Who drove them against each other? The crowd of workmen was drawing near, their songs swelled louder and louder, then the police advanced, step by step, a yard between each man. The singing gave way to an angry roar.

The clashes deepened the split between the SPD and the Communist Party, which indirectly advanced the goals of Germany's right-wing parties and the eventual rise of the Nazi Party in the German parliament. Even after the Nazis clinched power, Goebbels and his SA thugs had a difficult time cowing Wedding's militant inhabitants. Across the street from the Walter Röber Bridge, at Wiesenstrasse 29, is the former residence of a well-known local Communist of the time, anti-war novelist, Theodor Plievier (1892–1955).

The thirteenth child of an invalid rasp-file cutter (only seven of his siblings survived childhood), Plievier spent most of the First World War working as a sailor on a German battlecruiser before returning to Berlin in 1919 to start working as a critic and author. In the same year he founded the small anarchistic Publishing House of the 12, through which he published his first novel, a critical account of his naval experiences, titled *The Kaiser's Coolies* (1929).

Plievier's books were burned by the Nazis in 1933, and a year later the author fled to the Soviet Union. Following the German invasion of the USSR in 1941, Plievier became part of the National Committee for a Free Germany, a Soviet-funded Nazi resistance group made up mostly of German prisoners of war, for which he also worked as interrogator, interviewing newly captured Wehrmacht soldiers. Returning to Berlin in 1945, he used his experiences for his trilogy of books about the deciding battles of the Eastern Front – *Moscow* (1952) and *Stalingrad* (1945) – and the Battle of Berlin – *Berlin,* 1954. In *Berlin* he wrote:

Can this entire evolution, can this Berlin 'type' which finally emerged from the sand and the mud of the Spree simply be wiped out by the stroke of a pen? Is it no longer to exist because, due to a special constellation in home politics – and even more in foreign policy – a monster held the reins of government, and at the end of the war the three victorious Great Powers join together and declare that what is must not be?

Impossible! The Spree still flows through Berlin and will be flowing after the final collapse, even though the bridges crash in a last desperate and futile gesture of defiance.

Berlin is Berlin and will survive.

It will survive because of the Berliners. The ball is still rolling, the word is not yet spoken; no representative of any power – either in a Kaiser's cape, or in a President's frock coat, least of all in a brown shirt – can speak for Berlin. The Berliners with the cap, the ready-made suit, the blue shirt, the high-collared workman's pullover, the Berlin women in their little home-made frocks – it is they who will determine the city's fate. Hocus-pocus with pen or gunfire is equally futile. It is only Berlin itself who could surrender.

Plievier's war novel trilogy was published by newly formed GDR publishing house Aufbau Verlag and eventually translated into 26 languages. Despite his success in most Eastern Bloc countries, Plievier was increasingly concerned about the dogmatic style of Communism introduced in the GDR. In 1948 he left to undertake a series of readings in West Germany and never came back, eventually settling in Italy, where he lived until his death.

A 15-minute walk from Plievier's former home, across bustling Reinickendorfer Strasse, is Amsterdamer Strasse, the street on which Otto and Elise Hampel – the Nazi-resisting couple who inspired Hans Fallada's *Alone in Berlin* (published in 1947 as *Jeder Stirbt für Sich Allein*, or *Every Man Dies Alone*) – lived. The Hampels lived at No. 10 and maintained their ordinary, working-class lifestyle while waging a personal campaign against the Hitler regime after Elise's brother's died serving the Wehrmacht in France. For more than two years they secretly wrote and distributed postcards within Berlin, urging their fellow Germans to realise the war was useless and that there would never be peace under the Nazis. In September 1942 they were arrested, tried by a 'People's Court' and executed. In Fallada's version:

Then he picked up the pen and said softly, but clearly, 'The first sentence of our first card will read: Mother! The Führer has murdered my son.' [...] At that instant she grasped that this very first sentence was Otto's absolute and irrevocable declaration of war, and also what that meant: war between, on the one side, the two of them, poor, small, insignificant workers who could be extinguished for just a word or two, and on the other, the Führer, the Party, the whole apparatus in all its power and glory, with three-fourths or even four-fifths of the German people behind it. And the two of them in this little room in Jablonski Strasse.

Their story became known when Fallada was given access to the Gestapo case files, complete with interrogation records as well as examples of the postcards. The files also contained photographs which seem to have influenced the descriptions of Fallada's protagonists (called the Quangels in the book), though for some reason Fallada chose to base them in Prenzlauer Berg rather than the district in which they lived and operated.

Born Rudolf Ditzen, Fallada (1893–1947) chose not to emigrate after 1933. His world successes, *Little Man, What Now?* (*Kleiner Mann, was nun?*, 1932), the story of a down-and-out couple in a small German town during the Great Depression, and his prison novel *Who Once Eats Out of the Tin Bowl* (*Wer einmal aus dem Blechnapf frißt*, 1934), were considered to be critical of the Weimar Republic by the Nazis and he was allowed to continue publishing. Over the coming years, however, Fallada was increasingly seen as criticising the Nazi regime and in 1943 – unfit for military service after years of alcohol and morphine abuse – he was drafted into the Reich Labour Service and sent to France.

Returning to Germany a few months later, he was banned from publishing and retreated to his house in Mecklenburg-Vorpommern, where he lived until July 1944, at which point he was confined to a psychiatric institution near Feldberg in Thuringia following a drunken attack on his wife. He started working on the novel *The Drinker* (*Der Trinker*, published posthumously in 1950) while in the institution. In April 1945, after the Nazi authorities fled Feldberg, Fallada, as most prominent local resident, was briefly made mayor by the Soviets before returning to Berlin in September of the same year. In 1946, after another mental and physical breakdown, he was confined to the psychiatric ward of the Charité hospital. He was handed the Hampels' files by his friend, the poet Johannes Becher, who (rightly) thought the material would provide excellent inspiration for a novel damning the Nazis and immortalising the quiet resistance of the couple. Feverishly written between September and November 1946, the book was published posthumously in 1947, a few weeks after Fallada's death of heart failure.

A short hop across another of Wedding's busy main roads lies the Urnenfriedhof (Urn Cemetery), Seestrasse. Despite the roar of the nearby traffic, the cemetery is a surprisingly quiet and pleasant place, all manicured hedgerows and darting squirrels. Among the many locals buried here is one of the wittiest Wedding chroniclers, Jonny Liesegang (1897–1961), also occasionally known as 'Wedding son of the Muses'.

Born Johannes Haasis, Liesegang worked as a clerk at several Berlin publishing houses before being laid off in 1933 and starting out as a freelance writer. He eventually published three volumes of short stories that focus on the everyday life and people of Wedding, complete with dialogue in the almost untranslatable Berlin vernacular (Berlinerish) that was more common amongst the working classes during those times. The amusing titles of his books – *I Realised That* (*Det fiel mir uff*, 1938), *I Realised That, Too* (*Det fiel mir ooch noch uff*, 1939) and *I Nevertheless Realised That* (*Det fiel mir trotzdem uff*, 1949) – suggest their equally tongue-in-cheek content. Because Liesegang's works tended to abstain from direct political statements, he was allowed to continue publishing during the Third Reich – at least until he was drafted into the Wehrmacht in 1941. After the war, he continued living and writing in Wedding, and his sympathetic connection with the area made him something of a folk hero. He died at his home in Afrikanische Strasse in 1961.

Near Liesegang's grave, a large monument in the middle of the cemetery shows a man breaking out of the sandstone encasing. It stands in front of a communal grave where 11 of the victims of the 1953 uprising in the GDR (see Chapter 9) are buried. In total 55 civilians were killed by Red Army troops and tanks in the uprising.

Ida Siekmann, the first victim of the Berlin Wall, is also buried in the cemetery. Siekmann lived on Bernauer Strasse (see Chapter 10), which was part of the inter-German border from 1949. The buildings on the southern side of the street, where Siekmann lived, belonged to the GDR, while the buildings on the north side stood in West Berlin. When in August 1961 the border was closed and the Berlin Wall erected, GDR soldiers started walling up doors and windows of the Bernauer Strasse buildings while forcefully evicting inhabitants. Siekman, in a dramatic flight attempt captured by Western media, jumped from a third-floor window to her death.

For the next 28 years, Wedding existed in the shadow of the Berlin Wall. But unlike in Kreuzberg, no significant counterculture developed here. Rather, Wedding became a fairly prosperous place whose main shopping street, Müllerstrasse, became known as the 'Ku'damm of the North' and factories like the Wittler bread factory on Maxstrasse and the Rotaprint printing press provided employment not only for the locals but also, from 1961 onwards, the district's new Turkish *Gastarbeiter* (guest workers).

By the 1950s, the West German economy had started to grow again, thanks to the unabashed capitalism promoted by the Western Allies, but manpower was scarce. To ensure the continuation of the so-called *Wirtschaftswunder* (economic miracle), workers from outside Germany were needed, and the Turkish government signed an agreement with West Germany in October 1961 that allowed its citizens to move to Germany in order to boost the local workforce. The agreement limited the time a foreign worker could stay in Germany to two years, to ensure that the origin countries did not lose their entire workforce. However, German companies soon objected to having to train new workers every two years and in 1964 the restriction was lifted. Many workers began to bring their families over and, in Berlin, these families were often moved to areas closer to the Wall, where housing was cheapest. The guest workers were expected to leave again soon anyway, but they stayed for good, settling mainly in Kreuzberg, in Neukölln and in Wedding, where the largest Turkish communities in Berlin are still located today.

The West Berlin Senate also began to build new residential estates throughout these run-down 'Wall' areas, specifically to demonstrate its prosperity to its neighbours in the east. As East

Berlin writer Annett Gröschner writes in *City Spaces: Filling in Berlin's Gaps* (2015) about the changes in the Brunnenviertel, built between 1972 and 1980:

> When the Wall was built, the residents of the neighbourhood around Brunnenstraße had ended up in a dead-end, so the area lent itself to urban planning experiments. Here, in the Social Democrat Willy Brandt's constituency, it was full steam ahead for 'construction as symbolic politics.' For the reconstruction of Wedding, soon revealed as its eradication, a gigantic money-wasting machine was set in motion, private land was bought up by noncommercial housing associations, old houses demolished and new ones built that looked thin-skinned and made only for sleeping in, even from a distance.

German reunification meant that state subsidies for factories ended, and many businesses moved their operations away from Berlin. Wedding's unemployment rates increased up to 15 per cent and it began to garner a reputation as a wild, slightly rough place thanks to the emergence of Turkish street gangs and yet more gambling dens and shabby corner bars. In recent years the district has slowly begun to become gentrified, as an increasing number of expats have started to discover the cheap rents, and a smattering of small, independent businesses – cafés, galleries, small breweries – have opened up.

At Malplaquetstrasse 33, a quiet leafy street lined with tasteful Wilhelminian buildings, the American-run Tassenkuchen Café serves delicious home-baked cakes and cookies and organises occasional readings and acoustic concerts. Across the road, at No. 13, is Mackensen & Niemann, a cosy second-hand bookshop with hundreds of old and new books lining the walls of its three rooms, and typewriters for decoration. The shop also stocks English and French books and sometimes the German owner spins Tom Waits records on an old record player.

Some of the district's former factories and warehouses have also been appropriated as contemporary leisure and cultural spaces. The Uferhallen, a complex of modernist brick garages from 1929 that were formerly used by Berlin public transport company BVG, today houses artist and dance studios, a piano salon, a café and an indoor football pitch. On nearby Gerichtstrasse, the former public pool, Stadtbad Wedding, built in 1907, operated as a nightclub named Stattbad Wedding (a subtle play on words that means 'alternative' pool Wedding) between 2009 and 2015, before being closed down because of a lack of fire escapes. The community-run club and café Panke is also located in an old Siemens factory opposite the former pool.

A similar structure is the Osram-Höfe, an atmospheric ensemble of courtyards surrounded by the yellow-brick buildings of a former light-bulb factory near Seestrasse. Today it hosts several businesses and offices as well as contemporary German-language Wedding literature in the shape of the Brauseboys, who have been holding court in the Osram-Höfe's restaurant La Luz for the last decade. Every Thursday, this group of local writers presents a reading show with a variety of guests, each of whom casts a sharp and often witty eye on contemporary Berlin. Fittingly, perhaps, for the area, this is not highbrow literature but a critical look at both district and city from the viewpoint of ironic witnesses. Taking local lit to an extreme, the Brauseboys published *Müllerstrasse*, a book with stories centred on the nearby street in 2013. In his contribution to the collection, 'Walpurgisnacht Wedding', Heiko Werning writes:

> 'What is gentrification?' Ahmed asked.
>
> 'Gentrification is when people with more money move here.'
>
> 'This is good!' Ahmed said, 'when more people with money move here, we can sell more kebap. But here is no one with money. This is Wedding.'

Among published contemporary literature about Wedding, expatriate resident Paul Scraton put out *The Idea of a River* in 2014, a book about the 29-kilometre Panke river which cuts right through the district from north to south. Born in Liverpool, Scraton moved to Berlin in 2001 and runs the Under a Grey Sky website and, since 2015, a local magazine entitled *Elsewhere: A Journal of Place*. He has also hiked the Berlin Wall Trail for his Traces of a Border blog. In *The Idea of a River*, he writes:

> The fisherman sits on a squat stool, rod resting on a stand between his legs, his hat pulled over his head. He looks at peace, eyes cast forward across the calm waters of the canal, his thermos flask of coffee on one side, a cool box filled with supplies on the other. I can see him an hour or so earlier, stepping out from his nearby apartment, walking along the river to his regular patch on the canal bank. He's been coming here for years, since a time when no-one came to this corner of the city, when the neighbourhood was enclosed by the Wall and he could feel the eyes of the East German border guards on his back ...

Moabit

If Wedding writing is dominated by impoverished chroniclers living in shabby tenement houses, Moabit literature is characterised by prisons and prisoners. Bordering Wedding to the west, the district shares many historical traits with its neighbour, and is often seen as its geographical extension. In fact since Berlin's 2001 administrative reform, Moabit also belongs to the same borough as Wedding (Mitte).

The district underwent pretty much the same mid-nineteenth-century urbanisation patterns as Wedding, and developed a similar working-class community that, by the 1930s, also had a reputation as a Communist stronghold. Bombed heavily in the Second World War and relegated to a border district of West Berlin during the years of division – although where Wedding was enclosed by the

11   Moabit's Prison Memorial

Berlin Wall for a few decades, Moabit's borders have always been more aqueous: the Spree, the Westhafen Canal and the Berlin–Spandau Navigation Canal.

The area has been even less affected than Wedding by gentrification, to the point where Airbnb's Berlin online guide lists 'great transit' as one of its major draws – mainly because the Hauptbahnhof, the city's main train station, is technically based in the south-eastern corner of the district. That said, the 'island' does enjoy close proximity to the centre of the reunited city and its quiet streets and leafy riverbanks are slowly being discovered by new generations.

Colloquially, the name Moabit also refers to the central criminal court and detention centre, which deals with all criminal cases in Berlin. As mentioned, prisons and crime have always somehow influenced the writing coming from here. The Kriminalgericht (Central Criminal Court) at Turmstrasse 91, an impressive neo-baroque building complete with faux bell towers was, on its completion in 1902, regarded as one of the most modern buildings in the city due to possessing its own power plant, elevators and a separate telephone system. Defendants could be brought from prison van to courtroom by a series of corridors without being exposed to the public. A prosecutor once described the building as an 'Imperial punch into the face of Moabit's working class', and Ernst Haffner also mentions it in his novel *Blood Brothers*:

> Up stairs and down, round corners and into obscure nooks of the huge labyrinthine building. A large bright room on the ground floor. Trams whizz past outside. 'Go in there.' Ludwig is shown into a cage of loose wire, next to a whimpering little girl. Almost a child. Wonder what she's done? Whatever it was, she is measured, fingerprinted, photographed from the front and both sides, as though she is a dangerous criminal. Ludwig's turn next.

The Criminal Court was a haunt and inspiration for crime reporter and author Gabriele Tergit. Mostly know for her debut novel *Cheesebeer Conquers the Kurfürstendamm* (*Käsebier erobert den Kurfürstendamm*, 1931) about the machinations of propaganda and the advertising industry, she worked as the legal correspondent for the *Berliner Tageblatt* from 1925 to 1933. Fiona Sutton says of her in *German Novelists of the Weimar Republic: Intersections of Literature and Politics* (2006):

> The writings of journalist and novelist Gabriele Tergit during the Weimar Republic exhibit a powerful urge to chart and evaluate the conflicts arising from the shifting social and cultural values and from contemporary economic and political instability. Although Tergit wrote feuilletons, travel reports, and reviews, her main focus [...] was reporting from the law courts at Moabit in Berlin, because she felt they offered her insight into the essence of the age: '*Moabit ist seit einigen Jahren Quelle für die Erkenntnis der Zeit*' (For some years now, Moabit has been the source for understanding our time).

Not far from the Hauptbahnhof is the fascinating Geschichtspark Ehemaliges Zellengefängnis Moabit. Built in 1849 by order of King Frederick William IV of Prussia according to the 'separate system' – a form of prison management where prisoners are kept in solitary confinement – the objective of the original structure was to force prisoners into a state of penance through silent reflection upon their crimes. Four red-brick wings fanned out from a central administrative building, each containing 48 single cells across three floors that could be monitored from a single room in the main building. From *Blood Brothers* again:

All at once there's no more flowers or friendliness. Prison is gray-on-gray chiaroscuro. Sprawling up into infinity is a system of bare-iron staircases. Floor upon floor. Cell by cell, in a radial pattern, all dominated by the tall watchtower in the middle, where alarm bells go off at the least suspicion. Trusties in blue prison uniforms polish the linoleum floors of the corridors to an even deeper shine. The iron brooms scratch back and forth, back and forth. There's plenty of time here. Many months, if not years. Guards snoop through peepholes at their quarry, lawyers weighed down with files hurry into the consulting rooms to be taken to their clients – their murderers or black marketeers. Little squads of remand prisoners are marched off to the bathroom, to the doctor or to exercise. A prison full of bustle, but the human voice belonging to prisoner number so-and-so is just a shy whisper. Ludwig is taken to reception. Taken everywhere. Here in this well-secured prison, not one prisoner takes a step outside his cell without the law three paces behind him.

One of the most famous turn-of-the-century locals that served out their prison sentences here was Wilhelm Voigt, the 'Hauptmann von Köpenick', an impostor who in 1906 masqueraded as a Prussian military officer, rounded up a number of soldiers under his command and 'confiscated' more than 4,000 marks from a municipal treasury in Potsdam. After his release, Voigt became something of a folk hero and was eventually pardoned by William II.

Voigt's exploits were immortalised by writer and playwright Carl Zuckmayer in his most famous play, *Der Hauptmann von Köpenick*. Zuckmayer (1896–1977), who lived in Schöneberg until 1933, was one of the foremost playwrights of Weimar Germany and also worked as a dramatic advisor at the Deutsches Theater together with Bertolt Brecht. In 1929, he wrote the script – based on the novel *Professor Unrat* by Heinrich Mann – for one of the most iconic movies of the Weimar period, *The Blue Angel* (*Der blaue Engel*), which starred Marlene Dietrich.

Zuckmayer's works were banned by the Nazis on the grounds of being anti-militaristic and subversive. Unable to find work, he moved with his family to Austria and then the USA, where he worked as a scriptwriter and farmer. In 1946 he became a US citizen, and in the same year returned to Germany as cultural attaché while continuing to work as a playwright. His play *The Devil's General* (*Des Teufels General*), premiered in Zürich in 1946, had a main character based on Luftwaffe general and Nazi critic Ernst Udet, who had committed suicide in 1941. It became a major success in postwar Germany and was made into a movie starring Curd Jürgens in 1955. The Zuckmayers left the USA in 1958 and settled in Switzerland, where he died in 1977.

Among the better-known Zellengefängnis prisoners during the interbellum period were the socialist journalist Karl Radek, one of the passengers on the train that brought Lenin back to Russia in 1917; German-Jewish anarchist poet and playwright Erich Mühsam, who was killed in Oranienburg concentration camp in 1934; Bulgarian Communist politician and later leader of Bulgaria, Georgij Dimitroff; and Ernst Thälmann, leader of the Communist Party of Germany, who was arrested in 1933 and held in solitary confinement for 11 years before being shot on Adolf Hitler's personal orders in 1944.

After the Second World War had begun, and especially after the 20 July plot to kill Hitler in 1944, the prison was used as a detention centre for political activists and prisoners of war like Wolfgang Borchert. Borchert (1921–47) was an author and playwright connected to the so-called *Trümmerliteratur* movement – and Gruppe 47 – after the war. Borchert's stories were actually shorter than short: pieces such as 'Bread' and 'Dear Blue Grey Night' are tiny vignettes laden with a deep understanding of the human condition. A career at the theatre in Hamburg was cut short by conscription into the Wehrmacht. Catching diphtheria at the Eastern front, Borchert spent the years between 1941 and 1943 in various hospitals. After entertaining his comrades with a parody of Joseph Goebbels in late 1943 he was denunciated and incarcerated in multiple military prisons, with a final stint in Moabit from August 1944 onwards.

There, he witnessed the imprisonment of the members of the 20 July plot, and one of his fellow prisoners, a homosexual, features in Borchert's story 'Our Little Mozart' ('Unser Kleiner Mozart', 1947). He was returned to his unit in March 1945, and after they surrendered to the French, Borchert walked 600 kilometres from Frankfurt to Hamburg to be with his family again. His most famous work is the drama *The Man Outside* (*Draussen vor der Tür*), about a returning prisoner of war (see Chapter 1), which he wrote in the first days after the Second World War and which premiered in Hamburg in 1947, a few days before his death.

Borchert died of the late effects of jaundice, which he had contracted on the Eastern front, though many claim the real cause of his death was plain exhaustion: following his long walk home he had feverishly written one short story and play after another, only allowing himself to be admitted to hospital towards the end. He describes his time in Moabit in a 1947 poem named after the district:

> The Moon Lies
> Moabit
>
> The moon paints a grotesque pattern onto the wall.
> Grotesque? A bright square, hardly bent,

Pervaded by a number of dark grey
and small lines.
A fishing net? A spider's web?
Yet alas! The eyelash flutters
when I raise my eyes to the window:
It is barred!

A fellow prisoner of war at the Zellengefängnis was Musa Cälil (1906–44), the only Soviet Tatar poet to receive both the Hero of the Soviet Union award for his resistance fighting and the Lenin Prize for literature. Already an established poet and playwright before the Second World War, he volunteered as a political commissar when the war began and was captured by the Wehrmacht in the summer of 1942. Later that year, the Nazis started forming the Volga-Tatar legion, consisting of prisoners of war willing to fight for the Wehrmacht, and Cälil joined the propaganda unit for the legion under the false name of Gumeroff.

He immediately set up a resistance group which started circulating anti-fascist leaflets among the Tartar soldiers – which could be one of the reasons why the first legion battalion that was sent to the front mutinied and defected to the Soviet partisans. In 1943 the resistance group was arrested and Cälil was sent to the Zellengefängnis, where he began to study German and compile verses, writing when the prison guards hid from bombings or when fellow prisoners shielded him from the sight of the guards.

Knowledge of his impending execution filled his poems with a feverish energy and lines like 'My death will resound as a song of battle', which reverberated with many of his fellow inmates and, later, his countrymen. He and his group were sentenced to death in February 1944 and guillotined at Plötzensee Prison in August of the same year. His body was never recovered, but his notebooks were preserved and smuggled into the USSR by fellow prisoners and published in Kazan and Russian in 1953. Generally considered his most significant work, they were published in English as *The Moabit*

Notebooks in 1958, and in 1956 Cälil was posthumously awarded the Hero of the Soviet Union, followed by the Lenin Prize in 1957. One poem from September 1943 is 'Convicted':

> The verdict announced today:
> By death he was sentenced.
> Only the tears that were running high in the chest,
> All dried up … and he does not cry.
> Quiet in the chamber. On the night sky
> The full moon looks, grieving.
> A poor man thinks it will
> His child now will be an Orphan

On the night of 22 April 1945, when the Red Army had already surrounded the city, the SS gathered the remaining 16 political prisoners in the Zellengefängnis, marched them a short distance away and shot them in the back of the head. Among the murdered were resistance fighters Klaus Bonhoeffer, Rüdiger Schleicher and Albrecht Haushofer, who, like Cälil, produced an outstanding piece of writing while he was incarcerated, entitled the *Moabit Sonnets* (*Moabiter Sonette*).

Haushofer (1903–45), a geographer, author and sometime playwright, started teaching geopolitics at the Deutsche Hochschule für Politik (German Academy for Politics) in Berlin in 1933. When the academy was incorporated into the University of Berlin in 1940, he was made a professor at the Faculty for Foreign Studies and also served in the propaganda department of the German Foreign Office. Although he was somewhat unsuccessful as a playwright, his historical dramas *Scipio* (1934), *Sulla* (1938) and *Augustus* (1939) were all staged before 1945.

Haushofer joined the resistance centred on politicians Johannes Popitz and Helmuth James Graf von Moltke as well as contacting the Red Orchestra group, whose leaders Arvid Harnack and Harro Schulze-Boysen had also taught at the academy. Haushofer agreed that the only way to prevent complete military and political disaster was to kill Hitler, and he worked together with Claus von Stauffenberg and the other conspirators of the 'Valkyrie' plot to kill the Führer at his headquarters in 1944. After the assassination attempt failed, most of the conspirators went into hiding; Haushofer was arrested at a farm in Bavaria in December 1944 and incarcerated in the Moabit prison.

Murdered on the night of 22 April 1945, his body was discovered on 12 May by his brother Heinz, who found one of his sonnets, entitled 'Guilt' ('Schuld'), stuffed into the pocket of his jacket. Eighty more sonnets were discovered and posthumously published in 1946 as the *Moabit Sonnets*. They have since been translated into five languages. The poems are marked by their penchant for autobiographical details as well as descriptions of the prison and its inmates, who, one after another, were taken away to be executed:

> Guilt
>
> I am guilty,
> But not in the way you think.
> I should have earlier recognized my duty;
> I should have more sharply called evil evil;
> I reined in my judgment too long.
> I did warn,
> But not enough, and not clearly enough;
> And today I know what I was guilty of.

The prison survived the war relatively undamaged and was used by the Allies from October 1945 until March 1955, serving for a time as West Berlin's only execution site. Between January 1947 to May 1949, 12 people were killed here, including Nazi war criminals such as Helene Wieczorek and Berthold Wehmeyer, the last man to die under the guillotine before capital punishment was abolished in West Germany in 1949. The prison was torn down between 1957 and 1958, but restored in 2006 into its current incarnation, as a public park and memorial.

The original star-shaped layout of the buildings is today traced by lawns with concrete frames, while a walk-in sculpture reproduces one of the cells, right down to its original measurements and a concrete bench. When a visitor enters, a recording of one of Haushofer's sonnets is played, which lends an eerie soundtrack to the place. Paving stones set into the lawns indicate the location of the courtyards, and the central surveillance room is represented by another cubic sculpture. The design evokes the starkness and isolation of imprisonment, especially in winter, though since it is protected from the surrounding clatter of trains and cars it also serves as a popular relaxation spot in warmer months too.

The last place many of the writers and resistance fighters incarcerated in the Zellengefängnis would see was another prison in nearby Plötzensee (today located across the A100 circular motorway), which was used as a site of execution during the Second World War – and before, when it was the main execution site of Imperial Berlin). Plötzensee Prison (still in use today as JVA Plötzensee) was where executions were carried out by guillotine in a small shed in the prison yard. The condemned prisoners were kept in a large cell block directly adjacent to the execution shed and spent their final hours in shackles in special cells on the ground floor, before being led through a small courtyard to the execution chamber.

In late 1942, the execution chamber was also fitted with a steel beam with eight iron hooks to be used as gallows to speed up the execution process for the increasing number of prisoners sentenced to death by Nazi authorities. The first to die this way were the men and women of the Communist resistance organisation Red Orchestra in the same year, followed by the resistance fighters involved in the attempted coup of 20 July 1944, who were hanged with piano wire, on the personal orders of Hitler. Victor vom Gostomski and Walter Loch include an account in their *The Death of Plötzensee* (*Der Tod von Plötzensee,* 1993):

Normally the executioner came twice a week. His name was Roettger. He didn't so much walk as creep. He always wore a three-quarter length jacket. What did he think about? He had executed thousands. Innocent people. He had pocketed a bonus of 80 Marks for every head. And extra cigarette rations.

He always had a cigarette in his mouth. His helpers were big strong men. They had to bring the hog-tied victims to the gallows!

Two wardens led the condemned from the cell to the execution shed. Each of them got eight cigarettes for doing this. [...] A man named Appelt acted as overseer in the death building. The prisoners called him 'the fox.' He loved to pop up suddenly and check the bonds. He was always lurking around.

Today the site still functions as a prison but also contains the Plötzensee Memorial, dedicated to the German resistance against the Third Reich. After entering through a grey courtyard, again surrounded by prison walls, you reach the centrepiece of the memorial: a cold white room featuring a steel beam bearing hooks alleviated only by the few flowers and candles left by visitors.

Aside from this curious history of 'prison lit', Moabit has one more significant literary claim to fame: Kurt Tucholsky. Born in a small house at Lübecker Strasse 13 – which today houses the Kurt-Kurt arts space, a small public gallery and self-declared 'city laboratory' – Tucholsky (1890–1935) was a German-Jewish journalist, satirist and writer who also wrote under multiple pseudonyms (Kaspar Hauser, Peter Panter, Theobald Tiger and Ignaz Wrobel).

Already an established writer before the First World War, with articles published in the weekly satirical magazine *Prank* (*Ulk*) and the Social Democratic Party organ *Onwards* (*Vorwärts*), one of his first major literary works was the romantic novella *Rheinsberg: A Picture Book for Lovers* (*Rheinsberg: ein Bilderbuch für Verliebte* – see Chapter 4), published in 1912. After the First World War, during which he had worked at an army newspaper, he became editor of *Ulk* and a prolific writer of well-received feuilletons for major newspapers. His savvy ear for dialect and keen eye for detail made him highly popular, and he wrote everything from political stories and court reports to commentaries, poetry and cabaret songs.

In 1919 he wrote a wonderful assessment of the city and his fellow citizens for the *Berliner Tageblatt* under the title 'Berlin! Berlin!':

> A Berliner doesn't have time. A Berliner is usually from Posen or Breslau, and he doesn't have time. He always has plans, and he makes phone calls and appointments, and he rushes to his appointments – usually running late – and he has such an awful lot to do.
>
> People don't work in this city – they slave away. (Even entertainment is work here; they spit in their hands at the start and expect to get something in return.) A Berliner isn't really diligent, just constantly agitated. He has completely forgotten, unfortunately, why we're here on this earth. Even in heaven – assuming a Berliner could make it to heaven – he would 'have things to do' at four.

Tucholsky regarded himself as a left-wing democrat and correctly identified the threat of National Socialism. As a correspondent for *Weltbühne* (for which he also acted as temporary co-editor in 1926) and the *Vossische Zeitung*, he set off for Paris in the spring of 1924 and, like so many of his Weimar contemporaries, spent most of his time abroad, returning only occasionally to Germany. Yet even from a distance he remained a prolific writer on German affairs, mostly using *Weltbühne* to air his political views, as well as publishing works articles and books like his travelogue *A Book on the Pyrenees*.

In 1928, he went on a holiday to Sweden with his lover Lisa Matthias, which inspired him to publish the novel *Gripsholm Castle* in 1931. The novel had the same light-hearted tone as *Rheinsberg* and became his most successful, still in print today (and made into a movie twice, in 1963 and 2000). In 1929 Tucholsky had already fully migrated to Sweden and was living near Gothenburg. His fears of totalitarianism were confirmed when the Nazis came to power in 1933, his books burned as *Entartete Kunst* (degenerate art) and his German citizenship revoked. Plagued by constant health issues and his own self-doubt, on 20 December 1935 he took an overdose of sleeping pills and died. In Moabit a local elementary school and a library carry his name today.

🐻 8 🐻

KREUZBERG

During the Wall years, when Kreuzberg was all but synonymous with West Berlin for many people, the district was itself also divided into two halves by its postcodes. West Kreuzberg went under the code SW61 (South West 61) while the eastern part was SO36 (South East 36), and over time, these codes came to represent fairly distinctive differences between the two areas: the leafy, gentrified ambiance of the west, especially around Bergmannstrasse versus the vibrant,

12   West Kreuzberg's main drag, Bergmannstrasse

punky east, centred around immigrant-heavy areas like Kottbusser Tor and Oranienstrasse. Despite the postcodes becoming officially redundant after the fall of the Wall, the reputations have stuck, summed up in the contemporary rhyming colloquialism *36 brennt, 61 pennt* (36 burns, 61 sleeps).

In fact, the district originally comprised several smaller areas, namely Friedrichsvorstadt, Friedrichstadt, Luisenstadt and Tempelhofer Vorstadt, which were all brought together in 1920 by the Greater Berlin Act. Briefly named Hallesches Tor after its former customs gate, the district was renamed Kreuzberg in 1921 after Viktoria Park's Kreuzberg Hill, which itself had been named after the 1821 Prussian National Monument built on the top of the hill by Karl Friedrich Schinkel to commemorate the Napoleonic Wars.

Although Friedrichstadt, established in the seventeenth century, had long been a commercial quarter, the district was largely rural until the middle of the nineteenth century, when it was swept up in the push for industrialisation that transformed so much of the city. In 1852 the Luisenstädtischer Kanal – a canal connecting the Landwehrkanal in the south of Kreuzberg with the Spree – was opened, and the main train station of the area, Görlitzer Bahnhof, followed in 1866. Five large military barracks were erected in Tempelhofer Vorstadt in 1861, and throughout the area small and medium-sized factories opened up in the late nineteenth century. Business in Kreuzberg was mostly service-oriented, with many inhabitants working for the railway, the Prussian military or operating a small workshop in one of the many yards in the area.

One of the earliest literary names connected with Kreuzberg is that of E. T. A. Hoffmann (Ernst Theodor Amadeus Hoffmann, 1776–1822), who lived and worked between Mitte and Kreuzberg and is buried in the Friedhof III der Jerusalems- und Neuen Kirchengemeinde (The Third Cemetery of Jerusalem's Church and New Church Parishes) in west Kreuzberg. Born and raised in the Prussian city of Königsberg, Hoffmann studied law but also developed his creative passions for literature, drawing and music (the 'A' in his name stands for Amadeus, a reference to Mozart, which he changed from his parents' choice of 'Wilhelm').

Not only did Hoffmann become a renowned music critic alongside his day job, he also composed music and operas, and his writing is peppered with references to the worlds of music and painting. His impressive literary oeuvre spans around 50 works, ranging from light-hearted fairytales such as *The Nutcracker and the Mouse King* (which Tchaikovsky, among others, turned into a world-famous ballet) and *Princess Brambilla* (*Prinzessin Brambilla*, 1820) to darker, more Gothic material like *The Devil's Elixirs* (*Die Elixiere des Teufels*, 1814–15) and *The Sandman* (*Der Sandmann*, 1816). All these stories illustrate Hoffmann's fertile imagination, eye for detail and often disconcerting blurring of fiction and reality.

Hoffmann was also a noted drinker. He lived at Charlottenstrasse 56 in Mitte, a few doors down from wine bar and restaurant Lutter & Wegner, where he penned many of his most famous stories – including his final, partly autobiographical story *My Cousin's Corner Window* (*Des Vetters Eckfenster*, 1822). The tale is about a semi-paralysed author – Hoffmann was bedridden at this point – and his cousin, who together survey the Gendarmenmarkt below, offering a unique insight into daily Berlin life during the early nineteenth century:

> I've had my eye for some time now on an extremely puzzling figure: the man standing by the second, more distant pump, beside the cart on which a peasant woman is dispensing plum jam from a large barrel. First of all, dear cousin, do admire the woman's dexterity. Armed with a long wooden spoon, she first deals with the major purchases of quarter-pounds, half-pounds and whole pounds of jam, and then with lightning speed she throws a threepenny dollop to each of the greedy sweet-lovers who are holding out paper bags and sometimes even their fur caps to receive the jam, which they promptly devour with great enjoyment as a superior snack – the people's caviar! As I watch her dispensing the jam so skilfully by brandishing her spoon, I recall hearing in my childhood about a rich

peasant's wedding conducted in such splendour that a delicious rice-pudding, coated with a thick crust of cinnamon, sugar, and cloves, was dispensed by means of a threshing-flail. Each of the honoured guests had only to open his mouth cheerfully to receive his portion, and so it was just like the Land of Cockayne. But, cousin, have you got your eye fixed on this man?

Hoffmann succumbed to the dual effects of syphilis and alcohol abuse in 1822. With a nice touch of historical irony, the current Lutter & Wegner restaurant now stands where Hoffmann's former home once was. One story goes that Hoffmann's best friend, the actor Ludwig Devrient, with whom he always sat at Lutter & Wegner, was so devastated after his death that he had his coachman bring him to the cemetery, opened a bottle of champagne, drank half of it himself and poured the rest over his friend's grave.

During his Berlin years, Hoffmann also worked with other local writers such as Friedrich de la Motte Fouqué (author of *Undine*, 1811) and Adelbert von Chamisso, who were both part of the Hoffmann-led literary circle Serapion Brethren. Active between 1814 and 1815 (then named Seraphin Brethren) and again from 1818 until 1821, the group met either at Hoffmann's home or the Café Manderlee on Unter den Linden to exchange and review each other's work. The group name was also the title used for a four-volume collection of Hoffmann's novellas and fairytales, published between 1818 and 1821.

Hoffman's Serapion Brother Chamisso (born Louis Charles Adélaïde de Chamissot, 1781–1838) was a botanist, explorer and writer mostly known for his fable *Peter Schlemihl's Miraculous Story* (*Peter Schlemihls wundersame Geschichte*, 1814), about a man who sold his shadow. After being driven out of his native France by the Revolution, Chamisso settled in Berlin with his parents at the age of nine. In 1798 he entered a Prussian infantry regiment and studied natural science when his unit was stationed in Berlin.

When his family returned to France, Chamisso remained to continue his military career. Always interested in literature, especially short stories and poems, he began publishing his early works in the *Berliner Musen-Almanach* (a literary annual), which he co-edited with Karl August Varnhagen von Ense until 1806. In 1804 he founded the Nordsternbund, a society of Berlin Romantics and also frequented the literary salons of Rahel Varnhagen and Bettina von Arnim (see Chapter 2).

In 1806 he returned to France, only to find his parents dead and his estate gone. Offered a professorship at a *lycée* in the Vendée, he chose instead to join the literary circle of the famous *salonnière* Madame de Staël. He published *Peter Schlemihl* a year after returning to Berlin, partly to amuse the children of his friend Julius Eduard Hitzig, whose sister he married in 1819. In 1818 he was made supervisor at the Royal Botanical Garden (see Chapter 6) and an elected member of the Academy of Sciences, but continued writing ballads and poems, some of which were praised by Berlin poet Heinrich Heine (see Chapter 2).

From 1822 until his death (at the age of 57) he lived at Friedrichstrasse 235 in Kreuzberg, where he is commemorated by a memorial plaque. In his honour, the Adelbert von Chamisso literary prize has been awarded by Robert Bosch Stiftung since 1985. Although he is buried in the same cemetery as E. T. A. Hoffmann, a public place more associated with him is Chamissoplatz, a handsome leafy square in west Kreuzberg.

Close to the square was the Düsterer Keller, the well-known hangout of another famous Kreuzberg writer, Theodor Fontane (1819–98). This prolific German novelist and poet – one of the first German travel writers – was born in Neuruppin in Brandenburg. At the age of 16 he followed his father in becoming an apothecary, but indulged his passion for writing in his spare time. His first published work was a novella 'Sibling Love' ('Geschwisterliebe'), which appeared in the *Berlin Figaro* newspaper in 1839, and he continued writing articles for Leipzig newspaper *Die Eisenbahn* and others while working as an apothecary in Dresden and Letschin.

Upon moving to Berlin in 1845, Fontane joined a literary club called Tunnel über der Spree (Tunnel over the river Spree), where he met fellow writers such as Theodor Storm, Gottfried Keller and Berthold Auerbach. The club had been founded by writer and satirist Moritz Gottlieb Saphir in 1827 and existed until 1898 as a forum where members and guests could submit new pieces and get feedback. Today the LCB (see Chapter 5) uses the name for its yearly writer conference.

In 1851 Fontane began working for the Prussian intelligence agency and for several years worked as their official London correspondent. It was while based in the British capital that he became interested in old English ballads and in particular the work of novelist, playwright and poet Sir Walter Scott, whose style he aimed to emulate in *From England* and *Across the Tweed* (both 1860), his first collection of travel sketches. On his return to Berlin in 1859, Fontane became editor of the conservative *Neue Preussische Zeitung* newspaper. Always a keen hiker, he travelled extensively throughout Brandenburg in his spare time, which resulted in his five-volume non-fiction work *Walking through Brandenburg* (*Wanderungen durch die Mark Brandenburg*), published in 1863.

His historical romance *Before the Storm* (*Vor dem Sturm*, 1878) was followed by a series of successful novels that provided realistic sketches of everyday life in Berlin and rural Brandenburg: *L'Adultera* (1882), *Trials and Tribulations*, *Frau Jenny Treibel* and *Effi Briest* (1895). In *Frau Jenny Treibel*, a story about the intertwined fates of two local families, he uses an expensive Kreuzberg villa to issue a sardonic account of the wealth flooding into the city at the time:

> The Triebel villa was situated on a large property that extended spaciously from the Köpenicker Strasse to the Spree. Here in the immediate vicinity of the river there had once been only factory buildings in which every year uncounted tons of potassium ferrocyanide, and later, as the factory expanded, not much smaller

quantities of Berlin blue dye had been produced. But after the war of 1870, as billions poured into the country and the newly founded empire began to dominate the views of even the soberest heads, Kommerzienrat Treibel found his house in the Alte Jakobstrasse no longer suited to his times nor his rank – though it was supposed to have been the work of Gontard and – according to some – even Knobelsdorff. He therefore built himself a fashionable villa with a small front yard and a park-like backyard on his factory property.

Fontane died in 1898 at the age of 79 and was buried in the French Protestant cemetery on Mitte's Liesenstrasse. Though there are not many memorials to Fontane in the city, the apothecary where he worked between 1848 and 1849 has been restored and can be found inside the building that once housed the Bethanien Krankenhaus at Mariannenplatz, now known as the Kunstraum Kreuzberg.

This striking building, with its dramatic towers and a raised bell and cross high above the entrance, was built between 1845 and 1847 at the behest of King Frederick William IV, for the purpose of educating nurses and carers affiliated with the Society of Our Lady. It was used as a military hospital during both world wars and was closed in the 1960s before being saved from demolition by local protests. The building functioned for a while as a squat before being reopened in 1973 as a cultural and social centre.

In 2009 it came under the care of Treuhänder Berlins, a non-profit, non-government organisation, and some of the projects it instigated – the gallery and exhibition space Kunstraum Kreuzberg/Bethanien led by curator Stéphane Bauer, the BBK Berlin Printmakers' Workshop, and the Friedrichshain-Kreuzberg Music School – are in operation today. The Theodor-Fontane-Apotheke is located just down the hall from the gallery and is open to the public a few hours per week.

In the lead up to the Second World War Kreuzberg was, like most of Berlin, a fairly dangerous place due to the ongoing battles between Communists and Nazis who fought for control over the various neighbourhoods. At the same time it also succumbed to all the hedonistic and sexual temptations of the Weimar period. Christopher Isherwood, although more associated with Schöneberg, also rented apartments in Kreuzberg – one at Admiralstrasse 38, another at Wassertorstrasse 21a – and wrote about some of the district's seedy 'boy bars' in *Christopher and his Kind*, his 1976 memorial of his time in Berlin. One such bar was the Cosy Corner at Zossener Strasse 7, which became a model for the Alexander Casino in *Goodbye to Berlin*:

> Nothing could have looked less decadent than the Cosy Corner. It was plain, homely and unpretentious. It's only decorations were a few photographs of boxers and racing cyclists, pinned up above the bar. It was heated by a big old-fashioned iron stove. Partly because of the great heat of this stove and partly because they knew it excited their clients, the boys stripped off their sweaters or leather jackets and sat around with their shirts unbuttoned to the navel and their sleeves rolled up to the armpits.

Kreuzberg was also prone to the consumer impulses of the Weimar era. In 1929, a major commercial event occurred on the border with Neukölln (at Hermannplatz) with the opening of the Karstadt department store. Built in an Expressionist style by architect Philipp Schaefer, it was six storeys tall, encompassed 70,000 square metres and possessed roof gardens, a rooftop restaurant and – most impressive of all since they could be seen from afar – two 71-metre-high light towers. Even a complete new U-bahn station was constructed with direct access to the store – U-Bahnhof Hermannplatz today. Reviews of flashy new department stores often filled the newspapers and this one was no exception. The *Münchner Neueste Nachrichten* newspaper sent Joseph Roth there, resulting in an article titled 'The Very Large Department Store':

> The old, and merely big, department stores are small in comparison, not far removed from ordinary plain shops, although in essentials

the really big department store is not really all that different from the merely big ones. It has more stock, more lifts, more customers, stairs, escalators, tills, sales personnel, liveries, display racks, crates, and cardboard boxes. True, the goods seem to be cheaper. So very many of them are crowded so closely together that they can hardly help regarding themselves as of inferior worth. They are abased in their own eyes, lower their prices, and become more humble; cheapness is the humility of merchandise.

[....]

Therefore, the very large department store should not be viewed as a sinful undertaking, as, for example, the Tower of Babel. It is, rather, proof of the inability of the human race of today to be extravagant. It even builds skyscrapers: and the consequence this time isn't a great flood, but just a shop.

The store remained open until 1945. During the war it was used for food storage and the Heeresbekleidungsamt, the Wehrmacht Clothing Board, was housed here from 1943. Its massive construction made it somewhat impervious to the constant Allied bombing in the last years of the war, and also made it an excellent defence position during the Battle of Berlin, as described by Antony Beevor in *Berlin: The Downfall 1945* (2002):

With Neukölln heavily penetrated by Soviet combat groups, Krukenberg prepared a fall-back position round the Hermannplatz. The twin towers of the Karstadt department store provided excellent observation posts for watching the advance of four Soviet armies – the 5th Shock Army from Treptow Park, the 8th Guards Army and the 1st Guards Tank Army from Neukölln and Konev's 3rd Guards Tank Army from Mariendorf.

The department store did not escape destruction; to avoid it falling into the hands of the Red Army, German troops blew the building up on 25 April 1945. The department store was rebuilt in 1951 with a more humble, postwar design, and is still in operation today: the original staircase inside is one of the few elements to survive the war disaster intact.

A glimpse into the horrors of the local population experienced during wartime is given in Beatrice Colin's *The Luminous Life of Lilly Aphrodite* (published in 2008):

> The cart horse swayed and sank forward to its knees. The boy with the reins in his hands and the sob in his voice started to shout, 'Come on … gee up! … Move! Why have you stopped? Move! Please move?' He hit the horse's ridged brown back with his whip once, twice, three times. The horse flinched, showed the whites of its eyes, and then with a small moan, a letting out of breath, of steam, of life, it slumped and collapsed into a heap of angular bone and sagging skin. Lilly wasn't the only one standing on Mariannenplatz who was watching. No sooner had his head hit the cobbles than a dozen women appeared from doorways and alleyways armed with knives and bowls and cups. They ignored the boy's cries, his tears, his laments, and began to butcher the carcass, sawing through bone and slicing through veins to let the spurt of warm blood flow into their bowls. One woman, her face splattered with red, tried to hack off a ragged haunch with a penknife; another pulled out the tongue. In minutes, what was left of the horse would vanish completely.

It was after the war, and an extensive period of rebuilding, that Kreuzberg began to develop a more 'alternative' reputation, particularly in the eastern part (SO36), which was hemmed in on three sides by the Wall after August 1961. The buildings in the shadow of the Wall were, as in Wedding, often shunned by wealthier Berliners, though in Kreuzberg in the 1960s it was not Turkish immigrants who first moved here, but students availing themselves of the cheap rents. With this kind of demographic it was little surprise that by the late 1960s a fairly lively alternative scene was emerging. Jörg Fauser writes about a typical Kreuzberg bar of the era in his book *Raw Material*:

> Mister Go had rock music and a light show. The most popular images were snapshots from the Vietnam War. The walls flickered with GIs launching attacks and dying, monks on fire, Vietcong being executed. To a soundtrack with music that was new to me: The Doors, Jefferson Airplane, Cream, Jimi Hendrix. Dealers with flowing hair and Mao badges on their Indian shirts; wrestling types with earrings and musk aftershave; ethereal graces from Siemensstadt or Neheim-Huesten who wanted to swap their hairdressing apprenticeship for free love or a speed bomb, but instead woke up in a basement flat in Kreuzberg with a rusty needle sticking out of their arm; future political commissars with white nylon shirts and the collected works of Enver Hodsha committed to memory as well as complete lists of people to be lined up and shot; and street kids in search of their first rush – all of these huddled under the light show with its reminders of the Asian revolution, and The Doors trying to give the child a name: 'Father, I want to kill you.' When you left the building, there were the police cars on the corner, their flashing blue lights like a scornful commentary on the exploding collages in your head.

In 1966 the whole of SO36 was earmarked for destruction when the Berlin Senate planned to build an extension of the A100 motorway through the entire area. In the absence of any state support for landlords and investors, the postwar buildings were mostly neglected, and from the mid-1970s and early 1980s the area became a magnet for lower-income residents: artists, students, squatters, hippies, punks and military service dodgers (West Berlin did not formally belong to the Federal Republic of Germany (FRG) so was officially exempt from conscription). In his 2015 non-fiction book *City of Exiles*, a mix of journalism and memoir exploring the attractiveness of Berlin to outsiders, Australian author Stuart Braun writes:

I remember the first time I walked into the Kreuzberg Museum
and discovered that it was dedicated almost entirely to the
squatters and activists who stopped redevelopers from ripping
down the district's old tenement streets and putting freeways and
high rises in their stead. Around a hundred tenements were not
only squatted in Kreuzberg by the early 1980s but became base
camps in the fight against urban renewal. In the museum, I was
a little exalted by black-and-white photos of the old bullet-ridden
squats, *Wir Alle Bleiben* (We All Stay) slogans painted across them.
The images represented not some kind of anarchic hippydom, but
focused political action. And it often worked. It had been possible
to shape this city from the bottom up, something that had seemed
infeasible in Sydney, my home city where the developers always
won – or where people just didn't seem to care that much.

Philip Hensher writes in his novel *Pleasured* (1998), which is
set in pre-Wall Kreuzberg, about how the district created its own
mythology – one that continues to attract visitors and expats alike
in search of a more 'authentic' and 'alternative' Berlin:

Kreuzberg was a place more talked about, perhaps, than lived in;
it was a district better known to most Germans than whole towns
twice the size, a bleached witch of a place, a bleached witch in
a fairy story to scare the blonde good children of the West with
terrors, and which, seemingly, instead, only lured them in [...]
They told jokes about it – it was the third largest Turkish city in
the world – but mostly it was there to warn about what would
happen to Germany. What, in one corner, already had. It was
surprising no one ran coach tours there. But even within the
bounds of Kreuzberg, Kreuzberg was a place more talked about
than real, somehow; the people who walked in the Oranienstrasse
and sat in the Oranienstrasse bars seemed, if you judged by their
conversation, to think that the streets might vanish, might never
have existed, without the constant evoking of the name of the

square mile or so. An overheard snatch of conversation always offered the word Kreuzberg, brought in at some length; a town of lovers, it sometimes seemed, separated from their beloved, fated to go on saying the beautiful name, in the street, in a bus, inside their narrow walls, in the open air, to anyone who would listen and many who wouldn't, until the streets seemed filled with the nutcracker-noise of the name, Kreuzberg, produced by a thousand tiny yelling voices, a crowd of dwarfs, the hundred European accents of those same blond children who had heard of the walled witchy town from their warning mothers, and remembered. When they talked of it, people often liked to think of it as something interior, imagined; not bricks and streets, but, as they said, a state of mind.

The alternative scene was symbolised by the many artists and local bands that operated in the district, such as Sprung Aus Den Wolken, Malaria! and Einstürzende Neubaten. Australian musician Nick Cave moved here for a while too, living in an apartment at Dresdner Strasse 11, where he wrote music for his bands the Birthday Party and the Bad Seeds and also wrote his novel *And the Ass Saw the Angel* (1989), in between hanging out at local dive bars such as Risiko. In a documentary made by British artists and filmmakers Iain Forsyth and Jane Pollard, Cave explains how at the time:

> [T]here was no money so there was a level of existence that we weren't used to, a *quality* of existence actually. I worked all day and drank all night, and I would sit in my office space typing away at *And the Ass Saw the Angel,* and at night, or during the early hours of morning, we would go to Risiko, which stayed open 'til daylight. We would just sit there and wage this war against sleep.

While Risiko was legendary enough, the music venue that really put the district on the map was named after the local postcode: SO36. Set inside a Weimar-era cinema, it opened in 1978 and focused on promoting the punk sounds that were taking over the UK and Europe until German artist Martin Kippenberger expanded the programme to include a heady mix of new wave, post-punk and visual art. The venue is still going strong today with an equally dynamic mix of readings, Turkish gay nights, 1980s new wave parties and occasional punk and rock gigs. Hensher profiles the club in its 1980s heyday in *Pleasured*:

SO36 was a nightclub, of sorts; it resembled a large village hall, with a cloakroom at the entrance and a record player with a ferocious amplification system at the other end. Each night there had a different name. There was a night for ageing punks to jump up and down to their horrible music, called Hot Soup. There was a night for lesbians, which Friedrich had once gotten into by smoothing his hair down and gluing a monocle into his eye socket (using hair-gel for both purposes). In white tie and borrowed tails, he made, it was true, a credible lesbian. This night was called Rosa Klebb. The Friday night, which they were heading for, was loosely supposed to be fancy dress. They pushed Pierre Stifter, in his fur coat, forward. It had no specific limitations in clientele, no habit of exclusion, and one of the most inexhaustible of Kreuzberg's street proverbs was that sooner or later you saw everyone you knew, even your mother, leaning against the wall at SO36 on a Friday night. For this reason, the Friday night dance at SO36 was called The Inexorable Pleasures Of Polymorphous Perversity, and was packed. For none of these nights was much of an effort made in the way of changing the appearance of the club, except the punk nights, when all furniture that was not actually bolted to the floor was removed to a storeroom. The rest of the time, it was a long room, its floor, halls and ceiling painted a dull black; a colour which somehow amplified the always deafening music, which ricocheted in the space as if it were empty. It worked hard at an atmosphere of exhausted dreariness, and, to its appreciative customers, it achieved it.

There were other scenes aside from the post-punks too. Sven Regener's novel *Herr Lehmann* is also set in late 1980s Kreuzberg but describes a different 'slacker' scene that revolves around the low-key Markthalle restaurant (where the eponymous protagonist Herr Lehmann works) and the Prinzenbad swimming pool. Both venues are still thriving in Berlin today, and in fact the following description could have been written on any typical summer day in recent memory:

> People were running around on all sides, half naked people of all ages and either sex stomped through the footbath or stood in it, puffing and blowing under a cold shower. Pensioners shuffled past, Turkish youths yelled and guffawed as they belted each other with wet towels, little children hugged empty plastic bottles or stumbled along unwrapping ices on sticks, and the changing areas left and right of Herr Lehmann disgorged or swallowed up interminable streams of jostling figures. Further away could be seen the snack bar or kiosk area, where vast crowds were queuing up for something or already consuming it at seated tables. There were people everywhere, running or strolling, calling or waving to each other. and from the pool itself, which was partly obscured by ornamental shrubs, came shouts and splashing sounds and an unintelligible loudspeaker announcement. In the distance beyond, Herr Lehmann knew, lay a vast expanse of densely populated turf over which hung a faint odour of chlorine alloyed with a whiff of French fries.

Kreuzberg residents tended to have mixed feelings about the Berlin Wall, and how life might be on the other side of it. Many despised it and enjoyed scrawling their messages on it in paint or urine, but for others it was a fascination and, with access to the GDR being fairly easy for West Berliners, regular trips could be taken. When Herr Lehmann goes for lunch with his parents they exhibit a typical West German horror of the structure:

'Terrible.' His mother tucked into the bread. 'I don't know how you can live around here with that frightful Wall all around you. It's really terrible. I couldn't stand it.'

'It's not that bad, not for us. We can always get out.'

'But one feels so completely shut in.'

'Nonsense.' Herr Lehmann didn't feel like this Wall crap. It was always the same when outsiders visited Berlin. 'If a street in Bremen ends in a wall, you don't immediately think "Oh dear, I'm shut in."'

'That's quite different.'

'Yes, but it's the others who have the problem, the ones in East Berlin. The purpose of the thing isn't to stop us getting out, it's to stop them getting in. Except, of course, that they would regard it as getting out.'

'Yes,' said his mother, 'they'd all like to get out from the sound of it.'

During the 1960s and 1970s East Kreuzberg was also settled by a large influx of *Gastarbeiter* from Turkey, especially around Kottbusser Tor and Oranienstrasse, an area sometimes referred to as Little Istanbul. Before and after the Wall fell, many Turkish – and German-Turkish – writers have written about their experiences. One such is Yade Kara, who was born in Cayirli, Turkey in 1965 and moved with her family to Kreuzberg in 1970.

In Berlin she studied English and German and has since worked as an actress, teacher, manager and journalist. Her novel *Selam Berlin*, published in 2003, is a coming-of-age novel about Turkish-German student Hassan, who shuttles back and forth between Turkey and Berlin and bemoans the collapse of the Wall, which in his perspective somehow stabilised his whole family. The excerpt below refers to his father, who had a double life on either side of the Wall that was perhaps not uncommon during those divided years.

Baba's days in East Berlin were also the days he always put on his gray suit and carried his old attaché case. 'I don't want to attract attention in the East,' he always said. But he did attract attention with his black hair and the mustache that he had back then. Baba ate breakfast in West Berlin, hugged Mama and said goodbye to us. A few streets away from our apartment, he crossed at Checkpoint Charlie into East Berlin. Baba didn't need a visa because he had a Turkish passport in a black plastic jacket with a red crescent moon and star on it, that he always carried with him. He attended to his business, Rosa accompanying him. She was well-versed in the rules of the game of socialism. Then, after lunch, Baba probably explored the area between Rosa's legs.

Baba moved in two systems, on two stages, like an actor who kept his costumes and props ready for two plays. That's how Baba kept everything ready for performances in the East and West. Over the years he changed systems, his wardrobe, his bags, his women. It was daily routine for him and he had the security of the Wall. It stood there, and nothing could upset his life and his family in West Berlin.

Selam Berlin won the 'Best Debut' category of the German Book Prize in 2004, as well as the Adelbert Chamisso Promotional Award in the same year. In her acceptance speech for the latter, Kara made some astute parallels about her own life and that of fellow 'Kreuzberger' Chamisso:

My first student job was on Chamisso Platz. I played a passer-by in a movie about the 1930s. For an entire morning I sat with Mario Adorf on the top of a Berlin double-decker bus waiting for my cameo appearance on Chamisso Platz. Mr Adorf spent the time writing short stories, I spent it reading Proust's *A la Recherche du Temps Perdu*. Adelbert von Chamisso died on a late summer day in August, I was born on precisely such a day. He lies buried in the cemetery by Hallesche Tor in Kreuzberg. As a child I would play hide-and-seek in the cemetery with my cousins. I didn't notice the sign saying 'Dogs and children must be kept out of this place of rest' because I couldn't speak or read German yet.

Adelbert von Chamisso and I are like passers-by from different centuries, living and working in the same streets, squares and places in Berlin. Nowadays some people might define Adelbert von Chamisso as a Franco-German author or perhaps a multicultural writer, and find his rather different perspective interesting, etc. For me Adelbert von Chamisso is also an allrounder, as we can see from his work as an author, lyricist, and scientist. But most of all, I see him as a Berliner.

After the Wall fell, Kreuzberg maintained its alternative streak and its propensity for protest, rebellion and occasional outbreaks of violence, such as those that still take place annually on 1 May (Labour Day). This yearly tradition has its roots in a 1987 left-wing street parade that turned into a politicised trade union demonstration on Lausitzer Platz. The protests led to fights with police that involved tear gas, batons and shop lootings; more than 100 people were injured, many were arrested, and the event made international news.

These days Kreuzberg's anarchist communities have mainly dispersed and the May Day event (now called MyFest) is a four-day celebration of multicultural music and food organised by the city. But when the sun goes down, the police and lefties still square off around Kottbusser Tor and Oranienplatz – mostly for show, but occasionally with more injuries and arrests. Inka Parei's (born 1967) debut novel *The Shadowboxing Woman* (1999) offers an insight into the May Day celebrations in the 1990s:

It is a hot day, too hot for spring. The streets of Kreuzberg in the neighborhood of the Görlitzer Bahnhof shimmer with heat and sand. The sand blows over the remains of the train station – an unkempt expanse scattered with tracks. Aborted by the Wall decades ago, the tracks have lost their purpose and have relapsed to desert and steppe. It is late afternoon. The quarter begins to fill up. Turkish families in middle class cars, packed to the roof, look for parking spaces. People clamber out, bang the doors shut, drag tired children and the remains of their barbecues into houses still cool with winter. A little girl with blackened front teeth stares from almost every façade, the picture is frayed at the edges, wavy with poster glue. She shoulders a stick like a paramilitary, and offers passersby a speech balloon: Come out for the revolutionary First of May. Small groups, who have already broken off from the rally come over from Lausitzer Platz, walking toward me with apparent coolness, without haste. Only the way with which they keep, unfaltering, to their direction betrays tension.

Before the Wall fell, Kreuzberg's post-punk and New Wave scenes had begun to become slightly redundant in the face of the new underground electronic music that was exploding in the USA, the UK and Europe. Local clubs such as UFO (at Köpenicker Strasse 6) sprang up in basements and old factories, drawing a new generation into a similarly alternative lifestyle. Stuart Braun captures the atmosphere shortly before the fall of the Wall in *City of Exiles* (2015):

> The hybrid acid-house beats that pounded long into the daylight hours at Ufo were played by DJs who had no podium, who were not stars, who were on the same level as the audience. Ufo wasn't either a place to pick up, socialise and look good. It was a cauldron of pure dance where free spirits from across the city could jettison their pasts and identities. Facilitating the kind of liberating anonymity that had long attracted outsiders to the Spree, these early techno clubs were microcosms of Berlin.

After the Wall was opened, much of this scene moved to East Berlin, where there were more open spaces for parties and the living was even cheaper. Throughout the 1990s and 2000s, however, gentrification cleared many of the clubs from Prenzlauer Berg and the scene shifted to Friedrichshain and also back to Kreuzberg, where its alternative spirit is regularly channelled into live music and DJ venues like SO36, Bi Nuu, Magnet, Lido, Kater Blau and Farbfernseher. One of the biggest electronic music clubs is Watergate. Located right at the foot of the Oberbaumbrücke, it opened in 2004 and has since become a Mecca for clubbers all over the world – some of whom fly to Berlin for the weekend and spend it entirely on the dancefloor.

Journalist Tobias Rapp gives an insight into the post-Wall phenomenon of Berlin clubbing in his book *Lost and Sound: Berlin, Techno and the Easyjetset* (*Lost and Sound: Berlin, Techno und der Easyjetset*, 2009). In the following excerpt he talks specifically about Watergate on a Wednesday night:

It's not long after midnight and if the city is sleeping at all it's doing so elsewhere. The last U-Bahn is rumbling along the elevated steel track, about to cross the Oberbaumbrücke bridge into Friedrichshain. We're at Schlesisches Tor in Kreuzberg, Berlin. Not long ago this spot was anything but vibrant; the Wrangelkiez, a neighbourhood squashed in between Görlitzer Park, the Spree, the Landwehr canal and the traffic artery of Skalitzer Strasse was one of Kreuzberg's forgotten corners. This was still the case at the end of the 90s, when nightlife was centred around the Mitte district and techno was officially 'over'. Small groups of people are making their way along Falckensteinstrasse towards the river bank. Two ask the way. 'Watergate?' – 'The door over there, up the stairs.' It's Wednesday, the weekend is still two working days away, and the butterflies are already there.

彡 9 ⾭

FRIEDRICHSHAIN

Friedrichshain is similarly famed throughout the city for its vibrant
nightlife, which is centred mainly on and around historical Boxhagener Platz – in particular the 'party street' Simon-Dach-Strasse
– and most obviously manifested in its most famous techno club,
Berghain. Like Kreuzberg, it also has an 'alternative' reputation as a
magnet for anarchists, students and other left-wing revolutionaries,
though it stems mostly from the early 1990s when squatters – many
from Kreuzberg – moved into many of the vacated buildings in

*13   The Oberbaumbruecke, which connects the districts of Kreuzberg
and Friedrichshain*

what had previously been a neglected and run-down part of inner-city East Berlin.

Piecemeal gentrification as well as a concerted effort from the police and local authorities has all but cleared the district of its squats and more politically minded inhabitants, replacing them with a new demographic of professionals, middle-class families and more acquiescent students. Since 2001, the district has technically been part of the Kreuzberg-Friedrichshain borough, though anyone who knows these two areas knows that, although they share some overlaps, they also possess very different souls – not least due to their postwar locations on opposite sides of the Berlin Wall.

Originally a collection of small, neighbouring villages (Frankfurter Vorstadt, Boxhagen and Friedrichsberg) that were outside the city's customs and excise wall – the local custom gates were situated at today's Frankfurter Tor and the Oberbaumbrücke – the district was officially created in 1920 and incorporated into Greater Berlin. During the nineteenth century an influx of workers arrived in the district to work in the factories and cheap tenement buildings that were springing up, and large-scale industrial projects – the opening of a major railway line between Berlin and Frankfurt (Oder) in 1846 and the erection of the new Frankfurter Bahnhof station (Ostbahnhof today), the city's first waterworks at Stralauer Tor in 1865, the large Julius Pintsch machine factory in 1868 (which also later produced water and land mines) and a sprawling public slaughter house in 1881 – brought employment and money to the area.

Many of the district's entrepreneurs were actively involved in the First World War, something picked up by Kurt Tucholsky (see Chapter 7) in his 1916 poem – written under the pseudonym Theobald Tiger – 'The War Contractor' ('Der Kriegslieferant'):

> You live someplace in Friedrichshain
> And God has showered blessings on your marriage
> (six children). And your sour wines together
> with what you got from selling life insurance,

some racing tips, and playing 'war' for money
kept you and yours in bread up to this point.
By times you were broke, by times you had piles of Benjamins.
We often saw your wife sweeping the staircase.

But when the world from dreadful fear stops breathing
You bet it all on your brand 'Super Soup' –
Your ships came in! In your wife's stylish locks now
sparkle baubles on a silken band.

From Paulchen Thumann, Stöwer and Van Gocken
You've quickly grabbed the stuff you need
And when at last the peace bells ring for others:
What price Berlin? You've got it made, old friend!

While much of the area's industrial legacy was wiped out during
the war, it is possible to find traces of it scattered throughout the
district. The skeletal remains of the slaughter house complex,
designed by prolific city architect Hermann Blankenstein, has
provided the basis for a modern housing development in the north-
eastern part of the district, while the impressive Knorr-Bremse
brake factory on Neue Bahnhofstrasse – built by Berlin U-Bahn
architect Alfred Grenander between 1913 and 1916 – still stands.
Knorr-Bremse was founded in 1905 by Georg Knorr, a Berlin-based
engineer specialising in railroad technology who developed his
widely used compressed-air brake system. Just around the corner,
along Wühlisch Strasse, is the Knorr Promenade, a small street
lined with individually built houses constructed around the same
time to attract more wealthy people to the area.

Despite its industrial roots, the oldest part of the district –
indeed the place that gave the area its name – is the Volkspark
Friedrichshain, the vast green park located at the northern border
with Prenzlauer Berg. Planned in the 1840s to commemorate the
centenary of Frederick the Great's coronation (Friedrichshain

means 'Friedrich's Grove') the 52-hectare park predates the rest of the district by almost 80 years and remains one of the city's most popular and largest recreational spaces.

One of the oldest buildings within the park is the red-brick Krankenhaus am Friedrichshain hospital. Built between 1868 and 1874, it was one of the first hospitals in the city aside from the university hospital Charité. Next door to the hospital is the even older memorial cemetery, which hosts the graves of 183 revolutionaries shot by the Prussian military during the 1848 revolution. Historian Alexandra Richie describes the occasion in her history book *Faust's Metropolis* (1998):

> Berliners celebrated their successful revolution, and a huge funeral for the 'March Heroes' who had died in the fighting was planned. On 22 March a grand procession moved through Berlin, under trees and past buildings which had been draped with thousands of black banners paid for by the people of the city. Factory workers walked the route with professors, the mayor stood beside Alexander von Humboldt and Theodor Fontane, Poles and Italians marched together, each carrying their national flags, and Berlin societies and clubs sent representatives with ceremonial banners and wreaths. In all 20,000 people marched that day, and when they passed the palace the kings and ministers stood on the balcony and bared their heads. The bodies were laid to rest with much ceremony at the Friedrichshain cemetery, and the graves would become a site of pilgrimage for liberals, social democrats and Communists for that day on.

At the westernmost corner of the park, where Am Friedrichshain meets Friedenstrasse, a narrow lane leads to the park's literary showpiece, the Märchenbrunnen. This neo-baroque 'fountain of fairytales' was commissioned in 1893 and represents one of the city's first pieces of public art. Envisioned as a soul-enhancing sight for the impoverished residents living and working in the area (especially children), the fountain was designed by Berlin architect Ludwig Hoffmann and includes sculptures that reference well-known fairytales, including some by Berlin literary heroes the Brothers Grimm (see Chapter 7). Although nearly destroyed during wartime, the damaged sculptures were found hidden behind a nearby wall and the fountain was rebuilt. When it was first created, Max Osborn, a local art critic for the *Vossische Zeitung* and others, waxed lyrical about the fountain in a piece called 'Der Märchenbrunnen am Friedrichshain zu Berlin' (1914), describing it as 'a glorious chapter in the history of the promotion of the arts in Berlin':

> In a heavily populated part of the city, blessed with many children, an installation was to be laid out, the sight of which would refresh and delight the gaze of thousands of people during their day-to-day lives and in their hours of leisure. It was to appear in the corner of an old park that is hemmed in by streets [...] Here in the basin, the water gushes and flows across three shallow terraces, surrounded by monumental benches. Bubbly and frothing, the playful water springs with a merry murmuring from many small springs. Strange frogs perch among them, dominated by a goggle-eyed frog king. And around the edge appear eight charming figures, which we know well, yet appear new in the loving execution that Ignaz Taschner has brought to them, with an extraordinary sensibility for the laws of small-scale sculpture in a context such as this. We see Puss In Boots, Lucky Hans, Snow White, Sleeping Beauty, Little Red Riding Hood, and Cinderella, the Seven Ravens, and the little sister whose brother is turned into a deer. In the foreground, as droll harbingers of this fairy-tale parade, we see Hansel and Gretel riding toward each other on the downy backs of two ducks.

Due to the installation of anti-aircraft towers and bunkers in the Volkspark during wartime, it became a prime target during the war – not that you would know it today. Rubble from the park and surrounding areas was collected together to make the park's two large peaks, known today as the Grosse Bunkerberg (78 metres) and the Kleine Bunkerberg (48 metres), which look for all the world like natural hills and are popular with joggers seeking a bit of an incline, and people looking for a private barbecue or sunbathing spot. In 1983, the nickname for the park's rubble-filled hills, Mont Klamott (Rubble Mountain), was used by GDR rock band Silly for the name of an album and song of the same name.

In 1933, the entire Friedrichshain district was renamed Horst-Wessel-Stadt by the Nazis, a name that remained until 1945. Horst Wessel was an SA street fighter and activist during the 1920s and 1930s, but had also dabbled in music and lyrics. He was attacked by Communist fighters and shot in the head in 1930, dying from his wounds a month later in the Friedrichshain hospital. His alleged murderer, Communist Party member Albrecht Höhler, was sentenced to six years' imprisonment, but in 1933 was dragged out of prison by the SA and shot. In 1929 he had published the poem 'The Flag Up High, the Ranks Closed!' ('Die Fahne hoch, die Reihen dicht!') in the Nazi magazine *Der Angriff*. After his death it was set to the melody of a sea shanty and became a fighting song for the SA and other Nazi street fighters and, after 1933, part of the official Nazi anthem.

At the end of the war the flak towers in the Volkspark became the front line in the Battle of Berlin as the city was surrounded by Russian troops. A diary entry by 16-year-old Hitler Youth member Dieter Borkowski on 29 April 1945 describes the carnage:

We could already hear the 'Hurrah's from the attacking Soviet troops in Kniprodestrasse. There were dead and wounded lying everywhere in the five stories of the Flak tower, and an unpleasant sweet smell permeated the tower. We received the order to occupy the new front line in Höchstestrasse. The two Flak-towers now stand like islands in the sea for the Russians have long since forced their way past these fortresses [...] The provision of supplies and ammunition has become very bad.

After the war, the Volkspark ended up in the Soviet sector of the divided city. The GDR reconstructed the park, peppering it with memorials, most of which are still there today, along with a slew of newly added leisure facilities (a skate park and climbing wall, tennis and football courts, an outdoor cinema). As well as a memorial to the German volunteers who died during the Spanish Civil War, there is also one to the 1918 Red Sailors' Revolution and the Polish soldiers and German anti-fascist groups of the Second World War. The park's scenic lake also features a Japanese Pavilion and Peace Bell given to East Berlin by Japan as an anti-nuclear-war statement.

If the park is the oldest and greenest part of Friedrichshain, the district's heart is arguably Boxhagener Platz. Constructed in 1903 and named after a former Prussian fort (Boxhagen), it is flanked on all sides by graceful Wilhelminian tenements and was elegant enough to adorn postcards in the nineteenth century. In the northern corner of the square is one of the city's 30 or so remaining neo-Gothic metal *pissoirs* – nicknamed Café Achteck (Café Octagon) – built in the nineteenth century.

Boxhagener Platz did not fare well throughout the GDR years and became a haunt for local squatters, drug addicts and alcoholics in the years following reunification. The most famous book connected with the square is 2004's *Boxhagener Platz* by Torsten Schulz (born 1959). Set in 1968, the story centres on a young protagonist called Holger and his somewhat forthright grandmother, who is in search of her seventh consecutive husband.

The book was turned into a film by award-winning Berlin director Matti Geschonneck, who – like Schulz – grew up on the square during the GDR years. Today a dramaturg and director, Schulz began writing stories while a teenager, later enrolling in the HFF Hochschule für Film und Fernsehen in Potsdam-Babelsberg. His published works include *Revolution and Crabs* (*Revolution und Filzläuse*), a compilation of short stories published in 2008, and the novel *Nilowsky* (2013), an East German love story. *Boxhagener Platz* was translated into English as *A Square in East Berlin* by British poet Harry Guest, and describes daily life in the GDR, including the district's passive resistance to the state and the student revolts that occurred in the West that year:

On that day, as on most days, I was on Boxhagener Platz playing football with Jimmy Glitschie and Mirko Buskov. We were taking turns guarding goal but felt equally happy when the ball went bouncing away and we had to run and grab it before it landed on the main road.

'Holger! Come on! I want you.' My grandmother was standing behind me suddenly. She was carrying a rake and a watering-can so I knew all too well where she was off to.

'Can't go on playing now.' This meant I had to go with her. No excuses possible. No argument either.

'Another time then.' Jimmy's tone was sympathetic, while Mirko Buskov said, 'Have fun!' with unconcealed malice.

Gran pressed her beastly watering-can of grey lead into my hand and tripped away taking short, brisk steps. We got to the Karl-Marx-Allee in less than fifteen minutes. Just like each year on October 7th, tanks and rocket-launchers were rumbling down the avenue. Soldiers peered out of the cramped little windows acknowledging waves and cheers from the crowd on the pavement behind the cordon. It was embarrassing enough having to lug the wretched can around each time for her, but really horrible to be so near the parade now and not be able to behave like everyone else. My grandmother made the situation worse by complaining at the top of her voice. I must admit, though, she always added to my store of colourful vocabulary.

Now she was shouting. Angrily. 'Just look at that. The buggers have blocked the way to the cemetery.' The buggers referred to were the 'Commie bastards' or 'Ruddy Ulbricht's pack of thugs' as Gran described them on other occasions. She swished the rake around in the air as if to defy the tanks. Oh no! I thought. I hope there's no-one here I know!

Nowadays Boxhagener Platz is mostly a symbol of the area's gentrification. The ground floors of its surrounding houses are inhabited by trendy cafés and restaurants and its playgrounds are home to well-dressed kids munching on bio-brötchen purchased from local bakeries and the weekly farmers' market that surround the square on Saturdays. On Sundays the square hosts a flea market, which Chloe Aridjis portrays in her novel *Book of Clouds*:

> Another Sunday had arrived, one more notch in the unrelenting parade of Sundays, bringing with it the prospect of a walk. Rather than set out aimlessly, I headed towards Boxhagener Platz, the site of an animated flea market I hadn't been to in months. It would be good to circulate in a crowd, I figured, prodded on by strangers too caught up in the visual onslaught to pay much attention to anyone in their midst. The market was especially busy that afternoon. Long banks of furniture, outlandish clothes, a hodgepodge of crockery, vintage records: all was up for grabs, prices arbitrary (two euros for a skirt, twenty euros for a shabby belt) but negotiable.

Although Boxhagener Platz and its surrounding streets do not reveal much in the way of the district's GDR history today, the Karl-Marx-Allee remains one of the pre-eminent Soviet sights in the city. Built on the war-bombed ruins of the Grosse Frankfurter Strasse – whose rubble was cleared by the so-called *Trümmerfrauen* (rubble women) – the regime's most prestigious show street was originally called Stalinallee and was officially opened on Stalin's seventieth birthday in December 1949 – just a couple of months after the official founding of the GDR.

The boulevard's Soviet-style buildings, clad on the outside with expensive ceramic tiles, were deliberately monumental and presented ostentatiously as 'workers' palaces'. The height of luxury at the time thanks to such modern conveniences as lifts, heating and running hot water, they were initially available to workers too, until higher-ranking GDR officials began to claim them. The broad street was purpose-built for military parades and large-scale events like the annual May Day parade and the Third World Festival of Youth and Students, which took place in August 1951.

In 1953 it became one of the main sites of the rioting that took place across Germany after GDR leader Walter Ulbricht decided to increase working hours by 10 per cent for the same wages. Having deciding that postwar socialism was not working fast enough, he also hiked up the prices of bread and other basic necessities. On 16 June, 300 East Berlin construction workers marched down Stalinallee in protest; their numbers quickly swelled and a general strike and protests were called for the next day. The subsequent uprising spread throughout the whole GDR, gaining hundreds of thousands of participants until it was violently suppressed by Soviet troops and GDR Volkspolizei. Fifty-five protesters were killed, and the event was subsequently memorialised in West Berlin by renaming the large street that runs west from Brandenburg Gate the Strasse des 17. Juni (it had been named Charlottenburger Chaussee before).

In 1961, with Stalin long dead and buried, the name of the street was changed to Karl-Marx-Allee. Since building was still taking place along the eastern sections of the boulevard, the architecture correspondingly changed from the classic Soviet style into a slightly more relaxed modernist approach, and a slew of cultural venues – the Kosmos and Kino International cinemas (1962 and 1963) and the international restaurant Café Moskau (1964) – were built. Although many of the street's former establishments have today been transformed into minimalist galleries and trendy coffee shops, the street is a protected heritage site and its preserved buildings – and signage – still conjure a distinctly Soviet aura.

One stand-out sign is a large, curved orange one that heralds Café Sibylle at No. 72, a time-warp café that originally opened in 1953 and now hosts a small museum detailing the street's history. A few doors down at No. 78 is the Karl Marx Buchhandlung, also opened in 1953, whose own sans-serif sign has been seen in movies like *The Lives of Others* (2006) or *Goodbye, Lenin!* (2003). Today the bookshop has been replaced by media offices but Marx's image can still be seen on the wall inside, and the current company co-hosts the Salon Karl Marx Buchandlung, a series of up to four (mostly German-language) readings each month.

Since many books were censored in the GDR, the shop could not offer a truly diverse selection, but it was nonetheless popular due to cheap prices and its academic slant. As well as becoming associated with GDR intellectuals and authors like Christa Wolf and Bertolt Brecht, the occasional foreign visitor also visited the shop during its East Berlin years, such as German-born Jewish historian and intellectual Fritz Stern, whose family fled to America during the Nazi regime. Stern recalls a visit to the bookstore in his 2006 book *Five Germanys I Have Known*:

> I also repeatedly visited the stately, spacious Karl Marx Buchhandlung on Stalinallee, where one could buy inexpensive editions of the great 'classics of socialism' and translations of acceptable foreign works. The SED-controlled publishing enterprises produced a great flow of authorized books at low prices, hoping to leave no comrade behind. And in the secondhand section one could find 'bourgeois' editions of old classics at bargain prices: I bought an old four-volume edition of Herder's *Werke* with a modern stamp on the flyleaf: FROM THE GHETTO LIBRARY – no place specified. A grim irony: the works of an Enlightenment philosopher taken from the ghetto, perhaps the one place where he might have been read in the old spirit.
>
> I also purchased a big volume entitled *Deutschland*, translated from the *Great Soviet Encyclopedia*. Its editors, Jürgen Kuczynski and Wolfgang Steinitz, noted that this 'most comprehensive scientific work in the history of humanity' had been raised to a 'still higher level' in its 1950 edition, as decided by the Soviet Union's Council of Ministers. Of contemporary historical writing, it reported, 'After the destruction of Hitler's Germany

by the Soviet Union, German historians have gained wider perspectives in free scientific research ... However, reactionary ideas are once again prevalent in West German historiography, as Anglo-American imperialists conduct a policy of dividing Germany so as to allow the revival of fascism and militarism in West Germany.'

When the Wall fell, a large number of East Berliners moved to the West, leaving hundreds of apartment buildings throughout East Berlin completely empty. By 1990 approximately 200 buildings, mostly in Prenzlauer Berg and Friedrichshain, had been squatted. One of the most squatted areas in Friedrichshain was around Mainzer Strasse and Rigaer Strasse, which eventually became a focal point for violent battles between police and squatters. In a 2013 interview with author and co-director of Foreign Policy in Focus at the Institute for Policy Studies John Feffer, former squatter Dirk Mold told of his collective living experiences:

'On Mainzer Straße, there were 11 buildings squatted,' he related. 'Visually and culturally this was something new. The part of the street with squatted houses was 200 meters long. On the street there were several different groups. One house, for instance, had transvestites. The boys walked around with very hot female clothes. It looked like in a movie. They were wearing make-up and blonde little curls and short skirts, it looked really crazy. Other houses were really militant where they were always wearing black clothes and hooded jackets. All the houses were draped with flags and banners. Every evening, people would sit in front of their houses eating, chatting, and drinking.'

But the squats occupied only one side of the street. 'On the other side of the street, normal people were living,' he continued. 'The problem was that they had to get up early to go to work. Most of them didn't dare tell the squatters to please be quiet. If they called the police, the police said: "We are not stupid, we are not going in there." A street where the police doesn't [*sic.*] go? No state can tolerate this.'

In the infamous 'Battle of Mainzer Strasse' in November 1990, activists fought around 3,000 police over two days to prevent the forced eviction of 13 squats on the street. The incident prompted Germany's largest police deployment since the end of the Second World War; following the battle the city legalised many of the city's squats – some were let in exchange for token rents, while others were also forcibly cleared.

In Peter Schneider's 2000 novel *Eduard's Homecoming*, the eponymous protagonist – a Berlin-born scientist working at Stanford – has been living in California with his American family when he gets news that he has inherited part of a tenement in Friedrichshain. He returns to post-Communist Berlin to find the property occupied by militant squatters, a plot that allows Schneider to explore the theme of reunification and its attendant issues:

> He saw the city's body laid open like that of a patient on a gigantic, brightly lit operating table. Dark, stagnant fluids had oozed out everywhere to form lakes on which bulky construction plants floated amid ice floes. Seemingly airborne surgeons bent over the lifeless body with eye and instruments, probing the wound with remote-controlled arms, curetting it, making room for new organs, new sinews and arteries. Seated high above the open body or before their monitors in distant, darkened rooms, these unseen surgeons searched for the hidden tumors that had to be removed before the new heart could be implanted.

With the exception of a few squats, this heady part of Friedrichshain's past has all but disappeared, although its abundant nightlife and cultural spaces are often used as examples of its continued alternative spirit. Some of these spaces are indeed a direct result of the district's community and protest culture; for example the Raw-Gelände, an ensemble of heavily graffitied warehouses and industrial spaces that once made up a Prussian train repair yard right next to Warschauer Strasse, was in limbo for nearly a decade before local residents campaigned to resurrect it. Today it hosts several bars and nightclubs, a skate hall, an outdoor swimming pool and a dedicated street art exhibition area (Urban Spree).

On the Warschauer Brücke lies one of the city's most legendary techno clubs, Berghain, whose name is derived from its location close to the border of Friedrichshain and Kreuzberg. Housed inside a GDR power station built during the 1950s, its roots lie in the city's alternative gay and fetish scene, specifically in a previous club called Ostgut, which used to exist roughly where the O2 Arena is located now, close to the Spree and the East Side Gallery (i.e. where the Berlin Wall used to run).

In some ways, Berghain symbolises the district's history of anti-authority by refusing to sell out to lifestyle music trends: there are no VIP rooms, no mirrors in the toilets and DJs are encouraged to play ultra-long sets rather than short ones to discourage superficiality. The club is also committed to protecting the city's alternative culture by creating a safe zone for all kinds of people – and sexualities – to dance together. Their notorious ban on any kind of photography (stickers are placed over mobile phone cameras upon entry) is in place to avoid compromising such an environment.

Even more than Kreuzberg clubs like Watergate and Käter Blau, Berghain regularly attracts electronic music fans from all over the globe. Berlin resident Amy Liptrot, who was born in Orkney, compares the cavernous interior of Berghain to the dark shores of her home in her short story 'Diving into Berghain' (2015), published on the Somesuch Stories website:

> Entering this place is like swimming into a vast, echoing cliff cave and, once my eyes adjust to the dark, finding it full of rock doves and black cormorants, on shadowy ledges, darting past. I've found a complete ecosystem. Five hundred people or more, a bloom of

jellyfish, are drifting with the tide of music. Exquisite creatures appear from behind pillars and speaker stacks like rocks: fashion goths and techno gays, in leather and mesh and lycra and neoprene and swimsuits, every type of black. They are dancing with fans, topless in chain mail, showing off their tattoos. I am reminded of the beautiful and weird illustrations of Ernst Haeckel, the German naturalist and philosopher who, at the beginning of the twentieth century, made detailed studies of sea life including technical drawings of jellyfish and anemones.

Underwater, sound travels faster and objects look slightly magnified. Due to the refraction of light in water, they appear closer and larger. A similar effect is created in a club due to the smoke machine, the dark and the drugs. It is hard to tell distance, time or direction. I'm swimming in murky water. A white spotlight is like a shaft of sunlight reaching down to the seabed. There are red lasers and green exit lights. I can't tell how long I've been here.

A short walk from Berghain is the historical Oberbaumbrücke (Oberbaum Bridge), which today connects Friedrichshain with its sister borough Kreuzberg, but which between 1961 and 1989 served as a GDR checkpoint that kept the two districts separate. Originally built in the eighteenth century as part of the city's customs and excise wall, the current neo-Gothic red-brick structure was designed by architect Otto Stahn and opened in 1896. During the Battle of Berlin in 1945 it was partly destroyed by the Wehrmacht to stop the Red Army from crossing, but quickly reopened to enable foot traffic to cross, and in 1946 was repaired to allow the U-Bahn trains of Line B (U1 today) to continue running across.

In her memoir *Gone to Ground* (2015), Jewish Holocaust survivor Marie Jalowicz Simon recalls living – or rather hiding – in the area right across from the bridge:

> We went on foot from Schönleinstrasse to the River Spree. it was not far to the Oberbaum bridge yet I had never been in this area

before. I liked it very much at once. It had the typical atmosphere of Berlin. The Spree was my spree, my river. I fervently hoped that this might represent a long-term solution for me. The bridge led straight to a short street on the opposite side of the Spree (No 2 Am Oberbaum), where there were three apartment blocks in a row. We went into the middle one. I immediately felt at ease there, even in the front hall of the building. An old cardboard plate hanging on the banisters proclaimed that they were just polished, and I saw another such notice in the same hand, and like the first with spelling mistakes, that when the air-raid warning sounded the cellar doors must be left open. I relished the phonetic reproduction of a genuine Berlin accent on both notices.

She goes on to talk about life in the district, including the occasional walks she took around Friedrichshain and over the bridge to Kreuzberg:

I always had plenty to do during the day when Burgers was at work. I was now running the entire household. Simply doing the shopping and bringing it home took a good deal of time. I resumed my walks in the city. The area between the Oberbaum Bridge and Görlitzer Station, Stralauer Allee and Treptower Park became my main preserve [...] One night when we were all down in the cellar again we heard a frightful crash overhead. Soon it was obvious that our building had been hit by a high-explosive bomb. However, we hadn't been buried. We had only to move a little rubble aside to get out into the open. The three buildings that comprised am Oberbaum were still standing, but the facade that they all shared had been torn away and fallen to the ground. You could look into the separate floors like so many stage sets. The stairway was hanging askew and one banister rail was missing. Burgers ventured to climb up to our bombed out apartment once more to retrieve a few things. We had most of our stuff with us, in our air-raid emergency kits. I couldn't and didn't want to go up there myself. I was afraid of the climb. The desk – my desk – was partly hanging outside. I asked Burgers to bring my wax-cloth notebooks down for me, but he refused with obvious malice, laughing gleefully. That was his personal revenge on me, because he had always hated the desk and my reading and writing.

During the Wall years, West Berliners could cross into the GDR with a one- or 14-day visa, and the bridge was also occasionally used to transfer political dissidents from the East who had been 'bought' by the FRG (a common practice in which the GDR exchanged prisoners for Deutschmark to bolster its economy) into the West. After the Wall fell, the bridge was restored to its former appearance with a new steel middle section designed by Spanish architect Santiago Calatrava (1995).

Right next to the bridge is one of the longest remaining stretches of the Berlin Wall, the 1.3 kilometre-long East Side Gallery. Initiated by members of two German cultural associations – Bundesverband Bildender Künstlerinnen und Künstler (BBK, West Germany) and Verband Bildender Künstler der DDR (VBK, GDR) – after they merged in 1989, artists from all around the world were invited to cover the part of the so-called Hinterlandmauer (Inner GDR Wall) with art. The pieces painted included Dimitri Wrubel's famous *God Help Me to Survive This Deadly Love*, showing the brothers' kiss between Leonid Brezhnev and Erich Honecker, and Birgit Kinder's *Test the Best*, showing an East German Trabi car smashing through the wall. The 'gallery' was officially opened on 28 September 1990 but repainted – not without controversy – in 2009 for the twentieth anniversary of the fall of the Wall.

Today it is one of the most popular tourist sights in the city and has been featured in Anton Corbijn's video for the U2 song 'One' (1992) and Wolfgang Becker's movie *Goodbye, Lenin!* (2003). It is also mentioned in the lyrics of English band Bloc Party's single 'Kreuzberg' (2007).

❧ 10 ❦

PRENZLAUER BERG

The story of Prenzlauer Berg begins, as so many good tales do, with beer. Up until the 1860s, the area was located outside the customs and excise wall that demarcated the limits of the inner city (Prenzlauer Tor, located at the intersection of Torstrasse and Prenzlauer Allee, was one of that wall's 18 main gates) and known mostly for its farms and windmills, which earned it the nickname Windmühlenberg (Windmill Hill).

Following incorporation into James Hobrecht's 1862 urban plan, the district went through rapid and intense changes. Within a couple of decades, the farms and windmills had been replaced by tens of thousands of residential tenement blocks, and the discovery of underground drinking water and suitability of the area's hilly terrain for cellar-type storage had given rise to a series of Bavarian-style breweries that provided employment for the constant influx of workers.

Despite not getting a mention in Baedeker's 1905 guide to Berlin, Prenzlauer Berg was nonetheless very much integrated into inner-city life by the late nineteenth century and became increasingly entwined with the turbulent events of the twentieth century. As new breweries opened – there were 14 in Prenzlauer Berg alone by 1900, and some 250 across the city – and older ones expanded, they became increasingly significant for the neighbourhood, providing not only employment but also fostering the development of culture and politics throughout the area.

Prater, the oldest beer garden not only in Prenzlauer Berg but in Berlin, is still operating at the northern end of Kastanienallee.

14   *Cherry trees in full bloom line a street that leads to Prenzlauer Berg's Zionskirche*

To say the pub-restaurant and its beer garden have an 'old school' charm is an understatement, given that the venue has been selling beer since at least the 1850s, and probably a decade or two before that. In contrast with the trendy fashion boutiques and cafés that line Kastanienallee today, its courtyard garden has retained a strong community appeal, especially during summer when visitors and locals mingle, sip beer and munch on bratwurst below the chestnut trees.

Prater's original owners, the Kalbo family, gradually transformed the venue into one of the district's predominant leisure spaces, helped along by its easy accessibility from the centre of the city – initially via horse-drawn coaches – and capacity for up to 800 punters. As Thilo Zantke writes in *Der Berliner Prater* (1987), his in-depth history of the venue, Prater quickly became 'a public house, destination for day trippers, variety, people's theatre, ballroom, garden and place for political meetings'.

Beer and politics being such natural bedfellows, it is no surprise that such venues became meeting points for political groups. Prater's first organised meeting of this kind, which involved the Allgemeinen deutschen Arbeitervereins (General Union of German Workers), was held as early as the summer of 1871, while other events featured political readings and plays such as Albert Schweitzer's drama *Goose: A Dramatic Conversation on the Extension of the Female Job Market* (*Eine Gans: Dramatisches Gespräch über die Erweiterung des weiblichen Arbeitsmarktes*, 1869), a dramatic dialogue discussing female labour and at the same time satirising Karl Marx's *Capital*.

Over the years Prater continued to evolve. A new building added at the beginning of the twentieth century featured a large performance hall and fully operational theatre that put on plays such as Schiller's *Intrigue and Love* (*Kabale und Liebe*) and, after the war when the city's Volksbühne (People's Theatre) moved in (see Chapter 3), major cultural events like the premiere of Maxim Gorky's play *The Lower Depths*.

Stars such as the famous writer, singer and actor Ernst Busch also played the postwar Prater stage. Busch was famous for his interpretations of political songs by the likes of Weimar songwriters Kurt Weill, Kurt Tucholsky and Bertolt Brecht, and also appeared in the stage version of Brecht's *Threepenny Opera* as well as the 1931 film by Georg Wilhelm Pabst. He was also well known for his Communist leanings, which led to him fleeing Germany during the Second World War; he returned in 1946 to collaborate with Brecht and Erwin Piscator at the Berliner Ensemble and also founded the Lied Der Zeit GmbH record label – the forerunner to the GDR's official record company, Deutsche Schallplatten Berlin.

Thanks to its politico-cultural heritage, the local city council – by that point Prenzlauer Berg was part of East Berlin – named Prater an official district cultural institution in 1967. The beer garden was used for concerts and pro-SED rallies as well as by the district's counter-cultural network, which grew into one of the strongest dissident communities within the GDR. Groups such as Zinnober – an independent puppet and stage theatre collective that was eventually banned – staged productions at Prater, and in 1971 the venue published a notebook of poems that had been performed on its stage. Two years later, the venue opened a gallery exhibition showing the work of local artists that by 1976 had attracted some 40,000 people.

For all its long history and local engagement, Prater was one of the smaller breweries in the district. One of the largest, the yellow-brick complex today known as the Kulturbrauerei, also still stands around the corner on Schönhauser Allee. Founded shortly after Prater, in 1842, it was bought by Jobst Schultheiss in 1853, who opened a beer garden on the site. By 1860 the brewery was producing a seventh of all the beer sold in Berlin and was expanded to its imposing, fort-like form in 1887 by Franz Heinrich Schwechten, the architect responsible for the Anhalter Bahnhof and the Kaiser Wilhelm Church in West Berlin (see Chapter 4).

Like Prater, the Schultheiss brewery became an important and integrated part of the Prenzlauer Berg community, serving a purpose far beyond its primary role as a place of employment. Its owners were influenced by the social reform ideals of the nineteenth century, and from the very beginning built relationships with its workers and local inhabitants by providing them with subsided hot meals, coal deliveries and free workshops and community events. It even maintained its own fire engine service (which made practical use of unwanted beer water) and sent beer to German troops during the First World War.

In a chronicle of the brewery's history, Hans Ehlers describes it as 'a great company that is connected to the entire economic body of Germany with a thousand threads'. After surviving the turbulent Weimar years, the brewery became an official *Wehrwirtschaftsbetrieb* in 1938, which meant it was allowed to provide beer to the Wehrmacht. The brewery also opened a Hitler Youth training programme on its facility and used prisoner-of-war labour. At the end of the war, as the Russians surrounded the city, the brewery's tallest towers were used as defensive positions by SS sharpshooters; those who died fighting remain buried in the brewery's courtyard grounds. After the war, the brewery continued producing beer for a while, and from 1970 one of the towers was turned into the Frannz Club, a popular neighbourhood nightclub for locals that is still operating today.

The brewery was renovated in 2000 into the Kulturbrauerei (Cultural Brewery), hosting a more or less equal mix of cultural and commercial venues: a cinema and concert halls, an eco-furniture store, dance studios, a supermarket and – since 2014 – a museum featuring the permanent exhibition Everyday Life in the GDR, developed by the Haus der Geschichte der Bundesrepublik Deutschland. One of its crowning cultural glories is the literaturWERKstatt, which has been offering readings, contests, open mic events, poetry festivals and more since the 1990s. It also operates the website lyrikline.org, which offers recordings of international poets reading from their work, including Ingeborg Bachmann, Gottfried Benn, Paul Celan and Michael Ondaatje.

A third Prenzlauer Berg brewery worthy of note lies at the foot of Prenzlauer Allee. Founded in 1885 by landowner and investor Christian F. Bötzow, the brewery rivalled Schultheiss as one of the largest in the area. Following the war it fell into disrepair, its labyrinthine cellars occasionally used for events and club nights, though in 2010 it was bought by German entrepreneur Hans Georg Näder, who has been slowly transforming it into an upscale ensemble of luxury apartments, medical centre, exhibition space and cocktail bar Le Croco Bleu.

In the period before the end of the First World War and the Weimar era, its garden became a major meeting point for the left-wing Spartacist group. In 1919, during the Communist uprising in the city, the garden and brewery were a stronghold for the fighters, leading to their dramatic seizure by government troops. Count Harry Kessler recorded the event in his diary on 9 March 1919:

Yesterday Government troops seized the Bötzow Brewery, the Spartacists 'Fort Eichhorn'. Today the struggle is for the Frankfurter Allee. This is being kept under machine-gun fire by the Spartacists and 15.5 centimetre howitzer shelling by the Government. Flyers are participating in the struggle. It is a proper battle. In the afternoon took a walk through the centre of the city to inspect the damage caused by the most recent fighting. Generally speaking, it is less than the newspapers suggested but certain buildings are pretty badly affected, there is a lot of glass lying about in the streets and in some parts it is covered with a thick layer of pulverized brick. Police Headquarters has some fresh scars to add to its old ones. Every single window of Tietz is smashed. On the pavement in front of the stores is a pool of blood. The house opposite at the corner of Prenzlauer Strasse, is wrecked from the roof to two floors down, either through aerial bombing or shelling. In the Prenzlauer Allee, in the neighbourhood of Bötzow, the cemetery wall together with a tree and a lamppost has been flattened, evidently from a mortar hit.

The huge influx of workers to the breweries and other workplaces and businesses in Prenzlauer Berg created a cosmopolitan environment. Immigrants poured in not only from other parts of Germany but also from Poland and other countries like Italy. One of the largest immigrant groups were middle- and lower-middle-class Jewish immigrants, who by the start of the twentieth century made up around 10 per cent of the local community – enough to establish several Jewish schools, a community centre for the Jewish elderly and the Baruch Auerbach'sche Waisenhaus, a Jewish-run orphanage.

Prenzlauer Berg also had its own synagogue – the largest in Germany – which was dedicated on Rykestrasse, not far from the Schultheiss brewery, in 1904. Partially destroyed during the Kristallnacht pogroms of 1938, it reopened as early as July 1945 and was restored to its pre-war splendour in 2007, with political leaders and Holocaust survivors from around the world attending the re-inauguration ceremony. The interior, which originally held 2,000 people, now seats around 1,000 people, and access is restricted to services and cultural events such as the annual Day of Jewish Culture.

Only around 48 of the district's approximately 18,000 Jewish residents survived the Holocaust. One of the 1,700 so-called 'U-Boats' (Jewish residents who survived by going underground) in the city was Marie Jalowicz Simon, whose memoirs of the period were published in 2015 – in German as *Untergetaucht* (Submerged) and in English as *Gone to Ground*. Her remarkable story was told to her son Hermann Simon, a historian and director of the New Synagogue Berlin – Centrum Judaicum, after 50 years of silence on the subject. The interviews were recorded onto 77 tapes, the last of which was made just a few days before Jalowicz Simon's death in 1998.

Born into a home on Rosenthaler Strasse, close to the Hackesche Höfe in Berlin, the family moved around the Mitte and Prenzlauer Berg areas before the war. Just before the First World War they moved into Prenzlauer Strasse, and when she was old enough Marie was sent to school in Prenzlauer Berg's Heinrich-Roller-Strasse:

> It was 1928, the time of mass unemployment. Many very poor people lived near the catchment area of this school. All the same, my parents did not want to send me to an exclusive private school. I was to learn the social environment there, along with its Berlin dialect, and learn also to assert myself in those surroundings.

As the Nazis tightened their regulations on the city and the war got underway, Jalowicz Simon decided to escape their clutches by removing her yellow star and moving clandestinely from house to house. Over the years she moved all around the city (see Chapter 8), but often found herself in Prenzlauer Berg, at one point staying in Prenzlauer Berg's Lychener Strasse with a friend's former cleaning lady (and fellow anti-Nazi), Ida Kahnke, on Schönhauser Allee:

Ida Kahnke lived in the back part of what had once been a large and grand apartment. She really had only one room, the former kitchen, which was tiled and terribly uncomfortable. She had rented this room to a friendly young man. Unfortunately he stuttered and wet the bed. He dried his wet sheets in the room and it made the whole apartment stink. Otherwise there was only a small servant's room converted for use as a kitchen. Part of that room, again, was divided off as the toilet. The old woman slept in a kind of alcove in a back corner of the entrance hall, and I had perforce to share her big old wooden bed.

One of the oldest Jewish sites in the neighbourhood, the Jewish cemetery, can be found at No. 22 Schönhauser Allee. Built in 1827 it stands on the grounds of yet another old brewery (and dairy farm) and was constructed following the closure of Berlin's first and oldest Jewish cemetery on Grosse Hamburger Strasse in Mitte. Behind the cemetery, not immediately visible from the main entrance, runs a 7.5-metre-wide, 400-metre-long thoroughfare. Established in 1827, it is known as a Totenpfad, or 'Path of the Dead', and was built to provide separate access into the burial ground because – legend has it – the Prussian king did not want to see the 'miserable-looking Jewish mourners'.

The cemetery contains more than 22,500 graves and 750 family tombs as well as a couple of small memorials. One is dedicated to the 35 young Jewish men killed fighting during the First World War; the other to a group of deserting Wehrmacht soldiers caught hiding in the cemetery at the end of the Second World War. Discovered by SS officers, they were murdered for treason and strung up on the trees of the cemetery. The inscription reads: 'Den Tod anderer nicht zu wollen, das war ihr Tod' ('They wanted no more killing, and that meant their death').

Among the graves are many local Jewish notables: painter Max Liebermann, publishers Albert Mosse and Leopold Ullstein (see Chapter 1), composer Giacomo Meyerbeer, economists like

Ludwig Bamberger and entrepreneur, philanthropist and patron of the arts 'Henri' James Simon, who famously donated most of his significant collections to the Berlin State Museums (including the famous Nefertiti bust that today sits in the Neues Museum – see Chapter 2). The only real literary persona here is banker and art patron David Friedländer, one of the first people to translate the Hebrew prayerbook into German, based on the commentary of his friend Moses Mendelssohn.

Berlin writer Peter Schneider visited the cemetery for his 2014 book *Berlin Now: The Rise of the City and the Fall of the Wall*, writing that 'the most important message the gravestones convey is about the deceased's professions and the mark they left on the city's history.' He examines some of the personalities in more detail, such as Gerson von Bleichröder, banker to the Prussian court and financial adviser to Bismarck, underling how even an 'integrated' Jew remained an 'outsider in Germany's upper class'. At the end of his visit, Schneider sums up what has evidently been a poignant experience:

> I found myself alone in this vast field of graves under the rain, the chorus of all these voices, fallen silent so long ago, swirling around me like powerful music. All of them, everyone who was buried here, had once belonged to this city – had wanted to belong to it – had shaped, influenced and improved it through their work as doctors, publishers, lawyers, civil servants, workers, artists, scientists, bankers and entrepreneurs. Attesting to the lives and activities of Berlin's Jews as it does, the cemetery struck me as a wonderful memorial site that inspires awe and gratitude above all – in contrast to the guilt that memorials to murdered Jews inevitably elicit in Germans of my generation, which easily stifles empathy and admiration for their accomplishments, for what they left behind in their lives, and in the life of the city.

Thanks to its lack of strategic military targets and munitions factories, Prenzlauer Berg managed to emerge from the Second

World War relatively unscathed. Berlin's oldest water tower and one of the area's key architectural landmarks, the Wasserturm – nicknamed Dicker Hermann or Thick Herman – was one of the structures that managed to survive the bombs. Completed in 1877 – not actually 1856 as the text below states – and in use until 1952, the large cylindrical structure now houses much-coveted apartments, while the upper part of the connected former reservoir has been landscaped and now serves as a low-key relaxation area. Chloe Aridjis features the tower and its history in her novel, *Book of Clouds*, via a conversation between her narrator, Tatiana, and the history professor (Weiss) she ends up working for:

> 'What do you know about this Wasserturm?' Weiss asked.
>
> 'I've never been inside, but I think there are apartments, maybe a gallery.'
>
> 'That Wasserturm, Tatiana, was built by the English Waterworks Company in 1856. In 1933, it was used by SA troops for holding and torturing anti-Fascist prisoners. And now it is used, as you say, for "apartments with a nice view of the square" and for those pseudo-artistic spaces that have spread through Berlin like a virus.'

Indeed, close to the water tower and almost hidden by the abundant trees in summer, is a small memorial to this dark period of the district's past. The reservoir's former machine house was, in 1933, turned into one of the first concentration camps in Nazi Germany. Used mainly for the interrogation and torture of Communists and other political enemies, the building came to be known locally as the Turm des Schreckens (Tower of Terror).

One of the district's most famous pacifists and anti-Nazis was the artist Käthe Kollwitz (1867–1945), who lived just along the road from the water tower, close to the square she posthumously lent her name to: Kollwitzplatz. Known today for its leafy, cosmopolitan atmosphere and child-friendly ambience, the square features a couple of playgrounds, a small park and a large statue of Kollwitz in the centre.

Kollwitz was one of Germany's pre-eminent sculptors and artists. Born in Königsberg, she moved to Prenzlauer Berg in 1891 after marrying Dr Karl Kollwitz. Her home, destroyed during the Second World War, stood at what is now Kollwitzstrasse 56, adjacent to the square. Through her husband's work and their proximity to the area's working classes, Käthe came into continuous contact with the many sick and the suffering who lived in the overcrowded and smog-filled district during the late nineteenth century.

These local experiences were a big influence on her works, which spanned woodcuts, sculptures and lithographs shaped around universal anti-war themes such as sickness, hunger, war and death. As she notes in her diary, which she kept from 1900 to her death (published as *Diary and Letters* in 1988), 'It is my duty to voice the sufferings of humankind [...] the never-ending sufferings heaped mountain high.' Losing her beloved son, Peter, during the First World War only strengthened her pacifist resolve, as did the death of her grandson in the Second World War. In his historical sketch of Kollwitz in his book *Berlin: Imagine a City* (2014), author Rory MacLean describes the district around the end of the nineteenth century: 'crowded, pestilent Prenzlauer Berg is a place that can kill a man, joke local residents, as easily as if one uses an axe.' He imagines Kollwitz drawing patients in her husband's waiting room:

She holds to her breast – and against her heart – her sketchbook, the morning's drawings. Every day in Karl's waiting room Käthe registers the patients, drawing them out as she draws them: the cloth-cutter with severed fingers, the fierce tiler crippled by a fall, a battered tanner-woman recovering from her third miscarriage, the bow-legged twins wheezing with consumption. 'I meet the women who come to my husband for help and so, incidentally, come to me, I am gripped by the full force of the proletarian's fate,' she records. 'Unsolved problems such as prostitution and unemployment grieve and torment me, and contribute to my feeling that I must keep on with my studies of the working class.'

Following the war and subsequent division of the city, Prenzlauer Berg ended up in the Soviet sector. Although it had not been destroyed by bombing, many of its tenements had been shot to pieces by advancing Russian troops. More or less neglected by the GDR, which poured its money into the Berlin Wall, Karl-Marx-Allee (see Chapter 9) and its own high-rise housing blocks (*Plattenbauten*), Prenzlauer Berg was more or less left to its own devices.

Over time, the dilapidated buildings – almost 90 per cent of which were still heated with coal ovens and 43 per cent had no bath when the Wall fell in 1990 – were filled with a disparate mix of artists, unemployed, bohemians and squatters. By the 1960s and 1970s the neighbourhood's poets, songwriters, activists and authors began to organise an underground literary scene that was increasingly critical of the East German regime – much more so than previous generations, many of whom had bought into the Socialist project as a bonafide contrast to the horrors of the Third Reich.

This so-called Hineingeborenen (Born Into It) generation, which never made the same conscious decision to build an anti-fascist utopia, did not feel particularly compelled to conform to its restrictions. Anti-establishment zines, initially handwritten but later created on computers, carried names like *Anschlag, Ariadnefabrik, Bizarre Städte* and *Entwerter-Oder* and were distributed by hand; underground readings and punk shows were organised.

Given the all-seeing eye and merciless retributional power of the Stasi, these local dissidents took huge personal risks. But as well as support from official cultural spaces such as Prater and other bars and clubs in the area – many of them literally underground in basements and cellars – local churches such as the Gethsemanekirche on Stargarder Strasse were all too happy to engender criticism of an atheist system by providing a space for music rehearsals, shows and even public readings of banned authors such as Günter Kunert, who had been forced to publish his work in the West.

Despite the clandestine nature of these operations, Stasi personnel still managed to be present at most of these events. According to

Anna Funder's book *Stasiland* (2009), one in every six people was an informer in Berlin's inner-city areas, and in some cases this was an understatement: author and lyricist Lutz Rathenow discovered there were up to 53 people informing on him. In 1992 the *New York Times* published 'East Germans Face their Accusers', an article about the surveillance on Rathenow, noting how such reports 'are filled with details like how often subjects took out their garbage or where they stored their ironing boards [...] The Stasi even installed surveillance cameras in some public toilets, and agents were assigned, day after day, to monitor film of people entering, relieving themselves, washing their hands and leaving.' One specific report published on Rathenow recorded the following profound insights: 'Rathenow then crossed the street and ordered a sausage at the sausage stand [...] The following conversation took place: Rathenow: "A sausage please." Sausage seller: "With or without roll?" Rathenow: "With, please." Sausage seller: "And mustard?"'

One of the more significant literary works to emerge from the Prenzlauer Berg scene was a 1986 anthology entitled *Touching Is Only a Marginal Phenomenon (Berührung ist nur eine Randerscheinung)*, which included texts from most local protagonists, including Jan Faktor, Bert Papenfuss-Gorek, Rainer Schedlinski, Kurt Drawert and Uwe Kolbe. It was co-edited by Sascha Anderson, a songwriter, poet and author considered one of the scene's major ringleaders.

Anderson, an inveterate collaborator, was extremely active in terms of publishing regular newsletters, putting on – and playing at – punk and rock concerts, and also promoting up-and-coming artists. He moved to West Berlin in 1986, claiming that so many friends had already left that he could not continue his work. It later emerged, however, that he had been a Stasi informer, prompting a great deal of anger from his former friends and throwing into question the authenticity of Prenzlauer Berg's counter-culture movement.

Anderson wasn't the only one: it also transpired that another leading light on the scene, Rainer Schedlinski, worked as a double agent for the Stasi too. Interestingly, despite the furore that followed,

Schedlinski and Anderson managed to maintain the publishing house – GALREV (*Verlag*, publishing house, backwards) – that they had set up together in 1990, and which for a while was connected with a premises on Lychener Strasse.

Not everyone sold out. Lutz Rathenow continued writing his sketches and poems even though he was imprisoned; he also refused to emigrate. Uwe Kolbe, who attended the Johannes R. Becher Institute for Literature in Leipzig, the official school of poetry in the GDR, also criticised the regime without succumbing to Stasi pressure. Sometimes his views were made in public, but at other times they were more clandestine, such as the time he smuggled a poem into an anthology published by the politically conformist Mitteldeutsche Verlag. The poem was an acrostic whose initial letters formed the words *EUREM HELDENTUM WIDME ICH EINEN ORGASMUS / EUCH MÄCHTIGE GREISE ZERFETZE DIE TÄGLICHE REVOLUTION* (To your heroism I dedicate an orgasm / you powerful greybeards the daily revolution shall slash).

Kolbe revealed the prank afterwards, humiliating the publishing house and the regime, prompting a ban on his works for several years. He continued writing and translating for underground publications, however, as did Adolf Endler (1930–2009), the self-styled 'father of the oppositional literary scene' in Prenzlauer Berg. Also constantly harassed, Endler was thrown out of the GDR's official writers' association in the late 1970s. During the 1980s he continued to write for a series of underground magazines, including his own small, self-printed magazine *Sudelblätter*. In the 1990s, he published a volume of memoirs entitled *Tarzan in Prenzlauer Berg* (*Tarzan am Prenzlauer Berg*), which included a selection of his articles from *Sudelblätter*. From 1991 to 1998 he also ran a reading series named Orplid & Co, together with his wife Brigitte Schreier-Endler at the Café Clara in Mitte.

Much of Prenzlauer Berg's GDR literary activity took place on the streets around Helmholtzplatz, in particular Lychenerstrasse, Schliemannstrasse and Dunckerstrasse, whose nickname was the

'LSD Quarter'. The Duncker Bier-Quelle on Dunckerstrasse was one of the main hangouts of *Liedermacherin* (folk singer) Bettina Wegener and her husband, the writer Klaus Schlesinger, who is remembered by a memorial plaque here today.

Schlesinger (1937–2001) was born in Prenzlauer Berg. His father was a clerk at the Ullstein publishing house (see Chapter 1) and, after studying as a chemist, Klaus began working as a journalist at GDR newspaper *Neue Berliner Illustrierte*. He joined the official GDR's writers' association, published his first novel, *Michael* – an unpolitical coming-of-age story – in 1972 and organised a series of readings and concerts named Eintopp (Stew) with his wife at the Haus der jungen Talente youth club near Alexanderplatz.

In 1979 he was one of the signatories of the letter protesting against the expulsion of GDR protest singer Wolf Biermann (see Chapter 2) and was expelled from the writers' association, after which he moved to West Germany and published a short story collection about everyday life in Prenzlauer Berg called *Life in Winter* (*Leben im Winter*) via the S. Fischer publishing house. After the fall of the Wall he returned to Prenzlauer Berg and began working as a journalist and author, publishing *The Randow Affair* (*Die Sache mit Randow*) in 1996, a fictionalised account of the real-life story of Werner Gladow, the head of a violent youth gang that operated around Prenzlauer Berg and Friedrichshain (and the first man condemned to death in the GDR, in 1950).

Since the fall of the Wall, Prenzlauer Berg has undergone the most complete gentrification process of any former GDR district. The once run-down tenements have been lavishly refurbished and now command some of the highest prices in the city, and its leafy, wide streets brim with boutiques, coffee shops and restaurants. Its former residents, most of whom had left by the end of the 1990s, have been replaced with an influx of middle-class German and international expatriate families.

One of the few official traces of the GDR left in the area is the Bernauer Strasse Memorial (opened 1998), a preserved section of the former border strip that has been turned into an outdoor exhibition. Some 1.4 kilometres long, the memorial includes parts of the Wall as well as photo displays and a wealth of information points that detail the street's many fascinating stories: the successful escapes as well as the failed and fatal ones. At Bernauer Strasse 111 is the associated Documentation Centre – refurbished in 2015 for the twenty-fifth anniversary of the fall of the Wall – whose five-storey observation tower recreates the once-popular experience of peering into East Berlin from the West. Anna Funder visited the site during her time in 1990s Berlin and recounts in *Stasiland*:

> Today I walk from my place up Brunnenstrasse, past Frau Paul's tunnel to Bernauer Strasse where the Wall was. There is a new museum here. Its greatest exhibit is opposite: a full-size reconstructed section of the Wall, complete with freshly built and neatly raked death strip, for tourists. Right alongside it in Bernauer Strasse there are still some pieces of the real Wall, covered, as they always were on the western side, with bright graffiti. These remnants are behind bushes though, scrappy and crumbling. In some places the steel reinforcements in the concrete are bare as bones.

The memorial stretches north to the Mauerpark, a strip of landscaped green that was once the site of a stretch of Berlin Wall and the associated death-strip, but was turned into a public park in 1990. The park, scruffy but generally adored, is home to one of the city's best-loved Sunday flea markets, which draws a broad demographic of contemporary Berlin: hungover students, families, sleepless clubbers. Adjacent to the market is the Friedrich-Ludwig-Jahn-Sportpark and the Max-Schmeling-Halle, built in the 1950s and still hosting sporting events, and in warm weather a karaoke session in the park's amphitheatre ('bearpit') attracts equally large crowds.

The park has become a symbol not only for Prenzlauer Berg but for the reunified city, and is celebrated in the work of contemporary

15   Spectators gather round the singers during a karaoke session at Prenzlauer Berg's Mauerpark

German writer David Wagner (born 1971). A resident of Berlin since 1991, his prize-winning autobiographical debut novel *My Night-Blue Trousers* was published in 2000, and his book *Four Apples* was long-listed for the German Book Prize. His bestselling novel, *Lives*, won the 2013 Leipzig Book Fair Prize. Wagner often writes about contemporary Germany and living in the city during the 1970s and 1980s. He has also written extensively about Berlin in books such as *What Colour Is Berlin* (*Welcher Farbe Hat Berlin*, 2011) and *Berlin Triptych* (2014). In his 2013 essay collection *Mauerpark*, he writes:

> Mauerpark, I like your entrepreneurs, the bottle collectors scouting for deposits, the cake girls who sell home-baked produce on Sundays, the mini-kite salesmen, the soap-bubble man with his giant bubbles and the hula-hoop promoter with his dancing girls. And I like all the different musicians who play folk or anti-

folk behind propped-open suitcases – Mauerpark, at times I even love your drummers, who drum halfway through the night, so wonderfully annoying – that's just the way it is in a big city.

I like the fact that the Mauerpark creates an international public space, an audience European politicians can only dream of; this is where the youth of the world comes together, and it seems they simply leave behind a lot of rubbish. Burnt-out disposable barbecues, Tetrapaks and plastic bags. There are Sunday evenings when barbecue smoke drifts above the grass like a bank of fog, even though barbecues are actually banned in the Mauerpark, but Mauerpark, oh, I love your big grey crows that live off the leftovers. They've grown so fat they can barely fly.

CHRONOLOGY OF EVENTS

	Literary and Cultural Events	Political Events
1237		First recorded mention of Cölln, official year the city is founded.
1411		The Mark Brandenburg is given to the margrave of Nuremberg, the Hohenzollern Frederick VI, whom the emperor elevates to the rank of elector and margrave of Brandenburg as Frederick I.
1432		Berlin and Cölln merge to form a single municipality.
1443	The foundation stone of the Stadtschloss, the city palace, is laid.	
1486		The elector Johann Cicero makes the palace the permanent residence of the Brandenburg electors, the Hohenzollerns.
1647	An avenue is laid out between the city palace and the Tiergarten, the elector's hunting preserve, later becoming Unter den Linden.	

	Literary and Cultural Events	*Political Events*
1685		Frederick William, the Great Elector, issues the Edict of Potsdam, which encouraged oppressed Huguenots to emigrate to his nation.
1688		The population of Berlin reaches 20,000.
1695	The elector Frederick III has a palace built for his wife, Sophie Charlotte, near Lietzenburg. After her death in 1705, it is renamed Charlottenburg Palace.	
1701		18 January: Elector Frederick III has himself crowned Frederick I, King of Prussia.
1709		Frederick I decrees the unification of the five towns of Berlin, Cölln, Friedrichswerder, Dorotheenstadt and Friedrichstadt to form the capital and royal residence. The unified city has a population of 55,000.
1740	Berlin develops into a centre of the Enlightenment under Frederick the Great. Many representative buildings are erected around Unter den Linden: the Zeughaus (Armory), the Kronprinzenpalais (Palace of the Crown Prince), the Staatsoper (Opera House) and Prinz-Heinrich-Palais (the Prince Heinrich Palace).	

	Literary and Cultural Events	*Political Events*
1791	The Brandenburg Gate is officially opened, and crowned with Johann Gottfried Schadow's quadriga two year's later.	
1800	Many literary salons are held throughout the city, led by Jewish intellectual figures like Rahel Varnhagen, Sara Levy and Henriette Herz.	Berlin has around 170,000 inhabitants, 25,000 of whom are soldiers.
1805	The main cattle market and parade ground is named Alexanderplatz in honour of the Russian tsar Alexander I, who visits Berlin in October.	
1806		27 October: the French emperor Napoleon and his troops march into Berlin. French troops occupy the city until 1808.
1810	Berlin's first university, today's Humboldt University, opens in the Prince Heinrich Palace on Unter den Linden.	
1811	Heinrich von Kleist and Henriette Vogel commit suicide at Wannsee.	
1814	Adelbert von Chamisso publishes *Peter Schlemihl's Miraculous Story*.	
1830	The Altes Museum, built by Karl Friedrich Schinkel, opens.	
1844	The Zoologischer Garten is opened on the south-western edge of the Tiergarten as Germany's first zoo.	

	Literary and Cultural Events	*Political Events*
1846	Volkspark Friedrichshain is opened in the densely populated eastern part of the city as the first recreational area for all social classes.	
1848		Social hardship and the curtailment of political freedoms result in the outbreak of a democratic revolution throughout the German states in March. The revolution in Berlin is quelled in November by 13,000 Prussian soldiers. Most of the rebels killed are buried in a dedicated cemetery in Volkspark Friedrichshain.
1856	Wilhelm Raabe publishes *The Chronicle of Sparrow Alley.*	
1862	Theodor Fontane publishes his *Ramblings through Brandenburg.*	
1869	The new Berlin Town Hall is completed and, because of its red-brick construction, dubbed Rotes Rathaus (Red Town Hall).	
1871		Berlin becomes the capital of the German Reich and the empire's political, economic and scientific centre.
1874	The city planner James Hobrecht starts work on an extensive plan for the city's expansion.	
1877	Leopold Ullstein founds the Ullstein Verlag publishing house.	The population grows to more than 1 million.

	Literary and Cultural Events	*Political Events*
1882	The road connecting the city with the royal hunting lodge in Grunewald is revamped as the Kurfürstendamm. Housing in the 'new west' draws in wealthy residents, and the area around Kurfürstendamm becomes a popular place for artists and writers to congregate.	
1883	The Deutsches Theater opens on Schumannstrasse.	
1891–2	Mark Twain visits Berlin.	
1900		Berlin has a population of almost 1.9 million, over the following years it becomes the world's largest tenement city. In 1903 it has a total of 1 million apartments, 400,000 of which have only one room.
1906	Robert Walser arrives in the city and lives here until 1913.	
1911	In the years before the First World War, sciences, culture and business flourish. Figures like painters Max Liebermann and Walter Leistikow (who formed the Berlin Secession in 1898), scientist Rudolf Virchow, and poet Else Lasker-Schüler live and work in Berlin.	
1912		The population of the city climbs above 2 million.

	Literary and Cultural Events	*Political Events*
1914–18	During the First World War, it becomes increasingly difficult to supply the population, and many cultural figures leave the city for the front or into exile.	
1918		9 November: Chancellor Prince von Baden declares the abdication of Kaiser William II. Socialist Philipp Scheidemann proclaims the 'Free German Republic' from the Reichstag, while Communist Karl Liebknecht proclaims the 'Free Socialist Republic of Germany' from the Berlin Royal Palace. In the end, the Social Democrat Friedrich Ebert becomes chancellor. 30 December: Karl Liebknecht and Rosa Luxemburg found the German Communist Party (KPD).
1919		Early January: the Spartacist uprising of the KPD is crushed and Karl Liebknecht and Rosa Luxemburg are murdered in the Tiergarten on 15 January.
1920	The city is a thriving cultural centre. Artists like Otto Dix, George Grosz, Bertolt Brecht, Erich Maria Remarque and Joseph Roth live and work in the city, as does Nobel Prize-winner Albert Einstein.	1 October: the Greater Berlin Act creates the city with boundaries still in place today, and divides it into 20 boroughs. Berlin has a population of 3.8 million and is one of the largest cities in Europe.

	Literary and Cultural Events	*Political Events*
1922		24 June: German foreign minister Walther Rathenau is murdered by right-wing extremists in the Grunewald suburb.
1924	Thomas Mann's *The Magic Mountain* is published.	
1925		Berlin has a population of over 4 million.
1928	A total of 147 daily and weekly newspapers are published in Berlin. 31 August: Brecht's *Threepenny Opera* premieres at the Theater am Schiffbauerdamm.	
1929	Alfred Döblin publishes *Berlin Alexanderplatz*.	Due to the Great Depression, 450,000 people in Berlin are unemployed in February alone. Demonstrations and violent unrest follow; over 30 people are killed and hundreds injured during the 'Bloody May' protests in Wedding.
1932		The number of unemployed climbs to 630,000, and the streets of the capital see more and more violent clashes between left- and right-wing groups. Adolf Hitler's National Socialist Party emerges as the strongest party in parliament after nation-wide elections in November.

	Literary and Cultural Events	*Political Events*
1933		4 January: Adolf Hitler becomes chancellor of the Reich.
		20 March: all Communist members of parliament are removed; in July so are all Social Democrats.
		10 May: the National Socialists stage a large book-burning on what is now Bebelplatz.
1935	Kurt Tucholsky dies in exile in Sweden.	
1936	Walter Benjamin publishes *The Work of Art in the Age of Mechanical Reproduction*.	
	1–16 August: the XI Summer Olympics take place in Berlin.	
1938		9 November: during the pogrom known as Kristallnacht, members of the SA and the SS set fire to nine of the twelve synagogues in Berlin, loot Jewish-owned shops and arrest 1,200 Jewish citizens.
1939	Joseph Roth dies in Paris.	1 September: war is declared against Poland. The Second World War begins.
1940		August: Allied planes bomb the city for the first time.
1942		20 January: at the Wannsee Conference the administrative plans for the so-called 'Final Solution of the Jewish Question', the extermination of European Jews, are laid out.

	Literary and Cultural Events	*Political Events*
1943		The Allied air forces begin large-scale bombing campaigns against the city. Around 1 million residents are evacuated up until the end of the war, and more than 50,000 perish.
1944		20 July: Colonel Claus Schenk Graf von Stauffenberg's attempt to assassinate Adolf Hitler fails. Mass arrests and summary executions follow; 89 resistance fighters are executed at Plötzensee Prison.
1945		21 April: the Red Army reaches Berlin, and the Battle of Berlin begins. It ends with Adolf Hitler's suicide on 30 April and the surrender of the city on 2 May.
		8 May: The Second World War in Europe ends.
		In accordance with an agreement signed by the Allies, Berlin is divided into four sectors and administered jointly by the the USA, Great Britain, France and the Soviet Union.
1947	Gruppe 47 is founded in the Western sectors.	
	5 February: Hans Fallada dies. His *Alone in Berlin* is posthumously published in May.	

	Literary and Cultural Events	*Political Events*
1948		Conflicts between the Allies trigger a Soviet Union blockade from June 1948 to May 1949. The Western Allies respond with the Berlin Airlift, supplying West Berlin by air.
1949		23 May: the Federal Republic of Germany is founded in Germany's Western sectors. Berlin retains its special status as a territory under Allied supervision.
		7 October: the German Democratic Republic (GDR) is founded in the Soviet Sector, and East Berlin becomes its capital.
1952	February: construction begins to transform East Berlin's Stalinallee (Karl-Marx-Allee since 1961) into 'Germany's first socialist street'.	
1953		16 June: construction workers on Stalinallee go on strike, and on 17 June this develops into a GDR-wide uprising which is brutally crushed by Soviet troops.
1954	The Berliner Ensemble headed by Bertolt Brecht moves into a theatre of its own, the Theater am Schiffbauerdamm in East Berlin.	
1956	Bertolt Brecht dies at his Berlin home on Chausseestrasse.	

	Literary and Cultural Events	*Political Events*
1961		July: 30,415 GDR citizens leave the country for West Berlin, the highest monthly number since 1953.
		13 August: the GDR starts construction of the Berlin Wall along the sector border and seals the two parts of the city off from one another for the next 28 years.
1962	The city centre of East Berlin is outfitted with large representative buildings around Alexanderplatz.	
1963		17 January: Soviet leader Nikita Khrushchev visits East Berlin.
		26 June: US president John F. Kennedy visits the city and makes his famous 'Ich bin ein Berliner' speech at Schöneberg Town Hall.
1967		2 June: student Benno Ohnesorg is shot by a policeman during a protest against the visit of the shah of Persia, leading to massive violent student protests.
1970	Uwe Johnson publishes the first part of *Anniversaries*.	
1976	23 April: the GDR Palast der Republik is opened on the grounds of the former Stadtschloss.	
1984	1 October: the reconstructed East Berlin Schauspielhaus theatre, originally designed by Karl Friedrich Schinkel, reopens.	

	Literary and Cultural Events	*Political Events*
1987		12 June: US president Ronald Reagan gives a speech at Brandenburg Gate and demands: 'Mr Gorbachev, open this gate. Mr Gorbachev, tear down this wall!'
1989		7 October: the GDR celebrates its fortieth anniversary with a large military parade.
		18 October: GDR leader Erich Honecker resigns 'for health reasons'.
		4 November: more than 500,000 East Berliners gather at Alexanderplatz, demanding freedom of speech, freedom of the press and freedom of assembly. The SED leadership promises that restrictions on travel to the West will be eased.
		9 November: the GDR opens the borders and the Berlin Wall falls.
1990		12 September: the Allied powers and the two German states sign the 'Two Plus Four' Treaty, arranging for unification under international law. Germany is given full sovereignty, and Berlin's Four-Power status expires.
		3 October: the unification of Germany is celebrated with a state ceremony and large party in front of the Brandenburg Gate.

	Literary and Cultural Events	*Political Events*
1991		Berlin's governing mayor and Senate Chancellery move from Schöneberg Town Hall back to the Rotes Rathaus.
2000	Wladimir Kaminer publishes *Russian Disco*.	19 April: The German parliament holds its first session in the redesigned Reichstag building, making Berlin the capital of a reunited Germany again.
2005	10 May: Germany's national Holocaust memorial is unveiled.	
2006	26 May: Berlin's new main train station – the Hauptbahnhof – is officially opened.	
2009	The Neues Museum reopens with an exhibition of the world-famous bust of Nefertiti.	
2012	Berlin celebrates its 775th anniversary.	
2013	The reconstruction of the new Royal Stadtschloss begins.	Berlin has a population of 3,517,424.

SELECT BIBLIOGRAPHY

Aridjis, C., *Book of Clouds* (London, 2009).

Austilat, A., *A Tramp in Berlin, New Mark Twain Stories: An Account of Twain's Berlin Adventures* (Los Angeles, 2013).

Barry, K., *Dark Lies the Island* (London, 2012).

Beevor, A., *Berlin: The Downfall 1945* (London, 2002).

Benjamin, W., *Berlin Childhood Around 1900* (New Haven, 2006).

Beradt, M., *Die Strasse der kleinen Ewigkeit* (Frankfurt, 2000).

Binet, L., *HHhH* (New York, 2012).

Blücher, Princess E., *An English Wife in Berlin: A Private Memoir of Events, Politics, and Daily Life in Germany Throughout the War and the Social Revolution of 1918* (New York, 1920).

Borchert, W., *Gesamtwerk* (Hamburg, 1991).

Boyd-White, I. and D. Frisby (eds), *Metropolis Berlin: 1880–1940* (Los Angeles, 2012).

Braun, S., *City of Exiles* (Berlin, 2015).

Brauseboys, *Müllerstrasse* (Berlin, 2013).

Brown, D. J., *The Boys in the Boat: Nine Americans and Their Epic Quest for Gold at the 1936 Berlin Olympics* (London, 2013).

Clark, C., *Iron Kingdom: The Rise and Downfall of Prussia, 1600–1947* (London, 2006).

Colin, B., *The Luminous Life of Lilly Aphrodite* (London, 2008).

Deighton, L., *Berlin Game* (London, 1983).

Derbyshire, K. and H. Reyes, *Berlin (City-Lit Series)* (London, 2009).

Dimendberg, E. and M. Jay, *The Weimar Berlin Sourcebook* (Los Angeles, 1994).

Döblin, A., *Berlin Alexanderplatz* (New York, 1961).

Dodd, M., *My Years in Germany* (New York, 1940).

Eugenides, J., *Middlesex* (New York, 2002).

F., Christiane, *Zoo Station* (San Francisco, 2013).

Falkenberg, B., *Else Lasker-Schüler: A Life* (Jefferson, 2003).

Fallada, H., *Alone in Berlin* (London, 2008).

Fauser, J., *Das Schlangenmaul* (Frankfurt, 1985).

—— *Am Strand der Städte* (Berlin, 2009).

—— *Raw Material* (London, 2014).

Flannery, H. W., *Assignment to Berlin* (New York, 1942).

Frederiksen, E. P., *Bettina Bretano von Arnim: Gender and Politics* (Detroit, 1995).

Fritzsche, P., *The Turbulent World of Franz Göll* (Cambridge, 2011).

Fontane, T., *Wanderungen durch die Mark Brandenburg* (Berlin, 1863).

—— *Trials and Tribulations* (New York, 1917).

Funder, A., *Stasiland* (London, 2003).

Gerstenberger, K., *Writing the New Berlin: The German Capital in Post-Wall Literature* (Camden, 2008).

Grass, G., *Too Far Afield* (London, 2001).

Gröschner, A., *City Spaces: Filling in Berlin's Gaps* (Berlin, 2015).

Grosz, G., *A Small Yes and a Big No* (New York, 1946).

Haffner, E., *Blood Brothers* (New York, 2015).

Hamilton, H., *Every Single Minute* (London, 2014).

Hattemer-Higgins, I., *The History of History* (London, 2012).

Haushofer, A., *Moabit Sonnets* (New York, 1978).

Heine, H., *Almansor: Eine Tragödie* (Frankfurt, 1821).

—— *Briefe aus Berlin* (Frankfurt, 1822).

Hensher, P., *Pleasured* (London, 1998).

Herrndorf, W., *Arbeit und Struktur* (Frankfurt, 2013).

—— *Why We Took the Car* (London, 2014).

Isherwood, C., *The Berlin Stories* (New York, 1976).

—— *Christopher and His Kind* (New York, 1976).

Jalowicz Simon, M., *Gone to Ground: One Woman's Extraordinary Account of Survival in the Heart of Nazi Germany* (London, 2014).

Jelavich, P., *Berlin Alexanderplatz: Radio, Film and the Death of Weimar Republic* (Los Angeles, 2006).

Jenkins, J., *Provincial Modernity: Local Culture and Liberal Politics in Fin-de-siècle Hamburg* (London, 2003).

Johnson, U., *The Third Book About Achim* (London, 1967).

—— *Anniversaries* (London, 1975).

Jünger, E., *The Storm of Steel* (London, 2004).

Kaminer, W., *Russian Disco: Tales of Everyday Lunacy in the Streets of Berlin* (London, 2002).

Kästner, E., *Emil and the Detectives* (London, 1928).

—— *Going to the Dogs* (New York, 2012).

Kerr, P., *A Man Without Breath* (London, 2013).

—— *The Lady from Zagreb* (London, 2015).

Kessler, Count H., *Berlin in Lights, 1918–1937* (London, 1971).

Key, E., *Rahel Varnhagen: A Portrait* (Bremen, 2013).

Klein, C., *Escape from Berlin* (London, 1944).

Kollwitz, K., *The Diary and Letters of Käthe Kollwitz* (Michigan, 1988).

Kuehnelt-Leddihn, E. von, *The Menace of the Herd: Or Procrustes at Large* (Alabama, 2007).

Küster, B., *Max Liebermann: ein Malerleben* (Hamburg, 1988).

Le Carré, J., *Smiley's People* (London, 1979).

Ledig, G., *Payback* (London, 2003).

Lieberson, H., *Traveler's World: Europe in the Pacific* (New Haven, 2006).

Malina, J., *The Piscator Notebook* (New York, 2012).

Maron, M., *Geburtsort Berlin* (Frankfurt, 2003).

Marven, L., *Berlin Tales* (Oxford, 2009).

Matthias, B., *The Hotel as Setting in Early Twentieth-Century German and Austrian Literature* (New York, 2006).

Melican, B., *Germany: Beyond the Enchanted Forest: A Literary Anthology* (London, 2014).

Moorhouse, R., *Berlin at War: Life and Death in Hitler's Capital, 1939–45* (London, 2010).

Morris, J., *A Writer's World* (London, 2003).

Nabokov, V., *Despair* (New York, 1966).

—— *The Stories of Vladimir Nabokov* (New York, 1995).

Owen, R. J., *The Poet's Role: Lyric Responses to German Unification by Poets from the GDR* (Amsterdam, 2001).

Plievier, T., *Berlin* (London, 1969).

Rapp, T., *Lost and Sound: Berlin, Techno and the Easyjet Set* (London, 2010).

Reese, D., *Growing up Female in Nazi Germany* (Michigan, 2006).

Regener, S., *Berlin Blues* (London, 2003).

Remarque, E. M., *All Quiet on the Western Front* (London, 1987).

—— *Three Comrades* (London, 2013).

Roth, J., *What I Saw* (New York, 2013) .

Ryan, C., *The Last Battle* (New York, 1966).

Schneider, P., *The Wall Jumper* (London, 2005).

—— *Berlin Now: The Rise of the City and the Fall of the Wall* (London, 2014).

Schulz, T., *A Square in East Berlin* (London, 2012).

Scraton, P., *The Idea of a River* (Berlin, 2015).

Siepen, E., *Peeps at Great Cities: Berlin* (Bremen, 2011).

Simpson, J., *Strange Places, Questionable People* (New York, 1998).

Stern, F., *Five Germanys I Have Known* (New York, 2006).

Sutton, F., *German Novelists of the Weimar Republic: Intersections of Literature and Politics* (New York, 2006).

Sweet, P. E., *Neighbors and Enemies: The Culture of Radicalism in Berlin, 1929–1933* (Cambridge, MA, 2004).

Thiess, F., *Verbrannte Erde* (Frankfurt 1963).

Thomann Tewarson, H., *Rahel Levin Varnhagen: The Life and Work of a German Jewish Intellectual* (Lincoln, NB, 1998).

Tucholsky, K., *Prayer After the Slaughter: The Great War: Poems and Stories From World War I* (New York, 2012).

—— *Berlin! Berlin!* (New York, 2014).

—— *Rheinsberg: A Storybook for Lovers* (New York, 2014).

Twain, M., *The Chicago of Europe: And Other Tales of Foreign Travel* (New York, 2009).

Vassiltchikov, M., *Berlin Diaries, 1940–1945* (London, 1988).

Voss, K., *Reiseführer für Literaturfreunde Berlin* (Frankfurt, 1980).

Wagner, D., *Berlin Triptych* (Berlin, 2014).

Walser, R., *Berlin Stories* (New York, 2006) .

Winkler, H. A., *Germany: The Long Road West*, Volume 2 (Oxford, 2006).

Wraxall, N., *Memoirs of the Courts of Berlin, Dresden, Warsaw, and Vienna, in the Years 1777, 1778, and 1779* (Cambridge, 2012).

Wolf, C., *Was Bleibt* (Frankfurt, 1990).

Wolfe, T., *You Can't Go Home Again* (New York, 1940).

Zantke, T., *Der Berliner Prater* (Berlin, 1987).

Zuckmayer, C., *Als wärs ein Stück von mir* (Frankfurt, 1966).

INDEX